The Restaurant Owner's Handbook

**SUCCESS
THROUGH
MANAGEMENT
AWARENESS**

The Restaurant Owner's Handbook

SUCCESS THROUGH MANAGEMENT AWARENESS

By; Jack C. A. Drewes

POSH Publishing Company
The Sakari Building
509 Central Ave, N.W
Albuquerque, N.M. 87102

Published by: POSH Publishing Company
          Sakari Bldg
          509 Central Ave, N.W.
          Albuquerque, New Mexico. 87102

Cover Design by Chestnut House, Chicago, Illinois.
Cover Photographer: Mr. Ted Streshinsky
Printed in The United States of America

Library of Congress Cataloging in Publication Data
Drewes, Jack C. A.
The Restaurant Owner's Handbook.
1. Restaurant Management--Handbooks, manuals, etc. I. Title.
TX911.3.M27D74 1988   647'.95'068   **87-32697**

ISBN 0-945034-01-6 (Hardbound Edition)
ISBN 0-945034-00-8 (Soft Cover Edition)

DEDICATION

*This Text is dedicated to the established restaurant owner
who has shown the determination to continue on
past the two year kill period, seeking success through
self improvement.*

CONTENTS

Section IV Finance / Accounting 55-64

Section V Production / Operations 65-80

Section VI Purchasing 81-102

Section VII   Safety / Security / Insurance 103-124

Section VIII Health & Nutrition 125-164

Section IX Equipment 165-206

Section X Maintenance

Section XI Marketing

Section XII Advertising

Section XIII Consultants / Information Access

Section XIV   Computer Evaluation, by
S.P.E.   275-312

Section XV The FUTURE   313-326

Reference Section   327-332

Index   333-338

INTRODUCTION

This book was written and produced for the established restaurant owner. In most instances it is applicable to all types of independent restaurants, including small, medium and large sizes.

Management of the restaurant business is a serious task, and it is becoming more so each year.

The many management areas of the business need as much attention by the owner (operator or manager), as does his or her concern for the prepared foods coming out of the kitchen. This fact constitutes more awareness of every management activity. You can also say that management acumen is integral to what comes out of the kitchen.

What we believe to be fundamental and routine today, is not necessarily sufficient for successful business achievement tomorrow. The need for restaurant owners to increase their management abilities is imperative and this text is written and designed with that objective in mind.

This book is strong with authoritative research sources, strengthening the points which must be made.

The italicized story type examples are often humorous, however, the serious message is still obvious. The characters names in these examples are chosen to represent job descriptions and/or the personality which is sometimes seen by the owner.

This book has been organized so that the busy owner may read parts, return to the place where he or she left off, or quickly look up particular aspects of interest at the time.

Owners need to address management thinking through words that are clear and unwavering, hence the delivery of the authors work.

M.F. Seaton
Publisher

XIII

ACKNOWLEDGMENTS

Producing this text required extensive research from authoritative sources who offer excellence in experience to their specific field. The following list of companies, corporations, institutions, government agencies and trade associations, exemplify cooperation and a sincere concern for the foodservice industry. We are indeed grateful to the people of these organizations for their unselfish material contribution and their tolerant behavior in the face of a probing and often overly persevering author.

The American Culinary Federation, St. Augustine, Florida.
Ansul Corporation, Marinette, Wisconsin.
Alto-Shamm Corporation, Menomonee, Wisconsin.
Arctic Industries, Inc. Miami, Florida.
Brian Sill Associates, Seattle, Washington.
Business Computer Applications, Kirkland, Washington.
Bunn-O-Matic Corporation, Springfield, Illinois.
Center for Disease Control, Atlanta, Georgia.
Duke Manufacturing Company, St. Louis, Missouri.
The Educational Testing Service, Princeton, New Jersey.
Foodservice Consultants Society International, Seattle, Washington.
The Food and Drug Administration, Washington, D.C.
The Hobart Corporation, Troy, Ohio.
The Institute of Shortening and Edible Oils, Inc. Washington, D.C.
John Sexton and Company, Chicago, Illinois.
Keating of Chicago, Chicago, Illinois.
Metal Masters Corporation, Salem, Mass.
Manitowoc Ice Machines, Manitowoc, Wisconsin.
The National Restaurant Association, Washington, D.C.
The National Sanitation Foundation, Ann Arbor, Michigan.
Nobel/Sysco Food Service Company, Denver, Colorado.
National Restaurant Supply, Albuquerque, New Mexico.
Quality Books, Inc. Lake Bluff, Illinois.
U.S. Range/Alco, Gardena, California.
The Vulcan-Hart Corporation, Louisville, Kentucky.
Wolf Range Company, Compton, California.
Woods & Poole Economics, Washington, D.C.

PERSONAL ACKNOWLEDGEMENTS

To my brother Tom Charles Drewes, who was the initial motivator
in starting this book and who provided meaningful words of
encouragement and business help, merits my respect and love.
A special thanks to Dr. A.A. Gonzales who relentlessly listened to my barrage of
opinions and gave assistance at every turn.
Most of all the biggest thankyou to a woman named Mary Frances;
Friend, Strong critic, stabilizing force, editorial wizard, and loving wife,
I owe much tenderness.

THE OWNERS IDENTITY

I

WHO IS THE RESTAURANT OWNER?

Variables, in the types and kinds of people who are the owners of the restaurants and food emporiums in this great America, is the best evidence of a free enterprise system which will ever be offered by any segment of business or industry.

A non educated foreign immigrant, unable to speak English, is the owner of a restaurant. The super star entertainer is the owner of a restaurant. In fact, people from all walks of life, from other businesses and industry, all colors and religions, handicapped persons, athletes who are no longer in the game, retired attorneys, a steel worker who moved away from the heat of the furnace, an advertising executive who moved away from the heat of his constituents and clients, and a clergyman who left the cloth to serve mans hunger for food better than he could serve his hunger for spirit. It seems ironic that the number of differences in the owners of independent eating establishments is as great as the millions of cooking methods which produce an inconceivable amount of recipes.

This number of differences in a great number of independent owners, (Estimated by trade associations and economic authorities to be in the proximity of 470,000) should be the most difficult business to organize, what with all those owner opinions and such. Yet we see an industry which has grown each year without fail, and a mutual owners agreement that the consuming public shall be fed with the best hot dogs, pizza, hamburgers, spaghetti, fried chicken, N.Y. steak, prime rib, lobster, soft shell crabs, wild rice, Danish pancakes, eggs benedict, blackened red fish, and millions more, to be produced with an amount of pride and concern, that each owner agrees is the best served by anyone.

Would you consider an owners aptitude ?

You are in the restaurant business ? Oh' Your in the Food Service business, no matter, we identify those to be close enough for the same consideration. There are all too many overlaps in this business to quibble over this identification. The important point is that you are an owner of a restaurant or you are retailing the personal service to customers who come to your establishment to partake of prepared foods for digestible and nutritional consumption. *It is also important that you are not new to this business, meaning that you have gotten through the first two year kill period.* You are a veteran owner. One who has shown the guts to continue and not give in.

See if these questions have positive or negative answers for you;

1. Do I work well with others?

2. Do I get along well with people?

3. Am I consistent?

4. Am I able to stay cool during a crisis?

5. Do I have a good sense of humor?

6. Can I pinch pennies when necessary?

7. Am I willing to both learn and teach?

8. Am I afraid to get my hands dirty?

9. Can I be flexible?

10. Most important: Do I like people?

To be an ordinary restaurant owner you do not need to be concerned about any of the above questions. To be happy, financially successful and enjoy the business each and every day, you must be **very concerned** about these questions. A perfect score is the answer,"YES" to all the questions except number eight.

As you can tell, these questions deal with personality, humility, curiosity, temperament, responsibility and of course frugality. Most of us are not perfect, so the odds are almost sure that at least one of the above questions points up a doubt about ourselves. Should this be the case, then you will know what it is that you need to work on. Is this psychology you ask? To a degree, yes it is. It merely breaks down those things that make you the way you are to others in business, so that you can identify possible flaws which may be preventing you from achieving financial success, happiness, and your enjoyment of work.

These things of which we speak have to do with attitude and just how you come across to the employee, customer, vendor and other people, which your business brings you in contact with each and every day. Yes' these questions are important, but not half as important as your answers.

Owners are Generally:

ONE..........In most cases, the restaurant owner is a creative person with many frustrations due to varied talents that try to surface, however thwarted, because he or she has an impatience which makes for difficulties with people.

TWO..........In other instances the owner is a people person, attracts others because of a great personality, however lacks either the creative ability or the organizational savvy that is basic to a well run operation.

THREE........A creative hands on chef who cannot remove himself or herself from the kitchen because of the rewarding satisfaction of titillating taste buds. This type of individual often enjoys teaching others, however, the students usually need to be worthy before the owner/chef will give lessons.

FOUR..........Interested in money first; Quality and Service afterwards. Can not stand regulations of any kind. Mans the cash register due to lack of trust, even of relatives or partners. Is generally not a pleasant person because they do not like themselves.

FIVE...........The investor owner loves the restaurant because of the in-place it is, the attention, the profits or tax relief. They are thrilled with the entire operation until it no longer boosts the old ego, or one of the other elements needs a serious remedy which puts the restaurant down on their list of interests.

SIX...............The dedicated owner is a restauranteur through and through and just can't seem to get enough of the entire business. This owner is in the kitchen looking over or participating in the preparation of some culinary delight. Greeting the guests (customers), concerned about the piano entertainment and each employees appearance and behavior. With this owner the earning power comes after the quest for excellence because they know it naturally follows. Sometimes however, this person is overly trusting and would benefit by limiting financial and inventory control to others.

These six basic owner types cover a broad territory of owners, but there are many individual types which are a cross between the six very basic types and still thousands more who have a myriad of traits and behaviors which in the end, makes us quite a bit different from each other, a blessing not always in disguise.

Special, is the veteran owner

After the first two years of the restaurant business, you can separate the ones with the desire and those who can't cut the mustard. That is of course if the "New to the business start up entrepreneur" lasts that long.

The veteran restaurant owner is special and most are completely unaware of it. Why special? Because it takes more of all the elements of management and creative talent than just about any business. Not all veteran owners have the educational background that a neuro-surgeon has, yet they often have talents which show carving abilities, that the surgeon can respect when it comes to cutting out a niche for oneself. Why is this owner unaware of his or her abilities? Mainly because they are too busy to notice anything except the business. And that is as it should be.

A Typical Owner: No such animal exists

There is not a stamp made which can contain all the elements of
one owner and be perfectly applicable to another. There may however, be a few similarities from time to time.

A Dawning:

*Mr. Naive and his lovely wife sold their home, liquidated most of
their possessions, left the executive jobs and the eastern U.S. city
they also called home. With a rental truck, he and she took all they
had left and went west to start a new life. This new life had only
one main thought,"Do Not Work For Someone Else", start your
own business. It really didn't seem to matter to the Naive's which
business, as they both felt confident, and knew the Sunbelt was
where growth and change would be. After settling in to a new
home and in a new southwestern city, they both looked at more
than fifty different types of business's that were for sale.*

*Mrs. Naive finally said, "You know, people have got to eat, and
the restaurant we looked at downtown should be a good start.
Okay, said Mr. Naive, I'll take the kitchen and you run the front
end of the business. And so, with all their high level management
training and experience, they dove into a business they both knew
little or nothing about.*

Mr. Naive bulls ahead

*All the employee's inherited did not resemble the likes of any other
experience that the Naive's had witnessed. They didn't seem to be
able to read the memorandums pasted on the walk-in door, much
less follow basic instructions, plus they all moved at a snails pace.
The forth day of ownership came soon enough when Mr. Naive
put his fist through the kitchen wall, swearing and acting in a fit of
rage, and all because the second cook and dishwasher came walt-
zing in the restaurant, both drunk and two hours late. That wasn't
enough, the two promptly asked if they could get paid today,
which caused Mr. Naive to pound the walls some more.*

The routines that day were so far behind that it didn't seem possible that the lunch hour had a prayer. "Both of you are fired, now get the hell out of here", Naive exclaimed across the length of the restaurant. Then came,"find me some more help", which he shouted at his wife, while the customers, with frightened expressions seem to say, "The beast is attacking".

It is safe to say that the first year was pure, uncluttered , hell for Mr. Naive and worse than that for Mrs. Naive, because of Mr. Naive.

Mr. Naive had to do some serious soul searching if he was to survive much less be successful, as he had in other things. Why?, He asked himself, is it this simple little business is so tough and yet running large companies so much easier? After more questioning and needed bell ringing by Mrs. Naive, Mr. Naive got it through his head that working with people requires a lot more attention in the independent restaurant than it does with corporate experienced personnel, who respond to verbal and written communications with accuracy and dispatch.

Many veteran owners can identify with the Naive's beginning.

An example of change and terror that is totally unexpected.That is what the Naive's went through and many others find the restaurant business something other than a snap. Oh' don't worry, the Naive's are survivors with plenty of determination as you will see in the form of appropriate examples in some other sections.

An Entrepreneur

According to most authorities, the definition of the word "entrepreneur" seems to revolve around the word "risk", as in "risk taker". A successful entrepreneur is one who uses his imagination, together with good judgement, attitude and communicative skills. He or she also delegates responsibility while maintaining control.

Example: Showing the difference between Mr, Entree and Mr. Risk. Both individuals, had $25,000.00. Mr. Risk took the money and went to the gaming tables in Las Vegas. Mr Entree, on the other hand, took the money and bet on himself, by starting a business.

This example shows that believing in yourself, is integral to the meaning of an entrepreneur.

Owners identification/ Closing message

From these descriptions, a story, questions and facts, you should know you are a different person from the rest of the pack, and you should be willing to work at those little weaknesses which most of us find difficult to admit.

We find that over the years of communicating with many business folks who work with, or are in some way connected to, the food service industry throughout the country, that some opinions say, "Restaurant owners have great egos". We also hear that restaurant owners, "know it all". These opinions make little difference, as most successful people do have a healthy ego, and owners who are reading to learn more can hardly be dubbed," a know-it-all".

Before you read the following sections.

Know that each section in this text we call a handbook, covers much, but not everything there is to know about management and the restaurant business, no single text could ever accomplish that. Reading, learning and being decisive should be a continuing quest.

Know also, that each sections role in the restaurant business is vital to the truly successful owner. Luck does not count in the restaurant business as it might at the gaming tables, however, recognizing opportunities and knowing what to do with them, does count.

Who it is, can be a teacher..
Why is the identity, a preacher?..
Of every type and style we find..
An owner is of every kind..
Bewildered and befuddled..
Drawn to havoc and confusion..
If things go right from day to day..
You can pray, OK..
It will happen and all come together..
And in all kinds of weather..
He is up and down..
Also a clown..
And knows the PROFITS will be found...

MANAGEMENT

II

THE OWNERS CODE

Management; What is it? Most Simply put; The responsibility of a person or persons who insure that an operation runs smoothly and efficiently. This entails, setting the pace and following through. Now what is successful management? The answer only applies to those who want to work for it: **Skilled Direction.** There are many definitions, written opinions, and talking seminars, all good avenues to learn. All the types and kinds of labels which adorn management cannot escape the all encompassing, hard work ethic and common sense. To arrive at achieving the ultimate levels of these two aspects, will take most of a lifetime for the greater percentage involved with the responsibility of ownership. So let us not even begin to fool ourselves about management and the owners abilities, simply learn and apply what you believe works for you.

Drive and determination are the basic ingredients to maintain a most important element to this business; *CONSISTENCY* . If the entrepreneur/owner involved with the restaurant business will go to work each day and set goals, then be sure that *consistency* in service, quality and performance are a part of the daily diet. Enough cannot be said for *consistency* and it's importance to the business.

The next understanding we want to have is that of Management applications; When a person is the owner or in a management position (like the appointed restaurant manager), does it mean that person follows the regulations or routines laid out ? Yes', indeed it does. The example you as owner will set by your own behavior, directly correlates to what the employee will mirror. So, what is meant by management applications? Basically, the following, four categories :

OWNER MANAGEMENT IS;

Making the policy.

Implementation of the policy.

Handling the exceptions to the policy.

Leadership.

Policy making can be the job description of restaurant personnel or the methods used in purchasing food and beverage, it can be the guideline to cash handling, or the method of cleaning a grill in the kitchen. The various policies and routines should be updated and/or corrected when appropriate. Management also demonstrates the ability to understand that learning from ones mistakes, is not only intelligent, but gives management respect from it's employees. The fact is, when you admit to being human, people feel as though they can communicate with you and it is important to have that information link. This does not mean owners should make a zealous effort, however, when the appropriate occurrence arises, show some humility by letting those around you know that you too can make a mistake.

You have seen the results from top management types all around you, in the newspaper you read about them, on the television you see them in action, and you may even wonder what it is that they possess that makes them so damn good. Well, it is simply the basics which the previous paragraph touches on and the following indicates.

We know that *implementation of policy* is simply the method of communicating what the policy (rules and regulations) is. This is usually accomplished by written and verbal means. It's always best to have policy written down.

Exceptions to that original rule? Yes there will always be exceptions to policy, even the law of the land has it's alterations. The professional management type is one that handles the *exceptions*, because you know it is easy to follow what is already in place. *Exceptions* require a lot of common sense and quick thinking. Management must be on the alert. Changes to the policy, you know the ones;

Normally the waitresses in your restaurant clean the tables, except Chips the dishwasher was asked to help out and he did so for two solid hours because business was booming. Since Chips did this little extra chore (in addition to the rest of his dish-washing du-

ties), should the waitresses compensate him from the tips they took in? Should management give him extra? Should management say that this was part of his job because he is getting paid by the hour?

There is a change here, regardless which one of the three choices you take. Example: The rule (policy) is simply that "Waitresses will clear their own tables". The owner, manager or operator that addresses the *exception* will do so knowing that this is only one of many situations which require his or her daily attention.

Leadership is the most important element to management as it demonstrates loyalty in those who follow; When it takes a team effort to get through a rough period, because the street in front of your establishment is being worked on for the next six months, you need leadership qualities, otherwise the consistent service and food product could be seriously altered. During such a time you need your employees to pull together, cooperate with temporary changes, as you do not want to see that cohesive, well organized operation, you've built, turn in the wrong direction.

Leadership is, setting the pace and working with the people who are looking for ways they can feel apart of the companies effort, and most of us want to feel as though we are wanted and needed. So if you get your hands dirty doing some job that will help teach an employee some trick or simpler way, do it. On the other hand, if you stop to learn from an employees activity which you notice is something new and maybe different, work with him or her, show interest, and you will find a benefit .

REMEMBER;

Consistency

Making policy

Implementing policy

Handling exceptions

Leadership

Management Approaches

Whether by objectives (Goal Setting), or any of the other tactical-management methods which have been portrayed in hundreds of texts, management approaches or methods are as simple or complicated as you want them to be. Management savvy is as simple as riding a bike, once you get going.

Approaches to management are methods of organizing your time, the judgement of priorities, together with managing the personnel who keep to the routines and various functions of your business. The six common groups that make up management functions to all restaurant businesses are in the left column,in bold face, while the restaurant counterparts are adjacent, to the right;

I. PERSONNEL
Employee records
Training

Kitchen, dinning room, cashier (all employees). Performed by the owner, or manager.

2.PRODUCTION
Output

Kitchen, food preparation. Performed by the owner or chef.

3.SALES
Customer-revenue

Waitress,waiter, server, hostess,or host. Performed by manager or owner.

4.FINANCE
Bookkeeping
Accounting

Lending institution and CPA. Performed by the owner and / or the CPA.

5.PURCHASING
Goods to be resold

Vendors goods to be resold. Performed by chef, manager and / or Owner.

6. MARKETING
Advertising
Growth planning

Advertising and Growth planning, performed by the manager and / or owner.

Note; "Performed by" indicates positions responsible for management decisions.

People approach, Is that MANAGEMENT?

You can bet your walk-in it is. Mr. Naive didn't realize how important attitude and his words with the employees were until he caught on. When he did, his new name, Mr. Know was indeed appropriate.

A very important aspect to management and for that matter, to the entire world outside your family, is; "You are who people think you are". Therefore, your behavior will demonstrate to others the kind of person they believe you to be.

There was a dishwasher named Saint Nick, not because he was generous the last week in December, but because of the nicks in the dishes. When Mr. Know bought the restaurant, Saint Nick was one of the employees who came with it. Mr. Know made it known through his behavior, that he wasn't afraid of getting his hands involved with work. Mr. Know worked the cash register, waited tables, cooked, and yes, he did dishes too. Mr. Know was doing these things to familiarize himself with all the various operations, and to let the employees know that through his behavior, they could hardly feel less than anyone else in the restaurant operation.

Through all his self job training, he listened to the employees complaints and suggestions for improvements, however he made no commitments at that time. After two weeks, things were falling into place and more employees were doing better. The dishes didn't acquire more chips or nicks, in fact Saint Nick was doing things which no one could believe. The dishes looked clean , the pots and pans never looked so shiny and spotless. The other employees started referring to Nick as the dishwasher, and to top it off Nick built a special screen for the sink in order to keep the paper, tooth picks and other unwanted items from getting into the drain system. Nick upgraded the level of dishwasher and actually set an example which many of the other employees followed.

The hands on involvement by Mr.Know and his ability to listen and show interest in others, made such a success, that in the three years which followed, Mr. Know opened the doors to two other locations, plus an in-plant cafeteria contract with a famous computer chip manufacturer.

So; Is attitude integral to management effectiveness?

Is keeping your cool and demonstrating an interest in people beneficial ?

Yes, and yes again.

Leadership: A position of control

Reading about various techniques will give you ideas for consideration. It is important to use approaches which are comfortable to you. If you find something that makes you feel uneasy after you try it, and yet it works for others, you should look closely at why you react that way.

The highest level of management expertise

Good management techniques and approaches are helpful to successful ends. One indication of management expertise is the art of turning a negative situation around and making it work for you.

Example 1: The complaining customer who does so for attention. The elderly lady who lives alone, has no one to talk to. She comes in the restaurant faithfully everyday, however, everyday something is wrong with the food. The owner picks up on this situation immediately and says,"I'am so sorry, Chef Samuel in the kitchen knew you were coming in today and prepared this just for you".

The elderly lady's face lights up and exclaims; "especially for me"? From that day on, everything was superb, the staff could do no wrong in her eyes.

Example **2:** A server (waitress or waiter) calls in sick, and the three you will have for this evenings shift are use to their particular sections.

You could tell them that the fourth section will bring them that much more in tips, plus you could have extra bussing help from the dishwashers or other kitchen help, and have the hostess take a few customer orders, generally dividing duties. Then tell them, "lets prove we are the best in service tonight".

Putting that extra zing into motivational expression does have a positive affect. If the employees see that you are up in attitude, they feel better, and negatives can be turned around even easier.

How does leadership happen?

Have you ever noticed how some president, chairman of the board or other titular head comes across so calm, comfortable and in control? Sometimes you might even admire their position of success or status. Well, most of us have, after all this gives us something to compare to or shoot for.

Our management character is Ms. Arrived:

She did indeed arrive to a level of success that is admired by all who know her. It didn't seem to start out that way, in fact Ms. Arrived had more difficulties than anyone would ever have suspected.

In the first place a female gendered person wasn't suppose to be on the deans list and show such a genuine interest in business management. Her peers in school were jealous of her determination and high marks, and never seemed to pass up an opportunity to pose sarcastic remarks about her physical structure or negative comments about female weakness. During her sophomore year there was an instance where she stood up in class and shouted out what jealousies and ignorance certain students (she named them)

*had. She realized her mistake after her father sat down and lis-
tened to her emotional words, and dried her tears. Daughter, he
said, you must understand two very basic rules to the human race;
"You are what people think you are, and there will always be
those who are unhappy with themselves". Your efforts to try and
turn those people around who are not happy with themselves will
not be in vane, so long as you are listening to their cries. Once
you find your way and feel comfortable with yourself, your attitude toward others around you will develop to the point which will
motivate the potential you see in them, even if they cannot recognize it.*

*After her fathers words were spoken, Ms. Arrived broke through
a new level of self control, and all through school and various
jobs , she found that the meaning of her fathers words changed,
became stronger and all encompassing.*

*She only spoke well of others, gave a great deal of attention and
credit to those she worked with. Even when she was being rewarded for her excellence in food service management, she gave
the credit to others.*

*It is not surprizing that Ms. Arrived learned through listening, ad-
mitted her mistakes, and went on working with the people around
her, never saying too much, but always taking the time to share
with employees, regardless of position. To the summit of her
goals (president of one of the largest food service chains) she is
the person people want to work with and listen to, as when she
does speak everyone in hearing range pays close attention.*

Do you think that Ms. Arrived was right by standing up in class
and letting the boy's feel some of the barbs in return?

If you say **no** then you are correct. But why? We all want Ms. Arrived to kill the loud mouths; Quietly of course. However, She
should have kept quiet and in control because it is obvious she is
more intelligent and would lose any chance for a position of control. Even though the jealous boys taunted Ms. Arrived, they still,
underneath it all, respected her abilities. How is that? Because the
boys didn't feel they were as capable.

The lesson here is simple: People think you are what your behavior demonstrates. If you listen and understand what their problem is, in this case, jealousy due to a feeling of inadequacy, then you should make them feel good about themselves.

We are not suggesting that management awareness in this single example will solve all the problems you will ever come in contact with. It seems clear that if you believe a person is worth the effort (and many more are, then you may be aware of) then you should take the lead, and show interest in the person (employee), regarding their job. By doing so, you can increase your leadership abilities.

Guidelines you should find helpful:

1. **LISTEN** and keep your words minimized as if each one cost five dollars.

2. **SPEAK** to the positive aspects of others.

3. **GIVE** the attention and credit to the other guy.

4. **KEEP** your personal business, private.

5. **NEVER** complain more than once a year and then do it constructively.

6. **ASK** employees how they would handle the problem.

7. **SHOW RESPECT**, use the language properly.

8. **KNOW** there is always a better way.

TIME MANAGEMENT

Looking for more TIME ?

We just can't seem to find the time; Where does time go?

Why didn't Albert Einstein make more hours in a day? After all, he and his Time-Space-Continuum might have had a handle on it.

Most restauranteurs are doers and need accomplishment, however, many just can not find the time to do all the tasks that they feel, need to be done, plus those items which will help the organization grow. Over and above the business aspects, it would be nice to plan a vacation as well.

There are numerous books and articles on the subject of Time Management and most in depth are produced by the Harvard Business Review, but, this is not the easiest reading.

Pretend you are a salaried employee

To better manage your time is like making money; If you are used to $500.00 per week in salary, you can only imagine what it would be like to receive $1,000.00 for the same hours, doing the same thing. You do not think about it because you have already convinced yourself that working another job or two is out of the question, as there is no more time to spare.

If however, you were able to accomplish more productivity, eliminate other payroll expenses for your Restaurant- Owner- Boss, and do it in the same amount of time that your regular job called for; Do you believe that the boss would consider a salary increase? Suddenly the $500.00 increase looks surprisingly probable, unless the boss wants you to go back to the former situation.

What are TIME savings systems about?

They are about <u>selection</u> and <u>limitations</u>. Select the priorities you need to address first, then set time limits for doing them. You need to eliminate wasted time, but of course you can never be accused of that.

Wasted time examples;

1. Meetings

2. Telephone calls

3. Paperwork

4. Travel

5. Conversation (The idle kind)

If you adopt practices that cut back the time allowed for these offenders, you will make a start toward effective measures.

At meetings make sure the agenda is to the point and yields answers. Go on to the next agenda item and do the same. Do not include notices or directives, put them on the bulletin board.

When on the telephone, be sure your call is organized to the point that you know what you want and how to get it. Be brief but polite. Do not waste time holding on the phone, waiting for secretarial screening, leave a message, stressing the other parties benefit to return your call.

Paperwork can stifle some owners and drive them into seclusion and total unavailability. This happens because the tasks that are not particularly enjoyed are left unanswered too long, which finally produces near hysteria.

Make a note to spend 20 to 30 minutes a day on paperwork, and pick a time when you believe you will be able to concentrate.

Find ways of cutting down travel time. Make one trip do what use to take three.

By now you must be fairly serious about your valuable time; Idle conversation will almost automatically be eliminated through your new approach to habit forming time savings.

Age and Experience affect TIME

Since you are the boss, your flexibilities in time active duties are even more controllable than an employee who has tasks to perform which are not usually flexible.

If you are able to increase your daily management activities by just 15 percent, that $500.00 increase to the energetic employee we mentioned, would not be very much, considering the talents and abilities you have to parlay.

Time saving controls and habits are worth years of productivity. See Chart 2-One on page 25.

The time saving percentage increases between age 30 ,40 and 50 because the experience factor, coupled together with the knowledge factor increases. These time saving percentages are not based upon a scientific study, they are simply approximations. If between age 30 and 50, an average business owner hasn't increased his or her experience and knowledge at least 50 percent, then we figure that person has been rather inactive.

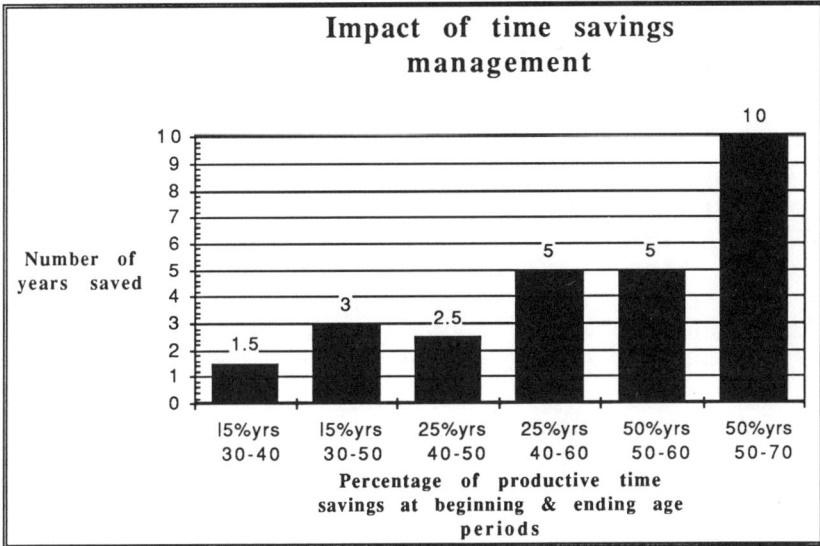

Impact of time savings management

Number of years saved

Percentage of productive time savings at beginning & ending age periods

	15%yrs 30-40	15%yrs 30-50	25%yrs 40-50	25%yrs 40-60	50%yrs 50-60	50%yrs 50-70
Number of years saved	1.5	3	2.5	5	5	10

CHART 2-ONE

Like the "Forest for the trees", it is difficult to see just how much time can be saved over a number of years. The previous table shows us just how many years can be saved if we manage our time effectively and efficiently.

There are exceptions who are like oak trees, who will have some difficulty getting started, but once they begin, even the most stubborn and set in their ways type, will draw upon their tremendous knowledge and do 50 percent more than they ever dreamed possible.

Identify wasted TIME

All of us do not fit into the same usage category, consequently we need to list the various habits, procedures and duties which make up a usual work day. Included should be those general items like; telephone use, travel time etc. Each day for the first two weeks you should make a list (like a diary) of all the time users. Next, put the amount of time it takes to do each task (the actual time spent). What you are formulating is a standards report of accurate time usage for yourself.

At the end of the two week period, you should compile the amount of time spent for each identifiable item and arrive at an average time spent for each. This will give you a representation of just how you are spending your time and from that you should see what areas need attention. If you think for one minute that this time study on yourself is less than serious, remember the years of productivity that you will be saving. If that is not like money in the bank, then what is?

Your Reaction at this juncture

After you have identified the many things that you actually do, and the written list is facing you, your reaction maybe; "Gee, I do all that"? "It doesn't seem possible." or, "I think I deserve a raise".

According to many phone calls which comprises a nationwide mini-survey, we found that most restaurant owners did not associate themselves as an object for time management disciplines. It seems as though owners do not look at themselves as a three piece suit executive working in an office building high in the clouds, whom they believe to be the type, time management is addressing. Boy, are they wrong. If ever there was a need for time management skills, it is the restaurant owner who would probably benefit the most.

Reason: The restaurant owner doesn't see himself or herself as a person in business who completes a list of functions, duties, and responsibilities which is greater than most any other position, regardless of profession or business.

Reverse Time wasting habits'

Keep a list of those compiled standards you put together. Now, as you go through the usual daily activities, (from telephone to checking on inventory depletions) you will see that the average time it used to take you, will almost force you to cut each activity shorter. It will also make you organize some particular activities better. The challenge of improving yourself when looking at the list should make you want to improve as it does when you stare at your score card at the end of eighteen holes of golf.

Procrastination (time waster)

There are three basic reasons for procrastination (to put-off or dawdle):

1.......... When a task is difficult. Like preparing for a business meeting with your CPA.

2........ When a task is distasteful. Like firing an employee that has been with you for ten years.

3........ When a tough decision presents itself. Like the two possible locations which are both ideal for your second restaurant.

A difficult task: Because the task appears too complex, what you do is simply get started by working on parts of it first. As you allow a certain amount of time for it, you will find that you are making head way, plus the more you learn about it, the more confidence you will have. The big item here is to get started, and keep at it.

A distasteful task:

These are the ones you do not want to do because they make you feel uncomfortable. This is a task that must be done first, don't wait. Look at this task from the positive point of view. In the case of an employee who must be terminated; Be objective, as the result is in the best interest of the restaurant and probably the employee.

A tough decision:

This one is generally caused by fear of making the wrong move. Thomas Edison made at least 4,000 wrong decisions when attempting to create a filament for the light bulb. Go with your gut feeling when the facts look so similar.

Final Time comment

Making up your mind to regiment yourself and form a habit through doing a time standards analysis, is not particularly easy for many. Knowing the result will save you productive TIME which cannot be replaced or bought, may motivate you.

Alcoholic Beverage

The management of beer, wine and hard liquor in any restaurant is a major responsibility at best. Accepting this responsibility appears to be a problem for some owners. If owners are willing to take pride in the food that is ingested by their customers, why is it difficult for management to show similar concern for alcoholic beverage consumed by their revenue source; The paying customer?

According to various surveys and statistics gathered on a national level, approximately 40 percent of the average (those who offer beer, wine and/or hard liquor) restaurants revenue (sales) represents alcoholic beverages. This also means some restaurants sell more than 40 percent and others sell less. In any case, beverage sales, may cause some owners to have a, " Sell all you can", attitude. Why not you say? After all, isn't that what business is all about? That is true, however, you want repeat customers who respect your property and the other people (customers and employees) who make your business successful.

Customers Vehicle, Alcohol, and You

If a patron wrecks his or her vehicle on the same evening after leaving your place of business, what amount of responsibility, if any, should the restaurant owner have? An important question to be sure, however, one that has not been completely and satisfactorily answered by legislative action, even though some jurisdictions do have enforceable laws.

What can an owner do?

Until the time comes when the definitive answers to alcoholic liability are both understood and generally acceptable by industry, and consumers alike, a common sense approach, with a sincere concern for the restaurant's drinking customer, is the best overall remedy.

Since owners and managers can not know the detailed medical condition of it's drinking patrons, it appears somewhat difficult to accurately judge, how much is too much. The following simple practices can make life in the drinking lane safer for all concerned:

1.

By keeping accurate bar tabs and/or guest checks that clearly indicate customers consumption, owners have evidence which may support possible liability questions.

2.

When you, or a management level employee, identify a customer whom you feel has had enough alcoholic drink, let them know quietly and as diplomatically as possible that; "It is your health and safety the restaurant is concerned about".

3.

When a customer is in, or rapidly approaching an intoxicating condition believed to be serious enough to impair driving skills; Try to locate and identify another member in his or her party that will manage the driving. If the person (intoxicated) is alone, call a taxi or contact a friend of the customers who can lend assistance.

These three practices are simple guidelines, and not total answers to a continuing complex problem. Adopting a healthy attitude and demonstrating genuine concern will provide the owner with some peace of mind, knowing he or she is protecting the business by helping to insure the customers safety.

III

Personnel Management; What Problem?

When you ask a restauranteur: What is the biggest problem in your business? Over half of the time the owners reply will be; "Employees". Certainly there is some justification in the owners answer.

If anyone believes that there are simple and quick solutions to an industry with over eight million employees, then every restaurant owner, manager, and operator will probably give the creator of that solution five minutes of silent prayer, every day of the National Restaurant Associations annual convention. What can be offered to restaurant owners is common sense approaches to motivation, reminders to keep cool, ideas on making routine paper work effective, and more.

Who gets the blame?

At one time or another in your restaurant experience you have found it justifiable to give a little hell to one of your esteemed employees. Most figure that is normal, in fact, many believe it is a part of the business. All the blame and fault finding, somehow doesn't seem to cure an awfully lot. Most of the time finding the culprit who misplaced a favorite spatula seems to evoke a little of Sherlock Holmes, and the owner becomes a super sleuth, trying to uncover the mystery. The only problem is that Sherlock wasn't an executioner.

Finding a reason for an employees mistake, putting him or her at ease and identifying the mistake to see if the system may need an adjustment, is a sure sign that the owner is on a track which can only lead to success. If on the other hand, the employee needs training; Why wasn't the employee trained first? The blame can be easily turned around on the owner, for he or she is the one with the experience and the responsibility.

Many owners think that training is mostly a waste of time because the employee turn over in the industry is relatively very high. Thank everything beautiful that many more owners do train employees, for they must realize that "what goes around, comes around".

What should we do to help control turn over?

After your organization is tuned up, by providing job descriptions, reasonable training programs (given the size of your operation), understandable routines, strong but fair rules and regulations, motivational ideas & practices, you will begin to attract employees who are less inclined to risk losing their job. Training an employee, who has been properly screened for the job is not wasted time. Even if you face a day where you are caught short handed, it is far better to train a new employee properly than face alternatives which could spell disaster.

Who should you hire?

There are those people in the work force who just don't care; About you, your business, other people and most of all, about themselves. Don't hire them, unless you don't care either. What a restaurant owner is looking for in an employee is results, not hard luck stories. If the owner doesn't agree with this view, then how will the restaurant succeed, and pay taxes, so that welfare can assist the genuine person in need?

The high standards of a restaurant who serves food and beverage to be ingested by the public, needs applicants for employment who are first of all;

Neat and clean in appearance

When this first criteria is met, then it is generally appropriate to consider an application. After the application form is reviewed, an interview should follow.

The application form and interview

Whether you use a standard application form which is available through the nearby stationery store or a customized version of your own, it is important that you incorporate questions that pertain to particular job openings.

<u>Waitress, waiter or other server:</u> Questions need to be addressed concerning their personality;

1. Do you like people? why?

Note; The servers ability to communicate with the customer in a pleasant manner is one of the most important elements to the restaurant business.The server represents you and the restaurant business.What ever comes out of the servers mouth, and is directed at a customer should be one of the highest concerns you have.

2. What is your reaction if you are faced with a day when you have twice as many tables to serve because another employee won't be in attendance? How will you handle the situation?

<u>Cooks, chefs, kitchen help and dishwashers, etc</u>: Questions about personal hygiene, details about experience and how they react to taking orders during times of hectic pressure due to unforeseen circumstances.

1. When you come to work, do you wash your hands and clean your fingernails? Why?

2. Do you use a hair-net under the kitchen hat? Why? If you do not, why do you think you should?

<u>Questions</u> which revolve around your greatest concerns that affect specific job descriptions are certainly important to your business, therefore you should ask those questions on the application form,

and during the interview when appropriate. When you read the answers to these types of questions you will learn more about the person, and this will provide you with a more meaningful interview. You will also learn how to tell the "movers from the shakers".

Note: Since there are legal sensitivities which concern the rights of people applying for work, it is important that your additional questions (appearing on the application form) are strictly involved with the performance of the position (job opening). It is generally wise to stay away from questions that do not apply to the job description, unless there is a good business reason.

Finding employee applicants

The most widely used methods are still the newspaper classified ads, and the unemployment office. The bulletin boards in schools, universities, public offices, membership clubs, and churches are often times more fruitful than traditional methods. Many times a restaurant will have a sign in the window; This is not a good idea as it conveys a negative connotation to the customer.

Mr. Naive learned that a certain Ms. Supreme had a very successful restaurant business which never suffered the short handed syndrome which he encountered on too many occasions. Ms.Supreme had 22 restaurant outlets and found that many young professional hopefuls who were seeking acting careers, or needed money for law school, or potential employees who were in school, etc, needed living expenses and tuition money to continue their quest for fame. Ms. Supreme devised a comprehensive plan which offered medical benefits, excellent pay and a "return to work deal", which afforded the employee a feeling of confidence and security should their professional job trial period or audition not work out. Together with high powered promotional opportunities, Ms Supreme managed to keep 85 percent of these employees plus a backlog of ready to work applicants. ....What Mr. Naive learned from this supreme example, (on a smaller scale) turned him into Mr. Know who opened a second restaurant near the university, which provided an excellent employee work force that he turned into a great success .

Whether your advertisement for help is through the newspaper, bulletin board or other printed message, keep it brief and to the point. Long descriptions are costly and afford the applicant more preparation than required.

Advertisement message information

l. Restaurant name (unless this will cause problems with present employees).

2. Address (where to apply for employment, not always the restaurant itself).

3. Phone number (only if the telephone does not interrupt business, otherwise applicants should come to the address).

4. Title of the position which is to be filled.

5. Part time or full time.

6. Time of day applicants should either telephone for an appointment or apply at the address. It may be applicable to indicate the convenient days.

7. Experience necessary or no experience needed. There is generally no need for in depth explanation as you need applicants. In some instances (few), more detailed information may be required.

Employee Records

In addition to the employees application form, and the payroll record, it is beneficial to have the employees record of attendance, job description, and notations of either awarding successes or failures. Whether you utilize a computer system or do paperwork by pencil and form, it is easy to keep an appropriate form-card attached to the payroll record or the same information filed in the computers memory. The time clock (if paid by the hour) data can also be integrated into the computer for the employee evaluation process.

If you are the owner of a large restaurant (which may include additional outlets) your employee records should contain more information about each of the employees and their performance over time:

Employee record:

1. weekly, monthly, quarterly and annual evaluations.

2. Evaluations: **Grading:** Indicate, Less than, meets, or exceeds regulations (job descriptions and rules).

   a. Hygiene
   b. Dress code
   c. Attitude
   d. On time (to work)
   e. Performance of duties
   f. Special notations:

   Example; This employee was leaving work when she noticed a customer out of gas, the employee siphoned gasoline from her vehicle and put it into the customers car. The grateful customer wrote a letter to the restaurant commending the employee and the restaurant.

The smaller restaurant can also utilize the employee record, however, it may be too much paperwork to implement all the details and frequency of evaluation which the larger business maintains.

Time cards and Clock:

If the employee is paid by the hour a time clock is a necessary tool that indicates what the hours worked should be. This information is compiled for payroll activities. Sometimes employees have been known to "clock in" or "clock out" for other employees. This behavior should never occur, and it is correct to have strict rules which alert employees to your company policy and even the consequences. To help avoid this practice, it is wise to have the time cards picked up immediately after shift changes. The cards are replaced prior to the next shift change. This way when someone is late, the employee is directed to the supervisor or person who keeps the cards when they are not in the rack next to the time clock, giving control of the situation to management(the owner).

Employee suggestion programs

Suggestion programs are very beneficial to growing restaurants, whether they are large or small. Admittedly it is somewhat of an extra amount of paperwork which the small restaurant owner feels he or she doesn't need, but just maybe this is another one of those steps which contribute to successful ends.

What are some benefits and reasons for a suggestion program?

1. Most employees need motivation other than a paycheck. Suggestion programs can produce a rise in employee productivity.

2. Often times, employees have ideas which result in time saving techniques, new menu items that are hot sellers, health and safety tips which can reduce insurance premiums and prevent injuries.

3. It even happens where an employee has increased business by addressing potential opportunities;

a.*The factory or large company needing a cafeteria which you might provide both work force and prepared menu items. An employee presented this one to his restaurant owner and the owner went with it, successfully. The employee found a new color television set at work, it had a red ribbon and a card with the employees name that said thank-you, signed by the owner.*

b.*The country club which lost it's previous food operator is looking for a replacement contract. An employee found out about it, worked up a basic scheme, presented it to her restaurant boss. She won a $500.00 cash award and the owner won a ten year contract, suppling the labor and management expertise for the country clubs food service needs.*

A small price to pay with one hell of an owners reward.

There are many such happenings as these, just call some of the more successful restaurants around the country and you will see. Not one of the restaurants which the author contacted (who had an employee suggestion program), had nothing but praise for it.

Guidelines for the suggestion program:

1. Be fair, don't do for one what you wouldn't do for another.

2. If you think that monetary compensation is appropriate, set up a $5.00, $25.00, $50.00 and $100.00 program. If the benefits are felt over a reasonable length of time, you can always increase the compensation reward.

3. Other rewards for beneficial suggestions: Tickets to ball games and other sporting events, three day vacations to sunny places, radios, television sets, etc....

4. When you start a program, do it with a little zest. Get the employees started by showing interest yourself. Tell them about the employee who located a business opportunity, or give them ideas about increasing productivity, safety, saving on utilities, laundry, garbage bags, mop heads, locating vendors who end up providing better products at better prices, etc.There are thousands of ways to make improvements which will benefit the restaurant business, and that is what you are doing, with the added help of the employees brain.

5. Use a suggestion box or tell the employees to deliver the suggestion directly to you. That way you can thank them for their participation and re-motivate again. The box is a little cold, however it does work.

6 . Put a suggestion program notice on the bulletin board periodically. When you get interest from the employees, tell them about it. If your not getting results as soon as you want, let the bulletin board show that "this month the $50.00 (or what ever compensation is appropriate) reward is going to a charity". That will tell them you are serious about the program and should stimulate interest.

7. Once you get things rolling, you must keep the program going with ideas. The benefits can be fantastic if you are the leader and smart enough to utilize the brains of all your employees, by getting them to work for you in addition to their everyday work.

8. Lastly; The successful suggestion program gives the employee a feeling of being a part of the overall picture, together with better prospects of promotions and pay raises. When the employee feels good about having a job, a major part of their security, is in knowing that the restaurant business is doing well, there-by contributing to the employee benefits through reward and a greater sense of job security.

Your ideas coupled together with your interest in your own **suggestion program** can be very successful. Many such programs in other industries have had their pros and cons which most of us have heard. Program failures are due to; 1.... lack of enthusiasm, 2........lack of perseverance, and, 3....lack of some imagination. Since the established restaurant owner generally has an abundance of these three elements, it would appear that restauranteurs should be capable of teaching the other industries just how a suggestion program really works.

Job Descriptions:
(Not an easy task, but well worth the effort.)

It is sure easier to give a new employee a typed up definitive outline of his or her responsibilities and authority, than to devote more of managements time constantly explaining and showing the new employee how things are accomplished. Certainly there is an amount of "show and tell", but with a complete job description, the employee knows the answer to a great many questions. In many instances it seems as though the new employee is, "in the way" more than helping the first couple of days on the job. This just isn't necessary.

Many restaurants put an employee to work right away by chopping onions (if in the kitchen) or another task which keeps them busy while the manager figures out some other near disaster. To justify his or her actions, the manager (owner in many cases) thinks that the new employee will learn as they go, or assumes so, because the new employee has worked the same job in another restaurant. This may be true, however; Does he or she do the job the way your operation is organized? But that isn't all there is to it.

Because there isn't a job description and a formal training program in most restaurants, the employee is seen doing very little, or nothing at all. When this happens and you the owner see it, you get angry with the person in charge, and they tell you that they are busy setting up for the rush hour and just don't have time to train the new employee right now. Job descriptions are worth the effort.

Definitive job descriptions help eliminate much of the first few days of nothingness and confusion for the new employee, because he or she can better understand the routine, compare to past experience, and see where help is needed.

It doesn't matter how small or large a restaurant is, taking the time to prepare for employment positions means that you must know what it is you want the future employee to do. The job description should do that. When you do not have to repeat the same verbiage over and over, and the employee needs minimal supervision, labor is utilized in a more effective manner.

On the other hand, we do not want anyone to believe that the job description will do everything that on-the-job training will accomplish. In all cases, new employee past experience and abilities vary, and so the attention which supervisory employees need to give will also differ from new employee to the next new employee. This is a normal condition and is to be expected.

The strongest reason for job descriptions

Once an owner has determined what his or her formula for success is, the owner would like to keep things organized and rolling in just that manner. When new employees come along, they are usually familiar with other restaurants and their procedures. You the owner want the new employees experience but you want the employee to "Do It My Way". This situation is often very discouraging to the new employee because they are confused in the first place, or confident to the point that they already know how they are going to change operations to suit their habits and likes.

If you have worked hard to establish routines and procedures that provide the performance you are truly happy with, the last thing you want is for a new chef to change everything around so that you can't find the melted butter for the toast, let alone the marinated Fajita beef (strips of inside skirt steak), or worse yet, you find that the chef has caused an unpleasant condition between other employees because of favoritism or confusion in operations due to changes in preparation procedures. There are hundreds of downside consequences which are the result of new employees being unaware, you know what they are, therefore a complete job description is of immense help.

Well defined job descriptions give the employee the basic parameters of the job they will be doing, and who they report to given particular circumstances. The restaurants procedures which affect that employees position are also included so that there is no misunderstanding. Deviations or changes to restaurant procedure, be they kitchen or dinning room oriented etc, need the approval of management (The chef, manager, operator, or owner, etc.), according to the owners designation.

If these elements (Job descriptions) are not followed in some organized and effective manner, the owner runs the risk of having his or her systems and procedures altered, which   produces owner fits of temper, unhappy customers and in turn can disrupt the entire operation.

Note; It is also appropriate that the employee be given access to company policies. These policies (rules and regulations) may be located on the bulletin board or printed sheets that are handed to the new employee.

What goes into a job description?

The following is a basic outline of elements that make up the job description. The larger the restaurant operation, the more detail is required because of the number of levels of authority, overlaps and amounts of responsibility:

1. _Employees Job Title;_ _Regular waitress, head waitress, regular waiter, head waiter, cashier, line cook, server, senior server,regular cook, cook, chef, master chef, executive chef, first dishwasher, regular dishwasher, kitchen helper, hostess, assistant manager, etc,etc_..

2. _Duties(Responsibility);_ _Describe all the duties this job entails by going through a typical work day in your mind, taking step by step._

Example: The dishwasher; On the day shift, you start work at 6:30 A.M. This means dressed with white short sleeved shirt, company tie (furnished), white paper hat (furnished), brown vinyl apron (furnished), and black or brown rubber sole shoes, and clean pressed solid color slacks (Brown, black, grey or dark green).Your shift is over at 2:30 P.M. when it is time to go home.
Hygiene : Specify hair length, and other personal hygienic aspects which are appropriate to the job and company policy.

Note: The concerns of public safety far outweigh perspective employees choice of their personal cleanliness-standards. Your right as owner to establish hygienic standards for the elimination and/or control of bacteria contamination (be they foodborne or other) comes before the employees choice of standards.

Procedure: Dishes are to be carried from the dinning room table stand to the dish-room sink stand using the bronze colored trays. The three well sink should contain the following:

Left sink; Hot soapy water (one cup powdered type-A soap), used for the purpose of soaking pots and pans from the kitchen.

Middle sink: Keep portable screen rack clean and in-place during dish-washing operation, as this prevents unwanted items like, paper, tooth picks etc, from clogging the plumbing system. This sink is used for final rinse of dishes prior to right -hand sink use.

Right hand sink; After food waste and garbage has been removed from the dishes, pots and pans etc, and the middle sink rinse has been preformed, you should soak the plates, cups, bowls and other china in this right hand sink. Dishes are then washed off and placed in the type 2 rack for the dish-washing machine process.

Silverware process: After removing the silverware (flatware) from the bussing tray , rinse it off in the middle sink and place in the silverware soak container. This container is filled with hot water and 3 ounces of type-3 liquid soap. When the silverware container is half filled , remove the silverware and prepare for the first dish-washing process. Place silverware in the flat Type rack with the screen insert. Run this rack through the dish-washing machine, then remove silverware and place each knife, fork and spoon in the type four rack (silverware stand rack) with the handles up. Important' The part of the silverware which is used to touch the food and the customers mouth , must be placed downward, so that at no time will any food handler touch that part of the silverware. When you have filled this rack properly, run it through the dish-washing machine for a second time. When dry, place rack at the dinning room stand in it's proper place.

Glasses: When removing glasses from the dinning room container, rinse them off in the middle sink before placing them in the glass rack (type 5). Lipstick marks on the lip of the glass must be washed by hand prior to placing the glasses in the type 5 glass rack. Run glasses through the dish-washing machine after the rack is full. After the glass rack is completed the wash cycle, place it on the drying shelf. Within l5 minutes the glass rack containing the clean and dry glasses can be brought to the dinning room glass stand.

Dish-washing-Machine-Maintenance: *The temperature gauge must show a reading of not less than 135 degrees Fahrenheit during the dish-washing machine operation. This is a low-temp type of process which utilizes a chlorination chemical dispensing action in addition to the soap and rinse cycles. If the temperature gauge dips below the 135 degree mark you are to notify your supervisor or the kitchen manager immediately. This machine has two removable catch-screens which need to be cleaned prior to the next shift, Ask your supervisor to show you where these screens are located.*

The dish-washing machine also needs to be wiped down, and checked by your supervisor once a day. Should the three chemical containers get low on their contents (Below level marks), you should replace them with full containers from the chemical storage area. You will be given assistance on this maintenance task when the need arises, thereafter, you will follow the routine on your own.

Placement of washed items: The kitchen area has specific places for all utensils , pots, pans, knives, etc. After your review of the places where these items are kept, you may have questions. It is important that you ask rather than put an item where they are not expected to be.

Other Duties: Rest room cleaning, trash emptied, area sweeping and moping, etc, etc...
And you would explain each of these and others as if you were approaching the job yourself.

3.Authority: *Here you are describing the limits on the employees authority concerning their duties,and when a question, problem or situation demands the authority of a particular supervisor or other company employee.Try to provide as many answers in order to minimize the amount of doubt.*

Job description summary:

To accomplish complete job descriptions is not an easy task, in fact it takes time, thought and typing, however, the rewards are more impressive than you may imagine. The following are five points to remember:

1. Once accomplished , the new employee will require less supervisory attention which provides for an employee who can get to a productive work stage faster.

2. Provides less confusion and better organization for all employees, therefore increasing productivity.

3. Less mistakes are made by new employees, which saves time and equipment.

4. After your first set of job descriptions are finished, all you ever need to do is up-date them and have copies made. If you choose to produce them with the aid of a personal computer, you will find it very simple and fast to make corrections and additions.

5. Job descriptions which are produced and used effectively, give the management (the owner) better control of employee activities as they are an accurate reference point.

It's not <u>one</u> that counts.

It is a good idea to be thoughtful and considerate of your employees, as this attitude makes it easier to obtain cooperation. When the little things slip by, often times they add up to a dollar figure which astounds you.

Example: The free soft drink program which you may have for your employees needs control. One more cola or other soft drink per employee can add up:

10 employees X 256 work days per year = 2560 servings.

Now if you charge a customer fifty cents for each serving, that is $1280.00.... That is just one per day.

35 employees X 256 work days = 8960 servings.

Now let us say that these 35 employees have an average of three servings per day more than you have allowed for:

Would you believe that comes to $13,440.00 (Dollars based on charging fifty cents per serving)?

The emphasis here is, " **it's not one that counts"**, it is all the others which are not paid for, except by the owner.

Most of the time employees do not realize how these little items add up, so you should post an annual accumulation of various expenses on the bulletin board. After you do that, be sure you control these expenses, after all, the set amount of cola or coffee, etc, you provide an employee should be enough, after that anyone can consume water or pay their way.

Use of the Telephone

It's not funny when you miss a call-in order for 28 dinners, just because the telephone was tied up. The same is true when potential customers calling in for reservations, find they can no longer wait, and decide to go elsewhere.

It's bad enough to lose any amount of business when poor service to the dinning customer is caused by an employee not paying attention to the job, but when you lose a customer that you haven't had the chance to serve, that's inexcusable, and yes, management is to blame.

In any size restaurant, the telephone is a very important link with suppliers and customers being the highest communicative priorities. This is particularly true when there is a limited number of telephone lines.

Employee use of the telephone should be restricted to instances of emergency. When employees are at work, they should not receive personal calls unless the call is a genuine emergency. This is not a case of being a hard-liner as some people may think. Business in the restaurant should be kept professional, and personal business should be kept away from the restaurant operation.

If an owner has limited telephone lines; Should customers be allowed to use the telephone? No. Do not interrupt incoming or out going business communications that are important to your restaurant. If the demand for customer telephone use is that great, have a pay phone installed.

Firing an employee

Letting an employee go is not always easy and is certainly not a comfortable thing to do.

You have all the reasons and explanations for terminating the employment of an employee, so don't procrastinate. Having an employee who is not a team member can cause harm to your business through his or her example to others, much less the deed itself, what ever it may be.

Termination of an employee from his or her job is something that should be done in private. Do not allow interruptions.

Plan a particular time of day (if possible) which is convenient for you and the business. Never show any signs that you are upset or emotional at all. Speak in a calm voice and show some interest in the employees behalf.

The most important aspect is, **"Not to burn bridges behind you"**. Like so many dealings with people in business you never want to leave a bitter taste in the other persons mouth, because you never really know what the future will bring. Many times restaurant owners have rehired an employee that they previously fired and found some work force relief. This is not generally a good idea.

Be honest and look the other person in the eye, like you really mean for him or her to learn from your words. Show that you care, even if you know they may not. Let them know that you are sorry that things didn't workout.

Lastly: Don't take more than 10 minutes to fire an employee. There is no point or gain for either party.

Managements actions to improve employee relationships:

Owners need to be aware of their conduct toward employees and the owners subordinate management staff (managers, chefs, hostess, etc) and their conduct toward other employees. The following five points provide the owner with some ways to improve relationships;

1. PRAISE WORKER MORE OFTEN: A most common management mistake is not praising the employee at all , much less not enough. You can't take good employees for granted and expect them to do high levels of work achievement. Often times, a little praise is better than a raise.

2. ACCEPT PERSONALITY TRAITS: The mistake in asking an employee to pay less attention to detail (who is meticulous by trait) will only alienate him or her. Learn to work around the situation unless of course the preoccupation really reduces effectiveness. You might consider use for this employees trait by providing beneficial assignments. The key is to distinguish opportunities for this type of individual.

3. PRONOUNCEMENTS: The desired result is to boost the workers enthusiasm so the objective is reached. Unless there is a plan of action, it is not wise to make pronouncements. The employee continues to work and is rewarded in the same fashion, but in time will believe the pronouncements to be meaningless. Make no pronouncements with out a planned back up.

4. CONTROL ANGER: If the head of the shed (boss) would realize that each time you show anger, respect for the boss diminishes. It is not easy to learn control of this anger which releases most of all when standards are not met, or stupid mistakes occur.

You might consider a private corner where you can punch a stuffed toy, or you may find release by running around the block at top speed, but do not show others how susceptible your emotions are.

5. EMPLOYEE PREPARATION FOR MEETINGS: When meetings are called and employees cannot possibly prepare, how can they participate? Allow enough time for employees to prepare for a meeting so they may make a constructive contribution to the business. If you wish to voice edicts, put them on the bulletin board, but keep them out of the meeting.

Elmo's Motivation

Elmo wants to get off from work, go home, get a can of beer, watch television and pretend that he is Lawrence of Arabia. If Ambition was gold, Elmo could be the world debt. He does work mind you, in fact, Elmo does very well at what he does, a cook with experience in most areas of kitchen preparation, except his limits to growth are limited as he does not see benefits.

In this case the owner was obtaining a loan for a major restaurant addition and he needed a head chef he could depend on. Elmo was called into the owners office and learned that Elmo had this fascination with Asia and travel. Near the end of the meeting, which was mostly small talk up to this point, the owner asked Elmo if he would consider the chefs job. The pay increase was nice, however er Elmo wasn't excited about the extra hours which would be required from time to time. Then the owner said," If you perform this job well for twenty four months, I'll give you a three week paid vacation with round trip tickets to Bombay India" . Elmo was hooked, he was so excited over the trip to Asia that the promotion was almost ignored.

Elmo's new job at the restaurant was performed with excellence, hard work and longer hours than required. The restaurant was very successful and Elmo made that trip. The owner learned quite a bit too, not the least of which was to find out more about your employees, then motivate them.

All Elmo needed was a chance at having a dream come true which he never believed would ever happen. The owner showed the employee a way of providing the dreams, and the employee performed.

If you give attention to employee management, from the moment of seeking help through the employees tenure, then the benefits will belong to all concerned.

The employee is dutiful ..
Sometimes even beautiful..
As I watch and learn..
I do a slow burn..
Up and down..
They run around..
Showing their stuff you know..
My temper does flair..
But I know I must care..
For payday is when they glow.
Sometimes I'm proud..
As I shout it aloud..
You know son you've done something well..
The very next day..
there is no son you say..
He's just told me to go to hell...
Forget it you owner, and try to relax..
there is another fine son coming in..
As he starts in to work..
You feel like a jerk..
As this one is better than him...

FINANCE/ACCOUNTING

IV

OBTAINING A LOAN;
IT'S A GOOD PROSPECT

Despite the often rumored comments about the failure rate or the little voices which seem to cry negative regarding the restaurant business, more loans are lender supportive of the independent restaurant owner, than most any other business. With 470,000-plus independent restaurant and food service establishments, is it any wonder that you may hear that there are more failures? In any case, the restaurant business failure rate is high where the beginner is concerned, not necessarily so with the two year or better established restaurant owner who has become a veteran.

If you put all the banks, savings and loan institutions, car dealers, printing companies and jewelry stores together, you would come up with less than half the number of independent restaurants, and that is being conservative. So where did all this business about restaurants being a poor risk come from? It is simply a matter of numbers and the more you hear about particular segments, one way or another, words are transmitted, related, inflated and generally taken for granted.

THE QUALIFIER

Banks and lending institutions usually have commercial specialties which they prefer because they have the most and best experience with them. Even with a lender who specializes in a different area, the qualified applicant, no matter what the business, can obtain a loan, yes, often with the proviso that the business is one in which the people at the bank or lending institution can relate to.

The emphasis is not on the business, but rather the individual who is applying for the loan. The importance that is placed on the business in the eyes of the lender is it's net earnings ability, it's past performance in gross sales compared to it's debt, and the fact that there are no liens upon the building or contents. Over and above that, the lender is looking for your credit rating, your amount of capital, the amount and forms of collateral you have and your character. The last requirement seems to get the least attention and yet can cause the most unsatisfactory results. Character to a lender means that you look and act the part of a successful, hard working, honest, well spoken individual, who projects positive thoughts.

A REASON FOR BORROWING

Reasons for obtaining loans are usually for business growth, and most generally can be substantiated. You may need the additional cash for equipment, because your productivity is hampered by severe increases in sales, or, expansion of the building and facilities, or, an additional restaurant unit needs to be constructed. Maybe you need to redecorate, put in new tables or booths. You could even decide to do 24 hour delivery service because the Air Force base near your location has given you a contract for particular food service, and you need delivery vehicles. The reasons for dollars needed for business growth are multi-numerous. All of the reasons are based on one main factor to the lender; They mean to increase the dollar income, giving you greater pay back ability. The banker (lender) likes that.

Suspect Reasons

Your business is down and you believe that an advertising program will do the job. This can be delicate, however, you should first evaluate the reason for the down turn in business. If your quality, service and price are in good shape, and people can get to your location without problem, then it may make good sense to advertise. Just be sure you are justified and not just trying to save a business which may be on the way out. It is always best to put dollars aside for advertising. Your success in obtaining the loan really depends on your relationship with your own bank.

You wish to consolidate debts to suppliers. Needless to say, you shouldn't allow supplier debts to accumulate. The supplier relationship and your debts owed will certainly be scrutinized by the bank or lending institution. If you intend to borrow money to pay supplier debts, it is most important to have a good rapport with the lender.

Other Loan Sources

You know that they are there; Credit card limits, second and third mortgages on the house, high interest lenders and the loan sharks themselves, so why don't you get your money through one of these means? Because you are too intelligent, and you realize that your income producing ability will be cut away just that percentage amount more and will usually cause greater financial problems. However, it's nice to know you won't need these sources if you stick to the rules of the game.

LOAN Preparation

When you are prepared, you are assured of some attention from the loan officer. Being prepared does take a little doing, however, each time you do it, like anything else, it gets easier and faster. By being prepared you will have copies of the following listed reports and forms;

1. Profit and loss statement for the last quarter.

2. A complete financial statement, listing assets and liabilities.

3. The last 3 years income tax reports which include profit and loss statements.

4. Projected financial balance sheets, for the next two years.

5. A type written explanation of your reason for the loan and the general marketing description of your business and how you expect to fare.

Even when you have a good relationship with a bank and you feel so confident about loan prospects, it is a good practice to be prepared, as the lender will only respect your professional behavior all the more. If you have computer assisted abilities at your disposal, producing these preparation forms can be fast and very inexpensive. If you can have the blank forms typed up, do so, as the least amount of work you give your accountant or CPA, the less expensive your costs to obtain a loan will be.

Financing a Large restaurant

Bigger projects demand large sums of money. If you plan to build a restaurant designed around your dream ideas and the concept encompasses everything from consultants to full POS computer assisted systems, plus state-of-the-art production equipment, and all the other elements, it is going to take more than the $150,000.00 you saved over the last 15 years. In fact, most complete full service restaurants with bar, lounge, 350 seat dinning room, decorations, full blown kitchen with top equipment, land including parking lot, brick or stone construction, landscaping, class "A" sign, total computer assisted systems, storage for all foodstuffs for one month during peak periods, a first class advertising program for a six month period, complete uniforms and training program for employees and stocked inventory, will run between a 1.5 and 3.5 million dollar average cost depending on location. These average cost figures include attorneys fees and services by a professional consultant.

Whether you form a corporation with many investors, find a venture capital financier who will back the project, acquire a limited partnership investment plan, seek low interest small business administration (SBA) loans and use them in combination with bank loans, real estate property investment shelters used with a limited partnership or corporation to buy the property and lease it back to the restaurant, plus many other financing schemes. A financial investment consultant can be of immense help.

Acquisition of funds for large projects like the dream restaurant mentioned is really a form of research and development. By that, we mean, finding the money is routine yet tedious, demanding patience and cool headed behavior. If you do your homework by providing a complete budget analysis, including the cost of the entire project, forecasts for gross sales and net income during the first and second year of operation, provide marketing statistics and demographic evaluations, plus advertising program planning with supportive reasoning for customer awareness and acceptance, then you will be considered a candidate for financial investment by lenders. Of course being considered a candidate also means that you're knowledge of the restaurant business is excellent.

If it costs $2,000,000.00 to produce a new restaurant as mentioned, how much do you think the average annual gross sales should be?

Considering a loan of $1,850,000.00, payable in 120 monthly installments. Using estimated figures, the following budget forecast might apply:

Annual gross sales..............**1,250,000.00**
Food and beverage cost.............................437,500.00
Payroll expenses incl taxes
                        & benefits............. 375,000.00
Payments on overall loan which includes;
   Total construction, land, equipment,
   legal fees,license & permits, decorations,
   consultants services,employees training,
   computer systems, signs, landscaping, initial
   inventory,main advertising program........... 240,000.00

Utilities..70,000.00
Insurance.. 65,000.00
Maintenance & repairs...................................18,000.00
CPA & Attorney 8,000.00
Replacement expense (china etc)...................7,000.00
Miscellaneous..4,500.00

Net income before taxes.............$25,000.00

At a **$2,000,000.00** annual gross sales the net income before taxes would be:......................................$263,000.00

At a **$2,500,000.00** annual gross sales the net income before taxes would be:......................................$425,000.00

At a **$3,000,000.00** annual gross sales the net income before taxes would be:......................................$578,000.00

Before you get excited and believe you are going to be very rich, very soon, understand this dream scenario we have proposed from a different view. In order to create an annual gross sales of $3,000,000.00 you should consider the following:

At an average of $10.00 per person, you would need **822** customers per day, 365 days a year.

At an average of $12.50 per person, you would need **658** customers per day, 365 days a year.

At an average of $8.00 per person, you would need
1,027 customers per day, 365 days a year.

Certainly 1.5 to 2.0 million dollars in gross annual sales is a more
reasonable and attainable range to work with, given the restaurant
statistics of the 1980's. This does not mean the higher sales figures
are not possible. It depends on many factors of which the most
important is location. If you need less capital, can manage to cut
expenses without affecting the quality or service, produce more
sales volume through more hours opened, offer catering service,
capture convention and other large volume events, etc, you can
certainly increase the net income over and above the example we
have shown. As you may be aware, many large restaurants do 5 to
10 million dollars in gross sales, however there is only one independent restaurant that does over 24 million dollars.

Accounting

Perspective

There are probably two or three owners who find accounting really exciting, of course there are those times when you can't wait to
see the figures of profit for last month.

You have either read or heard that attention to accounting is important to business. The obvious reason accounting is necessary has
to do with TAXES. You spend time and effort trying to shelter,
write off, depreciate and find ways of circumventing tax brackets.
Your CPA is trained to make sure you do not pay more tax than is
required. Let the CPA OR ACCOUNTANT do the work in that
area.

Your true benefit from accounting functions are the development of your restaurants data over various periods of time. Making comparisons of costs to productivity, and isolating areas which need management attention is the reason you should be interested in accounting.

The reports generated by hand or by computer are used to see what specific aspects of productivity are cost effective. Budget predictions and income statements are used for obtaining financing.

The four basic functions of accounting are:

1. **GENERAL LEDGER;** A record of all payments (cash or check) , categorically entered and identified.

2. **ACCOUNTS PAYABLE;** A record of invoice information which is the result of the restaurant purchases.

3. **PAYROLL;** A record of salaries and other forms of employee remuneration, taxes and benefits.

4. **ACCOUNTS RECEIVABLE;** A record of all revenues produced through the restaurants sales.

The amount of DETAIL which these four basic accounting functions can involve, varies tremendously between small and large restaurants. Certain detailed information of the four accounting functions are required, where other records of data may be calculated to generate forecasts, isolate specific productivity aspects, indicate food costs per menu item, show labor improvement or failure, indicate missing revenue by time, date, register, and the suspected responsible person, plus several hundred other available features.

In the "Computer Evaluation" section you will find more accounting information. It is difficult not to consider the use of the computer in business, just as it is difficult for most people to consider anything other than indoor plumbing in their home. It isn't only convenient, it saves time and keeps you healthier during stormy wheather.

PRODUCTION - OPERATIONS

V

OVERVIEW

Production-Operations is generally considered to be ways in which productivity is accomplished through the use of appropriate equipment and tools by trained personnel. This section is dominated by conditions concerning foodstuffs which are integral to successful production.

Food Preparation-Owners Responsibility

In the food service industry we hardly ever hear about the responsibility all of us have as preparer's of food for consumption by the general public. It is difficult to say the least, to find effective words that could result in total awareness on this subject. If however, the following simple explanation gives a few positive thoughts about the restaurant owners responsibility to the customer (consuming public), then something will have been gained.

Each and every day over a billion meals are served world wide. This is accomplished by cafeterias, hospitals, in-house company served meals, government operated mess halls and the chain of thousands of stock holder controlled eateries which seem to dominate all forms of advertising. Taking this number of places to receive a meal into consideration, we still come up with many tens of thousands more **independent restaurants.** This clearly puts a healthy portion of the responsibility of what is served to the public, on the shoulders of the independent restaurant owner.

Many times over the years we have read or heard about contaminated food experiences and unclean operating conditions in the industry of which we are apart. These acts do not help the consuming public or our industry.

We express such anxieties when waiting for our medical prescription being pulled from the shelf by a licensed and certified pharmacist, when all he or she may be doing is merely locating a red or green capsule. Such caution' and justifiably so. Yet, we take for granted all the billions of meals being served to us and other humans each and every day.

Future changes may control

Complaints galore about the water in the streams and the air we breath, all deserve attention. So, what about food that we prepare for daily consumption? The overwhelming majority of restaurant owners most probably would not vote to make changes in the industry that would critically control the food preparation operations. In fact most owners would no doubt state that there is already too much interference.

Changes will inevitably come to the industry, whether 10, or 15 years from now. The strong preventers of change will put up a strong and relentless defense, however, as in the past, the voting public will win over. No' you say, that can't happen, our industry is much too strong, too significant, and the independent restaurant is so much apart of the American way.

We do not wish to get political, only point out that if we do not take more pride in what we produce, then there may come a time when either stronger regulations, enforced certification requirements, or other controlling means will pervade our otherwise uninhibited kitchen practices. In addition, it is important to be aware of what most probably will come to pass, given the environment and specific circumstances which the restaurant owner will not be able to avoid.

The simple answer to minimize strict outside controls and keep production/operations effective and profitable;

Eliminate the reason for complaints about food contamination, unclean conditions and less than professional practices by implementing procedures which provide a consistent quality product with a minimum of waste.

If this has caused you to look deeper into rotations of food stuffs, proper refrigeration, keeping cooked batches in the best environments without mixing them, and the many other prideful practices, which all keep the customers happy and healthy, then you realize the intention.

The Health Inspector Calls

Mr. Naive wasn't exactly delighted each time the unannounced health inspector arrived. It meant that the inspector was there to criticize and generally pick apart innocuous points, which Mr. Naive had to listen to. Some learning took place before Mr. Know took over (body, soul and brain) Naive's self, but when it did, the transformation was complete to say the least.

On a following appearance, Mr. Know received the health inspector with a hardy handshake and an attitude of," How can you help me today"? The inspector really noticed this new behavior and began to show Mr. Know many things, like the nozzle on the milk dispenser (to be cut at a 45 degree angle) being cut to prevent collecting milk from drying and becoming contaminated.

Was it that the inspector was taking a new interest in Mr. Knows restaurant, or was it that Mr. Know was listening with a new set of ears?

In a matter of six months, Mr. Know and his restaurant crew had uncovered many potential problem points. They made several corrections in their production practices. Now, Mr. Know had a hell of a good feeling about what his operation was doing for the customer, and he still tries to develop better methods.

This fellow, Mr. Know seems pretty much like the boy scout who must do a good deed each day in order to face himself in the mirror. He seems a bit corny. However, it is hard to ignore his healthy attitude. In reality, we know that attitude toward unpleasant tasks can make the difference between someone we admire and someone, we hold in less esteem.

Handle the Health Inspector

If you do not have a naturally pleasant personality, especially when the health inspector comes around, that is normal. If you feel uneasy and nervous because intimidation sets in, that also is normal. In any case, the visit to your restaurant by the health inspector can be a less than comfortable experience for some.

What you do is turn the situation around, you be the one who is more interested in health and cleanliness. Make it a challenge so that the inspector will help you, not make an example of you.

"But Mr. Know, I need to go into your kitchen and do my job by inspecting temperatures and cleanliness". " Sorry Mr. Findit, but you must wear a hair net or head covering of some kind".

In this case Mr. Know not only accepted the challenge, but became proud and righteous about his restaurant ownership, and all anyone, including the health inspector could do is have respect for him. After all, the hair from the health inspector violates clean kitchen practices, just as it would if the hair belonged to anyone else.

This example does not mean we should set or lay traps, rather believe in having the most healthy food preparation and service restaurant around, through obtaining an education from the health inspector and the office where he or she obtains authority. After all, isn't that why they are there?

Once the people involved in the health inspection program see that you are serious about insuring the publics health and safety, you will win. It is not a matter of becoming gung-ho, it is simply another aspect of business which must be dealt with in a positive way in order to achieve, maintain and preserve success.

PRODUCTION METHODS OR PRACTICES?

Kitchen production methods are so numerous that to cover just the majority, we would need an encyclopedia of text material. Methods are a combination of equipment, recipes, and cooking techniques. If you consider the hundreds of small, medium and large types of equipment, multiply that times the number of recipes which fall into a general method category then you will arrive at a figure upwards of 2,550,000.

On top of that we have variables in chefs tastes plus the fact that different quantities of the same basic recipe often require changes. This is one of the main reasons why the restaurant business is so interesting, and why METHODS in kitchen food production and preparation are privy to each independent restaurant owner, hotel, motel, restaurant chain, institution, company and government mess hall, etc.

Even exacting methods can have differences in the taste of the final product. Why? Because the pizza produced in California does not have the same ingredients (produce varies the most), climate conditions, and cooks as compared to it's sister outlet in Maryland. This is true even though the equipment, recipe and cooking procedures are apparently identical. The most obvious proof to this statement is the big chain scenario.

Have you ever eaten or tasted the identical menu item at two or more outlets in the same chain of restaurants? More than likely you have. Now, whether these chains produce a hamburger, pizza, fried chicken, or fish etc, you can still experience taste differences (in most cases), and most likely you have said that you preferred the pizza at this location to the other spot, even though they are both in the family chain with the identical name above or in front of the building.

Now you may have a better understanding why your methods are so special.

PRACTICES IN THE KITCHEN

Methods may be too individually special and numerous, however, particular PRACTICES in the kitchen will save you time, money, and some embarrassment, through keeping your quality and customers health from deteriorating.

Temperatures

As much as we are aware of the move toward CENTIGRADE as a method of calibrating temperature readings, the following mentions of degrees in temperature will be in FAHRENHEIT, for it is still the most widely accepted and referenced measurement in the United States.

Refrigeration equipment (the freezer included) needs inspection of temperature readings at least twice in every 24 hour period. In addition, all kitchen employee's who utilize the walk-in's and other refrigeration equipment should constantly be aware (looking out for) of deviations in temperature.

The 34° to 38° temperature range for walk-in, reach-in and most other refrigeration equipment located in the United States is appropriate. What upsets this temperature range by producing problematic conditions with food (mostly produce) that is under a refrigeration environment, is humidity.

When is this ideal temperature range most effective in preserving the contents of the refrigeration container? When the humidity is no higher than 45 percent.

Dehumidifying   refrigerated   environments

If your restaurant is in an area where the humidity is usually higher than 45 percent (like, Florida, Louisiana, Georgia and other states), then it is a good idea to install dehumidifying equipment.

Dehumidifying equipment can be installed to accommodate the entire building, sections of a building, and in many cases, refrigeration containers themselves. Sometimes these dehumidifying equipment installations can be expensive, so it is important that you check it out first by obtaining quotations from qualified refrigeration professionals, and evaluating the dollar amount of loss you are experiencing due to produce, and cooked batches of food stuffs etc, which are deteriorating (going bad) faster than when better climatic conditions exist.

When considering food loss of items under refrigeration, be sure to include the volume purchase factor. If certain food stuffs were to last several days longer when refrigerated, would that mean you could purchase a greater volume at a better price? If your answer is yes, then this is an additional food cost factor to consider when evaluating the justification of humidity control installation.

Freezers usually fall into two types. The first keeps the contents at 0° to 10° below zero and is effective for most frozen items.

The second type keeps items at 30° below zero. Ice cream needs to be kept in the second or colder type of freezer, otherwise it will crystallize.

Questions about your refrigeration

Distributors and local sales and service companies are usually the only people owners call when a question or problem about refrigeration arises. Most often the local repairman or sales and service people make an in-person call. This costs them money, and of course you are presented with a bill. This seems to be a way of business life in the restaurant. In many cases the expensive service you receive can be avoided.

Most EQUIPMENT MANUFACTURERS are eager to hear from you the owner. Why? Because this is their opportunity to learn first hand what kinds of problems exist.

In addition, most equipment manufacturers have research and development departments or at least well staffed service departments who are extremely knowledgeable. Not only do they want to hear about the problems, but also the performance you have experienced with the equipment they manufactured.

Call toll free, but Call

How do you contact a manufacturer? First look in the yellow pages for the distributor, sales and service or even the repair service who works with the specific brand name in question. Then ask for the phone number. You may wish to explain that you have questions regarding your equipment. Most manufacturers have toll free 1-800 numbers, so ask for it. Even if your first call to a manufacturer is a long distance charge to you, the price of the call will be a great deal less than a service call.

We tend to forget that somewhere in the price of the equipment, the manufacturer needed to include his cost for maintaining service, research, and development personnel. So we are certainly entitled to call and ask questions, but somewhere along the way our conditioning suggested otherwise. Get to know the manufacturer and save.

Containers for storage

The containers of stainless steel and plastics are best for the vast majority of refrigerated and non-refrigerated items. Cartons are the exception when storing some produce and dairy products, although items like lettuce should not be kept in cartons for more than 24 hours.

Keep in mind that moisture contributes greatly to food deterioration

In the example of lettuce; Cartons are made of paper which is cellulose fiber and this fiber collects moisture like a garbage man after the Christmas parade. Yes' you are right, if lettuce heads are individually wrapped in cellophane prior to packing in cartons, then the carton should not be able to affect the lettuce.

Your question: Sometimes there are droplets of moisture inside the stainless steel container of sauce which was put into the walk-in refrigerator yesterday, why is that? Distilled condensation has formed because the hot sauce helped create that climatic condition. Not to worry, this is a normal occurrence and will not result in a problem, although it is best to use the sauce within 48 hours.

Rotation

This is one item all owners have experienced one time or another. As much as has been said about rotation of food items, it is too important and must be a strong part of the production/operations procedure.

Rotation of inventory in the dry storage area like canned goods should be maintained. There are several different checking systems to help insure proper rotation, one of which is as follows;

Mark the cans and cartons with an X, date received or other I.D.

When the next delivery is received, mark the cans or cartons with a XX,date or other *differing* I.D.

Doing this is simply a way of telling the old from the new. If you prefer numbers or other identification methods which suit your operation or computer system better, then use one of those systems.

The owner should spot check the inventory system at varying times.

Most importantly:

Prepared and fresh foods need rotation practices, whether it is a plastic five gallon bucket, or a stalk of celery wrapped in cellophane,etc. Whether you use opaque tape to indicate dates or rotation numbers applied by using a grease pencil.

It is essential that prepared foods, fresh meats, produce, dairy products, etc, are rotated for next item usage. This practice should be part of the production/operations procedure which is perpetually implemented with each and every food stuff movement.

BENEFITS TO PROPER ROTATION:

1. Keeps food from going bad.

2. Saves preparation time.

3. Minimizes waste.

4. Gives better consistency to the cooked product.

5. Insures better control of inventory.

BATCH TO BATCH

When cooked sauces, chili, gravy, stews, soups and other cooked and prepared items are stored in the refrigerator or freezer, it is important that each batch keeps to itself. This means that at no time should the previous batch of chicken soup be mixed together with the latest batch. Differing batches will not become bacteriologically identical.

When mixing among the same batch, be sure that you mix cold to cold or hot to hot. The same food temperature whether cold (coming from the walk-in) or hot (heated on the stove), must be applied to both parts of the same batch before combining them.

All too many cooks and chefs believe that mixing batches does not matter so long as you cook (heat up) the mixture to a bacteria killing 165°. This is not entirely true as there will always be a dissimilar amount of bacteriological culture which will cause a more rapid acceleration of bacteria growth.

This cause and affect simply means that the stew or soup, etc, will go sour faster than if the stew or soup were not concocted of two dissimilar batches.

AIR and WATER (Creators of waste)

Really fresh means you prepare from scratch, to order and from fresh delivered goods each day. There are not many restaurants like that.

Why do you think canned goods last so long? Yes' because the air and water can't get inside the contents of the can which had been heated to remove bacteria and vacuum sealed to remove trapped air. If you are able to apply that thinking to practice, then you should see why there isn't a need to use preservatives and whitening agents in the restaurant.

When you place foods into containers for storage be sure that any moisture is removed from the container first.

The following examples demonstrate how simple practices eliminate the use of whitening agents;

LETTUCE: When you use shredded lettuce, keep it in a tightly closed plastic bag, squeezing out the air, and then put the bag into a five gallon plastic bucket or other similar container with the lid secured properly. The lettuce (or a tossed salad) will keep for four days with out deterioration with most of the air removed and if properly refrigerated.

AVOCADOS: You can keep fresh whole avocados for seven days under proper refrigeration. The minute you peel an avocado, it starts to ripen like a banana. When you make menu items like Guacamole, mix all the spices in, but not tomatos, lemon juice or chili. Keep this primary mixture in plastic half gallon containers, full to the top with a waxed sheet of paper between the lid and the mixture. This primary Guacamole mixture will hold under proper refrigeration for at least 5 days. Draw from this primary mixture each day and add the remaining ingredients.

POTATOES: If you peel the potatoes, place them in a plastic bucket filled with cold water and a tight lid, they will keep for at least 5 days under proper refrigeration if you change the water each day. Whitening agents are not necessary.

IN-LINE PRODUCTION
(Sometimes referred to as ON-LINE production)

Producing menu items in the kitchen environment needs attention to the quality level of the item or items which the customer expects delivered at a level of service commensurate to the restaurants representation. IN-LINE merely refers to the natural order in which production is accomplished.

Achieving successful productivity requires methods which bring about effective results. IN-LINE productivity is a general application to all size operations. Rather than helter-skelter placement of both equipment and employee duties, IN-LINE production suggests orderly operations similar to that of the factory assembly line.

To maximize the results of IN-LINE production, you should consider each menu item, its preparation requirements, and the step by step process of putting an order together.

EXAMPLE: Six sandwich items need a meat product which is located seven feet away and behind another employees station. Consider moving the sandwich bar station to accommodate the location proximity of the meat ingredients. If the volume of specific menu items being put together at another employees station will be interrupted, then you should consider another alternative. Rather than move the sandwich bar station, you may consider increasing the stations ingredient capacity, which will allow for uninterrupted order assembly.

When foodservice consultants draw up plans for a new restaurants construction, production flow is always a primary consideration. Emphasis on placement of equipment, non interruption of cooks and other kitchen employee work patterns, are necessary to achieve maximum productivity.

Something borrowed something blue..
I married this walk-in for life, that is true..
What you do may bring you more..
So be good to this walk-in..
And shut the ---- door...

PURCHASING

VI

PURCHASING PERSPECTIVE

The words about purchasing in this section concern food (the ingredients to menu items) as it relates to quality, consistency, service and cost. It is assumed that the basic knowledge of purchasing utensils, equipment and other items which involve the restaurant are already apart of the established restaurant owners business experience. Additionally, the food purchasing aspect to the business is of much more importance than the determination of purchasing tile or carpet for the floor.

The number of variables in purchasing goods causes many concerns which affect the restaurant business. Why is that?

For Example; Lettuce, tomatos and other perishable food stuffs, are not consistently supplied by the same grower; there are climatic changes, soil erosion, insects, new developing agricultural areas, and other uncertainties which will affect the quality, availability and price.

Food distributors (wholesalers) of produce, grocery items, meats and most everything else which the restaurant purchases, are constantly searching for and planning future buys in order that the level of quality, price and service will be there for sale and consumption. Yet, this day in, day out, task of the distributor becomes a day in, day out task for the restaurant owner. Because of stiff competition and the variables which face the distributor, the restaurant owner must work at keeping his or her food costs (includes beverages) down.

Whether the owner or a designated employee does the purchasing, the procedures which are followed, the everyday awareness of prices, all contributes to your success factor. It is appropriate to note that daily pricing is not a usual process for each and every item by all types and sizes of restaurants. Some restaurants which order a large enough volume will normally qualify for national price list deals. These price lists can be incorporated into a contract between the restaurant and the distributor (also known as the vendor or supplier).

Keeping food costs down is important and relative to any type of restaurant. It is intended that the food cost as a percentage of the restaurants gross sales and as a percentage of each menu item, remains as stable as possible.

Many restaurants look for a food cost percentage of 25 to 35 percent and usually need to shop the distributors for the best prices. Fine dining establishments usually have food cost represented between 40 to 55 percent of their total gross sales. Many times the owner will think he or she is getting the best price, when in reality the case of canned tomatos at 20 percent less, will often yield 30 percent less than the better quality variety.

Price becomes a primary consideration only when you are comparing the identical quality and quanitity as offered between suppliers.

General Information on Distributors
(suppliers to the industry)

Food distributors who the restaurant owner often refers to as the "Vendor" or "Supplier", are the link between the manufacturer of the food product and the restaurant.

The restaurant owner is concerned about anything which may affect the supply of goods. Many suppliers today are buying manufacturing plants and other companies with financial interests are buying suppliers. In fact there is expansion, mergers, acquisitions, and internal company shake-ups in the past few years which many have difficulty understanding. Basically the reasoning has to do with growth in the food business and fierce competition.

Competition between the food suppliers has never been greater than in the 1980's and restaurant owners have for the most part, benefited significantly.

Since the restaurant customer is stressing quality and the restaurant owner has been putting demands on the suppliers for greater and consistent quality, the competition between suppliers is getting even stronger.

Food Distributors Consistency Factors

Quality is a Major Consideration

Before making purchasing decisions there are considerations which you should be aware of.

USDA standards specify for grading purposes, the net drained weight of fruits and vegetables.

Some packers, in order to reduce costs and be more competitive will have fewer people on the grading line. This results in an increased possibility for a less desirable product to slip by, and go into the pack. It can be a premeditated act on the part of the packer. A ton of raw material (fruits or vegetables) can yield many more cases of finished product if blemished or undersized (or oversized) cuts, sieves or pieces are allowed to be packed.

The farmer is concerned about how many tons of produce will be harvested from an acre. A packer is concerned about how many cases of finished product is obtained from each ton of raw material (fruits & vegetables). By not screening and grading as carefully as some packers do, the packer is increasing the yield.

The restaurant owner should be aware of how many servings and the acceptable quality level he or she is getting for the money. Vegetables and fruits that are of poor quality are turned back to the kitchen and to the garbage can which causes a double loss considering the customer may not return.

A number 10 can of fruit cocktail should weigh when drained, close to it's original packed weight. This will occur when all the various fruits in the fruit cocktail blend are at their proper maturity level when packed. It happens frequently where pears that are over mature at packing time are still used in a fruit cocktail. After several months in the can, the pears begin to disintegrate because of their softness at packing time. The result is; much of the pear solids break up into the liquid packing syrup, leaving less product in solid form. The difference can be 2 or more servings less per can, which converts to 12 or more per case. In addition, the overall quality-appearance and flavor of the product will also diminish. Any carry over (inventory at the packer or distributor) into the next years pack will be even less desirable and of less value, as the product continues to age in the can.

In a year when certain fruits are scarce at packing time, some packers will pack to the bottom of the allowable range of short items. Example; If pineapple or pears are short and therefore more expensive, the packer will utilize the minimum of the allowable specifications (USDA) range in a fruit cocktail product. The result is a product that can be overloaded with less expensive grapes and peaches, which produces less eye appeal, taste and general dinning enjoyment.

The restaurant buyers involvement

Owners or the responsible employee (cook, chef, manager, etc), should look for specific counts and count ranges on the labels of many products. Counts will vary with a lack of uniformity in piece size, which is undesirable. If the count specifications are not on the label, you should check the product to make sure that you receive what you paid for. Uniformity is critical too. Two persons ordering cling peaches and cottage cheese salads should get peach halves very close in size. One large peach half, the other small, doesn't speak well for the restaurant or the expertise of the person doing the purchasing.

Frozen soups are becoming very big in foodservice. Solids content is a critical factor that can help determine the true value of the soup purchased. Many soups on the market contain as much as a 22% to 33% difference in the amount of vegetables, pasta, chicken, beef or fish, that is, as compared from one product to another.

The quality-value difference in solids is important when you consider a "Cream of Broccoli" soup that contains primarily stalk pieces, with very little floret material. Also, vegetable soups can be woefully shy of vegetables, and vegetable colors may be unappealing.

Soup and gravy bases are another area where value received is not always on a par with prices paid. Many soup bases list salt at the first ingredient (THE LAW INSISTS UPON THE ITEMS IN GREATER QUANTITY CONTAINED IN THE PRODUCT TO BE LISTED FIRST ON THE INGREDIENT STATEMENT AND THE OTHER INGREDIENTS LISTED IN DESCENDING ORDER).

Salt is very inexpensive and one should weigh carefully what other flavor and color benefits a product provides when purchasing a soup base of this type. The best value of course, is the one which lists the meat, poultry, fish, or shell fish as the first ingredient. This means, that is the particular ingredient with the greatest amount contained in that product.

It is also important to consider yield. Some bases yield less than five pounds of broth when made up, where others may yield 2 to 4 times more.

Flavor is also critical. If a beef base lists beef first, what then about the quality of the beef going into the base? The quality of the beef can be very low, and thus affect the flavor of the finished soup or other recipe item.

Distributors Food Specifications

The specifications which suppliers incorporate regarding their buying practices from growers and food producers has reached levels of high standards never before attained. These standards do have consistency problems from time to time, however, most suppliers seem to be doing more follow up by trouble shooting isolated glitches and creating more stringent specifications.

To begin with, most food distributors written specifications have been regarded as classified information, privy to a few employees. It is believed that this type of information is increasingly becoming available to the suppliers' customers like restaurant owners, as a demonstration of concern for quality and value on the part of the supplier. Certainly the good customer restaurant owner should not be denied product specification information when requested.

The example of a thorough set of specifications is that of "Fresh Ground Beef". Since there are literally thousands of product specifications which the large suppliers work with, it would be to your advantage to find the time and check out those particular specifications of interest.

Prior to making a trip to the suppliers office, ask the salesperson to obtain specifications on one or two items. If the salesperson offers some excuse for not providing results, then call the president of the company and ask him or her, if there is a good reason why you should not know exactly what the specifications are on the products you are considering for purchase? If you do not receive cooperation on this, it would be surprising, however, it would seem awkward at best to do business with a company who will not explain fully, the contents of that which your customers ingest.

Title: Fresh Beef   Spec no: 2000

item I. Product: Fresh Ground Beef

item 2. Label Grade: Second line quality

item 3. Container Information;
    a. Box size = I2.0 X I0.8 X 6.5 (inches)
    b. Cubic area= 842.4 inches or 0.4875
    cubic feet.

item 4. Product code
    Number: 2000
    Pack amts: 2 each I0 pound units
    Description: Fresh ground beef (80 percent
    lean, 20 percent fat) 80/20.

item 5. Source of raw material
    a.) All formulations to consist of combinations of
    90/I0 lean meat trimmings and frozen 50/50
    trimmings Formulations will be derived "only"
    from **domestic, skeletal** meat sources.
    Furthermore, the 50/50 trimmings must meet or
    exceed USDA grade "GOOD" standards.
    b.) Bench trimmings from portion control operations
    or from previously aged or "cryovaced" meat,
    will not be allowed.
    c.) Other raw materials **Not to be included;**
    imported boneless cow meat, mechanically
    deboned beef, bull meat, meat with only parts of
    the fat removed from beef fatty tissue, re-worked
    product, added fat such as suet, cod fat, and
    meat from non-skeletal sources, as cheek meat
    and hearts.

item 6. Fat Percentage (precooked analysis)
    a.) 20 + or - one percent

item 7. Microbiological Standards (Counts
        are"not more than")
    a.) Total aerobic plate count   750,000 grams
    b.) Coliform   l,000 grams
    c.) Staphylococcus Aureus   250 grams
    d.) E. Coli   25 grams

item 8. Maximum Moisture/Protein Ratio
    a.) 3.8:l

item 9. Plate size of grind
    a.) l/8 inch

item l0. TVP percentage
    a.) "0" percent

item ll. Packaging and Labeling
    a.) The finished product will be packed in pure
        white, wax lined corrugated boxes with a
        minimum bursting strength of 275 pounds.

    b.) The label and production code dating system
        will conform to standards set forth by our com-
        panies "Quality Assurance" standard no. 23.

    c.) The finished product to be packed in a cryovac
        pouch with our companies logo per the quality
        assurance standard no. 32

item l2. Shelf life @ 28 to 34 degrees Fahrenheit shall
        be not less than l8 days. Shelf life is based on
        the packing date.

There are many other items for distributors specifications
to growers and producers, which of course depends on
the food product specified.

OTHER SPECIFICATION POINTS

Portion control requirements, slicing counts, muscle configuration, caloric information, batter/breading percentages, and chemical analysis, are some of the additional areas of specification
which concern meats, chicken, turkey, sausage, beef and pork.

Another example of some distributors specification inclusions is
orange juice.

Concentrated Orange Juice

Specification inclusions, depending on label quality,
        basically deal with such items as the following;

I. Style: Unsweetened

2. Variety: l00 % Florida

3. Quality: U.S. Grade or U.S. Fancy

4. Minimum score, including color, absence of defects,
    flavor, plus minimum score points which indicate
    levels of acceptance.
5. Detailed descriptions of Color, absence of defects and
    flavor, with degrees of Brix/Acid ratios and recover-
    able oil degrees.

**PLUS many   more specifications, however, you
can see from these examples, just how detailed
most distributors are.......**

Drained Weight

When you think about canned fruit cocktail, tomatos, onions, and other canned fruits and and vegetables, the term "Drained Weights" should come into focus. Why? Because this factor relates to the amount of solid product you are paying for in the can.

When you purchase a case of six number ten cans of tomatos at $12.00, is the drained weight relative to the $14.00 case from another supplier? Ask the salesperson and find out just what you are paying for. Sales people will seldom know the definitive answer, however, they should find out for you.

Research sources: The NOBEL/SYSCO Company, Denver, Colorado
The JOHN SEXTON Company, Chicago, Illinois

FOOD COST FORMULA BY MENU ITEM

The formula is very simple and most accurate for finding the per serving food cost.

The total COST of the ingredients purchased (include each ingredient) in a menu item, **divided** by the number of SERVINGS, equals the UNIT PER SERVING FOOD COST, of a particular menu item.

Finding the number of servings is most often accomplished by dividing the number of ounces which equals one serving, into the total ounces that makes a batch of a particular menu item.

If quality and consistency are a part of the requirements which you have determined as policy regarding the menu items in your restaurant, then this formula should have a significant meaning.

Forecasting Inventory

The methods used for forecasting restaurant foodstuffs are based on two control points. One is maintaining perpetual records of actual inventory, which includes daily orders received. Two is the knowledge of the amount of product sold. The more information presented frequently (daily), the more accurate the owners inventory will be.

All size restaurants, need to keep control over inventory in order to purchase with any degree of competence. Medium and larger restaurants should utilize both inventory and product sold information to purchase correct amounts and are of a size that provides justification for an appropriate level of computer assisted systems.

In relation to purchasing, the use of the computer is becoming essential for medium size restaurants and imperative for the larger establishments. The smaller restaurant may or may not find the aid of a computer both time and cost effective.

The main points which are appropriate to purchasing regarding inventory that benefits the restaurant owner are;

1. Not to run out of product necessary to meet the obligation to the customer set forth by the restaurants menu.

2. Not to overstock product inventory causing product to become stale, sour or spoiled.

3. Not to overstock product which uses space that costs you money.

4. Not to overstock product which causes a diminished cash flow.

For those who wish to invest in or already possess a computer system, there is software available which keeps the record of inventory by entering data when orders are received and when daily inventory withdrawals are made. This function can also be accomplished without a computer. Check the computer vendors for software.

The computer assisted system really proves itself when it automatically takes the items of specific product sold from the POS (Point of Sale) register and deletes the proportionate ingredients per sale from the amount of purchased inventory that was delivered the same day. These systems are expensive and therefore only justifiable where appropriate business dollar volumes are concerned. Refer to the Computer SPE section of this book for more information on POS systems and definitions.

Keeping track of inventory by hand means listing each item, it's location (dry storage, walk-in refrigerator, freezer etc) and being alert to a minimum amount kept on hand.

An example of a form which is used for manual entry is as follows;

INVENTORY LIST
and ORDER SHEET "DRY STORE ONE"

Item	Amt on hand	Amt min	Amt to order	date	Supplier	Date Del
___	___	___	___	___	___	___
___	___	___	___	___	___	___

Figure 6-one
Sample of a partial inventory and order sheet in tandum

The <u>item</u> may be canned green beans.

The Amt <u>on hand</u> may be 4 number ten cans.

The Amt <u>min</u> (minimum) may be 6 cans.

The Amt <u>to order</u> may be two cases.

The <u>Date</u> is the date you are taking inventory.

The <u>Supplier</u> is the name of the company which will
        fill the purchase order.

The Date <u>del</u> (delivered) is the date the order is
        scheduled to be delivered.

The form described above (Figure 6-one) is basic and multifunctional in that both inventory and a record of items to be ordered is utilized on one form. You can incorporate product identification numbers and different storage locations on the same form, Like; "FREEZER ONE', TWO, THREE and "DRY STORE ONE", TWO, THREE, or "WALK-IN ONE" etc, etc....... Or you can keep a form for each storage location mounted to a clipboard, all depending on your specific setup.

Note: If you or your chef are aware of what you have on hand, there is a better chance the inventory will be used, as opposed to learning of old foodstuffs which were buried in the shelving system.

Placing Your Order

The salesperson

Usually the sales representative of the suppling company to the foodservice industry is the order taker. In a few instances the order is telephoned to the supplier. Use of the telephone for orders will probably be increased as a method of ordering. Also, this will be accomplished by use of the computer and a modem. Personalities should not be a factor where the salesman is concerned, however, personalities have caused problems between the salesman and the restaurant.

If you think that you as a restaurant owner are having personnel problems, try to sympathize with the supplier for a moment and realize that the majority of new people coming into the food distributors business are not of the same caliber which was the case a few years ago. Restauranteurs who have been in the business for sometime, remember when each and every salesperson couldn't do enough for the restaurant owner, plus they were knowledgeable about the products they sold and, offered intelligent suggestions which were sincerely in the best interest of the restaurant.

The better salespeople who work for the distributors are naturally going to attend the high ticket customers, which means the largest restaurants, institutions, hospitals, government installations, chain operations etc. This leaves the small, medium and some larger re-

staurants who are often serviced by less experienced sales people.
Why you ask? Because the distributors world is changing. The
food distributors (suppliers) are finding more and different companies (in or related to their business) expanding, merging, acquiring
growers and producers, etc, which creates greater competition and
less financial margin to operate on. This being the case, training
programs for sales people does not receive the attention it once
did, nor is there the overall enthusiasm there once was for the
salesperson's job.

Most certainly there are exceptions, however, changes in social
environments, technology, and economic shifts are steering many
would-be sales candidates to other professional endeavors, like,
opening a restaurant, video store, or getting involved in the computer industry, etc.

Now, when you deal with the salesperson who is not the total
super-sales-oriented representative, you should understand and
appreciate the person and todays situation. If you are fortunate
enough to have an experienced sales person who is sincere in his
or her efforts to provide you the quality, service and price you
have come to enjoy, consider yourself lucky.

Demeanor with salespeople

Always be pleasant, and courteous, however, you or whom ever
does your purchasing, should stick to business. That means no
fun and games. It should also be a standard practice to keep from
fraternizing with salespeople after business hours. This only
creates feelings of obligation and distorts the business relationship. Some people think this practice a bit stiff, that is until they
have to move to another supplier which can cause bad feelings between so-called friends. Yes; there are exceptions, but as rare as a
2 carat flawless diamond found in the subway station.

Rumors and vendors

One thing that hasn't changed over the years because of human nature and a desire to be first to tell it, is the rumor. Rumors get started from sources which have negative designs, sources that have great imagination and those devilish pranksters. Once in awhile there is a rumor, whose source had some credibility except it grew out of proportion with each hand it was passed to.

Restaurant owners hear rumors that are sometimes designed to cause a feeling of competition, so that the purchaser will increase the order.

The bottom line is; Pay no attention (ignore) to rumors, and if something is said which needs verification, call the person who should know, directly. Never believe a story, check it out if it affects you, otherwise leave it alone.

The Written Deal

Regardless if the order is given to the supplier by purchase order or verbal communications, you need to have a written form to let whom ever is receiving the order know what is expected. The simple form which is shown in "figure 6-one" under the heading "Inventory List", is adequate for these purposes, although you may add more information which could help your particular operation.

Upon occasions deliveries have mistakes, and you should not have to pay for them, with your time or money. When you are given credit for that case of corned beef hash you didn't order, your money is being used for that period of time, free of interest, when it could be better used in your business. When you use a form that indicates the date and time of expected deliveries, the description of each item, the amount of each item, and the agreed-on price, you minimize error and time consuming paperwork.

If you are using the purchase order system, then you are probably incorporating the necessary elements for receiving orders by providing a copy of the purchase order to the responsible employee doing the receiving.

When wrong items are shipped, you simply refuse delivery. There are instances when a supplier will ship a substitute item because of being out of stock. Many times this alternate product shipped is done so in case you are in such need that you will be happy for a replacement. If you do not need the replacement item, return it then, do not allow the delivery person to charge you for it. If you develop a good rapport with your supplier, then they should contact you well ahead of time, when deviations from your placed order exists.

Receiving Goods

Not enough attention is paid to delivery times, and yet this aspect of the purchasing process can cause unnecessary problems which left unchecked, produce wasted time, less than adequate inspection of goods received, plus additional paperwork and sometimes spoiled goods.

Mr. Can't (cousin to Mr. Naive), ran a medium sized restaurant with 70 employees. During one hot summer when the tourist trade was delightfully brisk, his deliveries from the main supplier were being made by the driver, Mr. Myway. Mr. Myway usually made his presence known during the lunch rush hour or at 6:00 P.M. when dinner was underway.

Sigfried the head chef was responsible for signing for goods received during the day shift.

One fine day, Mr. Myway broke through the back door with a load of ordered items, then he unloaded the hand truck, here, there and everywhere. In the middle of the lunch hour, Sigfried tore himself away from the hectic pace of the kitchen, signed for the goods received, however neglected inspection, after all, he was glad the french fries got there to see him through his shift. Sigfried groaned and barked at the driver for being late. Mr. Myway stood there blocking the aisle, making excuses, which seemed to blame the rest of the world for his lack of education and less than intelligent behavior.

Sigfried asked the dishwasher (Nick) to put the order away as he hurried back to the kitchen and Mr. Myway went on his way. With all the activity going on, the rest of Sigfried's shift went by quickly and he soon forgot about the delivery annoyance, unfortunately he also forgot to follow up on the delivered goods and their proper placement into storage.

When the dinner shift arrived, Mr. Can't met the dinner chef in the aisle where he noticed the delivered goods that had not been put away. The Frozen pies had thawed out, the wrong type of ham, three broken cases of individual jellies, and two cases of canned tomatos, were sitting on top of the 40 count ripe Haas avacadoes, which were crushed to the point of becoming prepared Gaucamole.

That evening Mr. Can't had to spend time sorting out the differences in the invoice and the order sheet, putting the wrong and damaged items to one side and preparing a letter to the supplier and a memo to Sigfried.

Mr. Can't learned the importance of stressing delivery procedures to the vendor and to his staff to help prevent similar occurrences from happening.

Delivery times and relative procedures on the part of staff employees and the vendor's drivers should be spelled out and reinforced on a regular basis.

Things you can do to help alleviate delivery problems:

I.
Post a sign at the delivery entrance indicating times of day when deliveries will be accepted.

2.
Ask the vendor (supplier) to put the delivery times on the invoice which accompanies the driver.

3.
Establish a good rapport with the salesperson and customer service people who can alert you concerning late deliveries. Have their telephone numbers kept nearby.

4.
The first time a new driver (delivery person) shows up, be sure to meet the new Mr. Myway, establish your ground rules, which may include; ringing the door bell, who to ask for, where to put items, how to stack them on the hand truck, etc... Make a strong but fair impression.
Whether it is the breadman, or the person who delivers pastries, milk, beverages, potato chips, meat, produce, grocery items, or many other products; It is in the best interest of your restaurant to install a vigilant receiving procedure.

Paying for Goods Received

The watchword phrase is: "Pay for what you ordered at the agreed upon price". If you think that paper work confusion and time spent on locating information for orders which took place three months ago is efficient use of your management expertise, forget it. Rather allow the procedures you put into place work for you. Unless your restaurant organization is large enough to support a complete and thorough purchase order system which can nail down all the possible errors before paying for them, you are better off giving the delivery person a check before departure.

Mr. Naive thought that doing business by paying for goods on 30 day or more terms with a vendor was smart use of his financial prowess. Because his past experience in working for large companies taught him the purchase routine including the use of terms, he believed that his cash flow would be utilized better through this extension of the 30 day curse.

Statements came in and he tried to make comparisons to the invoice. He located the invoice references which appeared on the statement, made ajustments for credits and price changes that the salesman said would be made, and finally determined that the supplier was out to get him for some unknowing sin. After six months of heated debate with the suppliers credit department, he decided the communications between the salesman, the credit department and himself was so frustrating and problematic that it became necessary to change his payable system.

Naive changed to a "Preferred C.O.D." method which saved time and paperwork, gave him better knowledge of inventory, increased his reputation for payment to suppliers, and kept the power of the buying relationship on his side.

The experience which Mr. Naive had, doesn't mean that payment by terms is wrong for all foodservice, but rather that "terms" (like 30 days after delivery, etc) are best suited to those restaurants who can afford the time and effort and will find it cost effective because they have both the volume and staff, enabling efficient and beneficial results.

SAFETY / SECURITY / INSURANCE

VII

SAFETY

Preventative measures, that is what safety is all about. If you think about all the possible accidents that your operation could produce, and you make a list of them, you will be making a major contribution to the safety of all concerned. It is as simple as that, because awareness of potential hazards is half of the preventative action.

To be included in your list of safety elements that will obviate accidents, should be the laws, regulations, and guidelines that have already been set forth by the Federal, State, and Local governments. There are reasons for safety laws and it is your job to find out what they are, plus the appropriateness of these laws, to your particular restaurant business. All food service operations under certain jurisdictions are not necessarily affected by each law (or regulation) in the same manner, that is why it is important for you to seek out the answers.

Example: The garbage removal from defined institutional food service operations (like hospitals and universities) may be required to have the Wet Garbage Dumpster emptied each day. Because someone thought they understood the laws intention, restauranteurs heard rumors through the grapevine which were picked up by the news media , and before Sam could ask Sally for a date, many restaurants thought their garbage removal expense would greatly increase, and that wasn't the case at all.

Sometimes we are confused by the way laws are written and people take it for granted that the particular law in question, is meant either for them or that they are exempt, when the truth is otherwise.

If an owner reads an article in the morning paper concerning signs hanging in front of the building, and the owner knows that the new four foot extension law should not apply to him or her because the owners sign was installed years ago and therefore "Grand Fathered-in"; Should the owner find out what safety aspects the law makers may have had in mind? Of course he or she should, because conditions (materials, climatic changes and methods of installation, etc) may exist, leading to an accident.

Mr. Naive did not know that the awning in front of the restaurant was working it's way loose. One, day when the winds were whipping around the building and pedestrians were holding onto their hats, two people got out of their car which was parked near the walkway in front of the restaurant. The entire awning, com-

plete with metal framework came down, missing the people, but damaging the hood of the customers car. It was a blessing that no one was hurt, and the restaurants insurance policy took care of the car. Now Mr. Naive periodically checks the new awning.

The fact that you never know when or where an accident will occur, and that is obvious, because if you could see in to the future, there are many other ideas which would interest you. What does one do? MINIMIZE the possibilities of accidents ever happening in the first place.

What you can do

Here are a few simple thoughts, provoking ideas to get you started, after which you can put together your own more comprehensive list:

1. When a waiter or waitress tries to carry too much at one time, help them immediately, then quietly instruct the employee why it is unsafe.

2. When lettuce or other food falls to the floor, particularly during preparation times, instruct the appropriate employee to "pick up these things immediately ".

3. Keep floors clean and dry.

4. Knives and other sharp implements of the trade, should be kept sheathed, plus proper instruction should be given kitchen employees regarding their handling.

5. Keep brooms, mops and mop buckets in an area away from halls and traffic lanes (walkways). Preferably outside.

6. Use non-slip strips on ladders, steps and appropriate elevating devices.

7. Keep the parking lot and sidewalk areas clean and free of ice, snow and debris, well lighted when applicable, etc.

8 . Have employees wear non-slip rubber sole shoes to prevent slipping.

9 . Post signs: "Do not touch", "Wet floor", "Fire extinguisher", "Close walk-in door","Low ceiling","Watch your step", "No smoking area", etc.....

KITCHEN SAFETY

One does not need more excuses for employee absenteeism, and you do not wish to see another human being hurt.

Cuts, bruises and burns are not funny, to the person who is on the receiving end, or to the restaurant business where it happened. You cannot in all probability, eliminate burns, cuts and bruises altogether, but you can MINIMIZE the number of occurrences through good safety practices and procedures.

Basically the burns come from cooking equipment, like the handling of hot stock-pots, pressure cookers, or brushing up against a heat lamp, or, pouring hot water or cooked soups, etc. One simple measure you can take is to invest in quality super lined mitts for the employees, and then make sure they are used properly. The money spent for this safety measure, will come back to you time and time again.

The SAFETY CALL

In the restaurant, employees are constantly moving and they are usually carrying something. Whether you say;" Behind you", "Coming through", or "Excuse me, this is hot", etc, the important thing is that you teach your employees to use some code or signaling means to communicate to the others, not to make any abrupt moves, thereby preventing another accident.

Fire Safety

Insurance companies are well aware of the facts concerning restaurant fires. Most fires start in the <u>kitchen</u> because hot grease, open flame, electrical wiring and concealed duct-work present formidable fire hazards. Small fires are an inconvenience and large fires often result in a restaurant that is never to be re-opened. Total insurance coverage, if you can afford the premium, will not pay for customer regeneration and every single item you forgot to claim, plus, replacement cost on a $9,000.00 (new price) piece of equipment, or other items like tables, chairs, booths, etc, means you will usually receive market value, not the amount paid for when new.

Insurance cannot compensate for all that is lost due to a fire, therefore there is no reason why restaurants should not protect themselves with the professional installation of quality fire suppression equipment and have an active fire prevention program.

Fire prevention

The important elements the restaurant owner should insist upon, begin with keeping the area clean. The balance of concerns is a 14 point program to be self-inspected as often as indicated.

1. Keep hoods, grease removal devices, fans, ducts, adjoining wall surfaces and other accessories free of grease build-up. Ninety percent of all serious fires occur in these areas. *To be accomplished twice weekly in one shift operations and four times a week in restaurants operating two or more shifts per 24 hour days.*

2. Never use flammable solvents or cleaners. Flammable residues are extremely hazardous. *This point should be reinforced periodically by responsible supervision.*

3. Operate your exhaust system whenever the appliance is pre-heating, heating, cooking or cooling. This helps to prevent excessive heat buildup which may otherwise actuate the fire suppression system._Kitchen employees should be cognizant of this point every work day, plus responsible supervision must be on the daily watch to be certain of adherence._

4. Never operate filtered equipped exhaust systems without the filters in place. Excessive grease may build up in the hood and duct system. _Responsible supervision should make sure this does not occur._

5. Never restrict air intake passages, this can reduce the efficiency of your exhaust system. _When your exhaust system is serviced or any work is being done with regard to the exhaust system, responsible supervision should make sure blockages do not occur._

6. Operate all U.L. tested grease extractors by manufacturers instructions to ensure effective grease removal from the hood and duct systems. _Responsible supervision should make sure of adherence to this point on every occasion._

Make sure your fire suppression system is maintained;

7. Never use corrosive cleaning solutions on fusible links or cables, as over a period of time this could result in enough deterioration to activate or prevent activation of the system. _Responsible supervision should maintain adherence._

8. Have metal fusible links replaced annually. Deterioration of these links can cause the system to actuate or to malfunction in case of fire. The quartzoid bulb-type link need not be replaced annually, but must be cleaned at each semi-annual inspection or more frequently if conditions are applicable. _Responsible supervision should maintain adherence._

9. Never tamper with the fire suppression system. It is a complicated piece of equipment that is for professional attention only. *Responsible supervision should maintain adherence.*

10. *Periodically check* your system for loose pipes, which could interfere with the flow of extinguishing agents. Check for missing or grease covered nozzle caps, which can cause blockage.

11. *Periodically check* your visual indicator to make sure the system is cocked.

12. Have your system inspected by an authorized factory representative who seriously knows and understands the fire suppression system and it's application to the restaurant business. *This should be done at a minimum of six month intervals, and immediately after major hood and duct cleaning.*

13. If you add a new appliance, be sure you add fire suppression equipment if applicable. *This should be checked out and added if necessary before operation of the new appliance.*

14. Posting operating instructions of fire suppression equipment, including the hand held extinguisher is a must. *Make sure selected employees understand the operation of equipment and procedures in case of fire. Do this on a regular basis.*

In case of FIRE

I. Evacuate others from the premises.

2. Pull station manual actuator ring-pin to activate the fire extinguishing system.

3. Call the fire department.

4. Standby with a hand held extinguisher;

    a.) If you need to use it, pull the pin.

    b.) Stand back about ten feet from the fire itself.

    c.) Aim at the base of the fire, squeeze the trigger-handle while using a sweeping motion (back and forth).

The LIQUID fire suppression system

A sodium bicarbonate dry chemical agent, has been and still is an effective fire suppression agent when used in accordance with properly maintained equipment. More than 20 years ago this agent, together with appropriate equipment was developed for the restaurant industry by Ansul Fire Protection, of Marinette, Wisconsin.

The LIQUID fire suppression system is recent and is a superior system because of the following reasons:

1. The size of the pipe network is simplified, making it easier to install and revealing less exposed pipe.

2. Fewer nozzles may be required.

3. The liquid agent (like Ansulex) reacts with hot grease and oil to form a foam blanket. It makes soap (saponification) out of grease and oil which cannot burn, thereby further reducing the possibility of re-flash.

4. Should a small fire occur, the liquid agent is many times easier and faster to cleanup, thereby reducing down-time.

5. The liquid system is more concentrated on the specific hazard area.

Figure **7-1.** A diagram of an installed liquid (dual-tank) R-102 restaurant fire suppression system.

Figure **7-2.** Shows the installer setting the automatic detection and control device which will discharge the restaurant's fire suppression systems, should a fire occur.

Figure **7-3.** The LIQUID R-102 system has three major components in addition to piping and nozzles. From the left is the liquid extinguishing agent, the Automan regulated release mechanism, the three gallon stainless steel tank which stores the liquid agent, and the nitrogen cartridge (shown in front) which pressurizes the agent tank and discharges the liquid onto the fire. The system employs different nozzles (shown right-front) depending on the hazard.

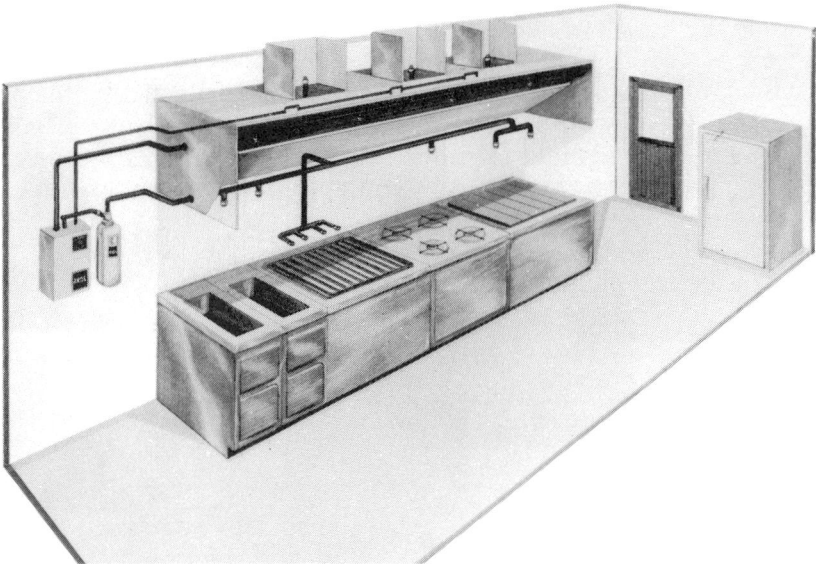

Figure 7-1

Figure 7-2   Figure 7-3

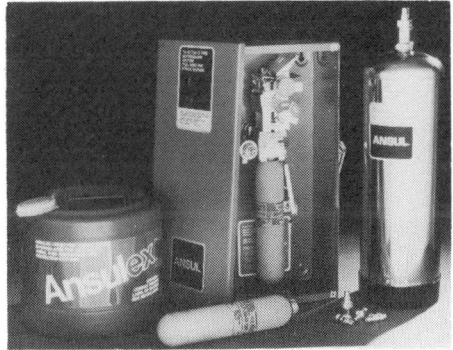

Source: Ansul Fire Protection, Marinette, Wisconsin

Final comment

Safety is not the most popular subject for management or employees to get excited over, yet it's importance cannot be overlooked. When the owner addresses the subject of safety, he or she can better motivate the employees by letting them know that their safety is of great concern. If the owner shows that he or she is interested in the health and well being of the employee, then it should be difficult for the employee not to take a keener interest.

SECURITY

Handling Cash Transportation

The cash register is a central location for financial transactions, with the exception of company checks. If you have a routine for daily bank deposits, it is a good idea to vary the times for delivery of monies to the bank and disguise the money pouch in a paper bag or other method of concealment. Do not walk or drive to the bank using the same route each day. This may not be possible in some rural locations. The main concept is to keep movement of currency varied in the time of day and routes taken for deposit.

Safes and Services

When the restaurant has a safe it generally makes it easier to vary the times of currency movement, although it is best not to accumulate currency for periods any longer than twenty four hours. High volume establishments should move cash at least twice a day. In some cases where cash is accumulated in greater amounts, it may be wise to check into armed guard pickup and delivery services. The expense of these uniformed delivery services needs to be carefully weighed against that portion of the insurance premium which deals with theft. Usually the insurance premium that covers theft will be lowered when the insurance company (through your agent) understands your use of an armed guard service. When considering the cost differentials of the guard service, be sure to factor-in the time it takes management or another employee to make the cash deposits. It is certainly important enough for many restaurants to check it out.

Controlling the Register

Regardless how sophisticated you believe your money checking system is, there is an element of trust that cannot be overlooked. In smaller restaurants you can trust yourself to handle the register. If you are fortunate to have a marriage partner or a business partner (the vested kind) working with you that helps. In any case, whether you feel confident about your cashiers trustworthiness or not, a mathematical system which shows what amounts were ordered and paid for by customers, and comparing that total with the cash received is fundamentally necessary.

The Point of Sale (POS) computer systems for restaurants do a very respectable job in this cash and trust situation, however, access codes can be obtained by employees if you are not careful. Those owners who have the benefit of a POS system, should not get over confident, as these systems do not allow for employees selling menu items to their friends for cash, without touching the register (computer enhanced or the conventional register).

Note: See the Computer Evaluation section for more information on POS systems.

Building Security

Unless your business is operated from a truck, van, or moveable stand, you will have a building with equipment, inventory, furniture, and many other things of value. Alarm systems seem to be a part of business and it only takes one burglary to justify having a system for the preventative reasons. Alarm systems of any kind have a limited deterrent effect, because, anyone wanting to get into a restaurant can do it if they want to badly enough. The big trick here is to make it troublesome enough for a perspective thief or burglar so they will not attempt it in the first place.

In light of all the information which comes to us about security systems, they do offer an element of peace of mind to the owners who have them. If you couple the appropriate insurance coverage with security measures, it will certainly provide you with a high degree of assurance that you have done most everything you can.

In some cases however, insurance premiums are too high to consider. Alarm systems that notify the police department and are battery backed up, provides a remedy for some. Since there are a number of security alarm companies today, and the growth of that industry is rapid, you need to be selective by shopping, comparing, and checking references of perspective vendors.

Checking the alarm system vendors:

1. **Check for the length of time the company has been in business.**

2. **Call at least three businesses which have the vendors system.**

3. **See what you can learn from the businesses who have the vendors system. a) Has the alarm prevented a burglar from continuing his nights work? b) Has the system malfunctioned causing false alarms? c) What ways has the system helped? d) Did you ever need service to the system, and if so, did the vendor respond quickly?**

What you do to secure the building besides alarm systems maybe equally important. The thief looks at the amount of difficulty he or she has to endure before they decide to go for the gold. The more difficult you make the perspective thieves entrance to your building, the better the odds are that they will try somewhere else.

Other measures you may consider:

I. **Fences and walls with locked gates.**

2. **Outside lighting.**

3. **Foot locks, head locks, dead bolts, sliding bars, are used to reinforce doors to the outside.**

4. **Posted notices of trespassing, alarm notices, and other applicable notices with words of prosecution consequences.**

5. **Wrought iron (or metal) window and door coverings.**

Use your own judgement considering your particular circumstances, which may be similar to what Mr. Know did.

Mr. Know had an urban area restaurant and his building was a two story brick structure, while all the others in the block were three or more stories high. When he first learned that burglars were using his building to climb up on, he decided to make the burglars exercise a little more difficult. While staying well within the legal system, he painted the drain spout with grease, put wire covered flood lights up high on the wall, and then chain link fenced the open space which faced the alleyway. He then put up a sign that indicated "Trespassers will be prosecuted". Since that time, no one has gone to the trouble of scaling his building, for any reason.

Dumpster Protection

In many cities and towns you can, upon request to the waste removal superintendent and for a small increase in your monthly charge, receive keys to special padlocks which are welded to the body of the metal dumpster. The benefits of this measure are worth the effort, as now you can better control access to the dumpster, keeping vagrants, insects, rodents and the like, from pulling the tied garbage bags apart, spilling everything onto the ground, which makes work for the employees and accumulates rapid growth of disease breeding bacteria.

Employee Theft

Employee theft is a difficult thing for an owner to face, yet it is all too often a reality. Inventory, whether dry storage or under refrigeration, needs to be accounted for on a perpetual basis.This means that only certain employees should be allowed to remove inventory and a control system (by pencil or computer) must be used.The smaller restaurant may require the owner to implement the control system, while the owner of the larger restaurant should oversee the trusted employee who actually does the supervision. In general, a control system begins with a purchased number of items and what was received according to the ordered items. After items are received and prior to appropriate storage, it is important to identify the box, can, bottle, etc. You may consider using a grease pencil, stick on label, taped I. D. patch, numbered or lettered stamp, or other method of applying identification.

This I.D. labeling exercise can serve three basic tasks: One; It should keep the rotation of foodstuffs in order.... Two; Keep track of inventory quantity (particularly for reordering).... Three; Identify missing items which narrows down the suspected thief or thieves. Locked doors and access to storage of inventory needs to be limited to selected employees. Periodic checks during each work shift should be visible to other employees.

This general outline of preventative employee theft measures can be applied to most restaurant organizations, however, it is equally important that the employee knows that thievery will not be tolerated. A simple message (notice) on the bulletin board should take care of that. When you follow a system of identifying and checking be sure that it is not openly talked about. The biggest advantage you have is silence, as people fear that which they do not know and are less likely to attempt stealing. Once the employees know that the owner is serious about employee theft and he or she uses methods to identify missing items routinely, the chances of an occurrence are severely minimized.

Once you catch an employee with the goods, or by confession, you should not hesitate to make an example of this employee by calling the police and signing a formal complaint. Do not let the employee off the hook, as this is a sure sign that your inventory is open season to all that have the nerve to steal from you. After the first example, which includes termination of the employees tenure, it is doubtful that other employees will think you less than serious about your restaurant business.

Armed Robbery

The best advice regarding the armed robber is compliance.

For the first time in your life you feel helpless and scared to death, if not for others, for yourself. You want to be like some movie hero, but you can see the pointless side more clearly than trying something foolish.

Mr. Know stood there at the edge of the counter near the door to the kitchen, he knew that all the alarm systems, security procedures and tips he had learned over the years were helpless against the shotgun being pointed at him. "Lay face-down on the floor", said the masked intruder."We will cooperate with your demands", said Mr. Know. The robber wanted all the cash. The robber worked fast collecting his booty, while his accomplice waited near the front door. From his prone position on the floor behind the counter, Mr. Know was facing one of five silent alarm buttons placed around the premises. He moved slowly until his finger tip just touched the button. In the next 30 seconds the robbers were gone and Mr. Know was on the phone to the police.

The police were already aware of the robbery. However Mr. Knows description of the robbers and the white panel truck they sped away in, helped. Mr. Know then called his insurance agent, who indicated the losses would be covered. The most important thing was that no one was hurt, Yes' the robbers were caught three hours later and everything was returned.

Certainly divine providence stepped in and helped out a bit, however, cooperation with the robbers themselves, and the silent security alarm system which automatically calls the police station, was equally beneficial. Not every restaurant can afford fancy security systems, although some modest types should be considered. The most important aspect of armed robbery is to remember that the safety of people (customers, employees and yourself) is paramount, as no amount of cash or other valuables is worth the maiming or death of a human being. Cooperate quietly.

Security Conclusion

Checking with your local fire and police departments on a regular basis often proves to be a wise action. These authorities keep records that show the number and types of crimes (including arson) which pertain to your geographical area. This information allows you to know the trends in the world of crime, and gives you a chance to prepare for those sometimes unexpected changes that may affect different communities. In addition, these authorities usually have updated security methods and ideas which can lessen your current risk of burglary, arson, robbery and employee theft.

It is a good idea to look into security alarm and deterrence companies. Even if you decide against a new type of alarm system, as an owner, it is to your advantage to learn as much as possible from each vendor (security company). To call these vendors and ask for an on site inspection should not cost you a penny.

INSURANCE

A General View

Insurance companies are in business due to their careful analyses of statistics and the offering of predetermined protection which allow the insured party or parties an assurance of fiscal security in case of specified events or happenings.

To the restaurant owner, insurance is generally very complicated because of a number of precisely written words that he or she cannot fully comprehend. The fact is, insurance is complicated, and is best served by specialists who comprehend and articulate their niche. Having an insurance agent who knows his or her business and completely understands your requirements, is important. In addition, if you can harbor an agent who will offer financial prudence regarding appropriate coverage, a sincere interest in the success of your business, and an ability to explain the "Bottom Line", then you should covet this agent-relationship as you would your best friend.

Too much coverage is almost as detrimental to the success of your business as not enough insurance coverage, which is a good reason you and your agent should periodically review the current policy as it applies to;

I. **Business changes in the restaurant.**

2. **Insurance coverage changes.**

3. **Changes affecting the underwriters of insurance.**

4. **Changes in the law.**

In the main, restaurant insurance has to do with the building, it's contents of material items, and liability protection regarding the safety and health of customers and employees. There is insurance for cash loss due to robbery and burglary, special liability insurance for restaurants serving alcoholic beverages, earnings replacement coverage, window glass breakage, and coverage for that bulky, however creative sign, which is suspended 60 feet in the air, etc.

Insurance naturally has limits to coverage and deductible amounts which converts to additional reasoning for differences in premiums. <u>Maintaining the appropriate amount of coverage for your particular needs, demands close scrutiny and periodic evaluation.</u>

WORKERS-COMPENSATION

Workers Compensation is a legal business requirement where employees are concerned. Penalties for failure to insure varies from jurisdiction (state, district, territory etc,) to jurisdiction. Fines can be as small as ten dollars or as large as fifty thousand dollars, or more.

Imprisonment is another penalty which can result in years of confinement. In particular instances employers can be liable to suit with defenses abrogated (nullified). Additionally, there are jurisdictions which may enjoin (prohibit) the employer (as is the case in the state of New Mexico) from doing business.

The most severe penalties currently belong to Alaska, which considers a $50,000.00 fine and ten years imprisonment, or both, and the employer may be liable to suit with defences abrogated, plus the individuals in charge of corporation activities are liable for monetary compensation.

Ohio, West Virginia, North Dakota, Nevada, Wyoming and the state of Washington, are six jurisdictions which actually handle the Workers Compensation policy to the extent that the business owner cannot obtain this insurance in any other manner (Monopolistic; Required in a state fund).

Governmental authorities representing all 50 states, Canada, and U.S. Territories including; Guam, American Samoa, Puerto Rico, and the Virgin Islands, all treat Workers Compensation seriously.

Restaurant owners should understand the implications which this type of insurance entails. For specific information dealing with the restaurant owners jurisdiction, it would be wise to have your insurance agent explain necessary details. You may also contact your state insurance authority or the UNITED STATES CHAMBER OF COMMERCE to obtain,"Business Insurance Chart of Laws and Requirements".

HEALTH / NUTRITION

VIII

Health and Nutrition

A subject most owners do not find particularly exciting, however, one which is probably the most important.

EDIBLE OILS: FACTS NOT CONFUSION

Overview

The owner wonders: "What should I put in the deep fryer?"

How long until restrictions limit shortenings to nothing but particular vegetable oils?

Is it true, that the people of Crete do not die of heart disease because they use olive oil and none other?

Common sense dictates that supportive facts plus reoccurring events utilizing identical elements and data will produce a "cause and effect" pattern.   Since owners are protective of their business, anything which threatens it will mean a slight internal panic. Hence we tend to believe what we hear before checking it out.

Shortening and oils............ The implications which chemistry and it's technological advances produce each year, are all evolving. Findings from one scientific group to another seem to make the news media stand up and take notice. And why not? News keeps the editorials going and the media in business. The problem with the last thirty years of developments, scientific discoveries and the like is that some apparent successes, often cause reactions not anticipated.

Examples include, agricultural insecticides, acid rain coming from the tall chimneys, and medical cures which work for some but not others. The intentions were honorable, however there were some aspects which only later, after public acceptance, did the problem surface.

Sure, there are many more positive benefits which the scientific community has given us, and we are grateful, however, this does not mean that the mistakes should be allowed to fall through the cracks, causing differing opinions and confusion.

What edible oils are used for ?

Edible oils fall into a number of usage groups;

All purpose shortenings

Cake and Icing shortenings

Specialty cake shortenings

Specialty Icing shortenings

Puff pastry shortenings

Yeast raised dough shortenings

All purpose margarines

Specialty margarines

Margarine substitutes (spreads)

Solid frying shortenings

Liquid frying shortenings

Lards and tallow

Liquid Dressings

Salad and cooking oils

Confectionery and non-dairy fats

Solid shortenings for food processors

Emulsifiers and stabilizers

What are the sources?

The main source of edible oils come from MEAT FATS (10.09%) and VEGETABLE OILS (89.91%). In figure 8-one the 17 usage groups (previously mentioned) are represented by 3 basic categories. The following (**figure 8-one**) allows you to see the percentage of edible oils used and what they are used for.

Soybean oil tops the list, with a whopping 74.0% usage. Meat Fats (the animal portion of A/V shortening) is responsible for 10.09% of all edible oils produced each year.

Historical oil pattern

On a per capita basis, about two thirds the visible fat consumed in the year 1940 was from animal origin and about one third from vegetable origin. In the year 1966 only one third of the fat consumed was from animal origin and two thirds was from vegetable origin. In 1981 this trend continued further and vegetable oils contributed 80% of the visible fat in the diet. Thus, over the past forty years, animal fats have gone from a dominating position to a very subordinate position as far as the visible fat portion of the diet is concerned. This information is based upon the quantity of fats purchased for consumption by the civilian population.

Definitions & Terms concerning
Nutrition & oils (fats)

Cholesterol: A crystalline, fatty like alcohol which occurs naturally in animal fats and tissues. Cholesterol is produced by the human body and is necessary to transport fats and fatty materials from the intestine to the blood. Cholesterol can deposit in the arteries as plaque (atherosclerosis) resulting in heart disease (heart attacks).

EDIBLE SOURCE OILS

FATS & OILS USED IN DOMESTIC FOOD CONSUMPTION IN THE U.S.
(Indicated by percentage of annual production for 1985)

	Baking & Frying Fats	Margarine	Salad & Cooking Oil	Total
Vegetable Oils				
Soybean	26.8	12.0	35.20	74.0
Corn	-	1.54	3.86	5.4
Cottonseed	1.27	.06	2.83	4.16
Palm	1.70	-	-	1.70
Peanut	-	-	.81	.81
Olive	-	-	.79	.79
Other	1.84*	.30**	.91*	3.05
TOTALS	31.61	13.9	44.4	89.91%
Meat Fats				
Edible Tallow & Lard	9.58	.51	-	10.09
Butter****	-	-	-	-
GRAND TOTALS	41.19	14.41	44.4	100.00%

(100% is representative of 13,510 million pounds of annual production for 1985)

* Includes; corn, peanut sunflower and safflower oils.
** Includes; peanut, coconut, palm, and sunflower oils.
*** Includes; coconut, palm, safflower, and sunflower oils.
**** Butter is not counted as it is a direct use.
        Note: The total fats and oils used in food does not include export products.

Sources: Economic Research Service of the U.S. Department of Agriculture.
The Institute of Shortening and Edible Oils, Inc.

Figure 8-One

ONLY ANIMAL FATS CONTAIN CHOLESTEROL. ALL
VEGETABLE SHORTENINGS CONTAIN NO CHOLESTE-
ROL . A typical order of french fries fried in Beef Tallow (A/V)
contains about 1/35th the cholesterol as there is in one egg.

Fatty Acid: A chain of carbon and hydrogen atoms which ends in
an acid group (carboxyl). Three such acid groups form a fat or oil
(triglyceride) when combined with glycerine. FATS AND OILS
ARE A MIXTURE OF TRIGLYCERIDE MOLECULES.

Essential Fatty Acids: Specific fatty acids required for proper
body growth and crucial for good skin and hair quality. These fatty acids cannot be manufactured by the body and must be consumed in the food we eat. These fatty acids are polyunsaturated.

Saturates: Fatty acid in which all the carbon atoms are filled to capacity with hydrogen. These are typically the highest melting fatty
acids and form the highest melting fats with one exception; the exception is lauric fats like coconut oil which are highly saturated
but relatively liquid.

Studies have shown an association between increased intake of
saturated fatty acids and increased serum cholesterol. Increased
serum cholesterol, in turn has been associated with increased coronary heart disease.

Polyunsaturates: Fatty acids that contain much less hydrogen than
monounsaturated or saturated fatty acids. These are typically the
lowest melting fatty acids and are liquids. Fats comprised of polyunsaturates are LIQUID OILS.

Recent studies suggest moderation in consumption of polyunsaturates in a healthy diet.

Monounsaturates: Fatty acids that contain less hydrogen than saturated fatty acids but more hydrogen than polyunsaturated fatty acids. These fatty acids are typically liquid, but when combined with
some saturates can form solid products.

Although previous research suggests monounsaturates had a neu-
tral effect on serum cholesterol and ultimately coronary heart dis-

ease, more recent studies indicate, monounsaturates may actually have a beneficial effect.

Fat Soluble Vitamins: Some vitamins are soluble only in fat (lipids) in the body. These vitamins are; A,D,E, and K. Fats in the food we eat carry these vitamins and fats in the blood and are necessary to transport and store these vitamins in the body.

THE CONTROVERSY: Fats and oils

In recent years scientists have studied the relationships of fats and oils with regard to diet and human health. Specific areas of concern have been that of CANCER, plus, HEART and CARDIO-VASCULAR DISEASE. Reports of studies have been confusing, because some scientific groups provide their basis for belief and still others demonstrate an opposing view. It appears as though most of the questions raised years ago, remain unsolved and may require decades to achieve mutual consensus among the scientific community.

From time to time the news brings attention to apparent meaningful results derived from studies and what are called findings.

OLIVE OIL and Crete. The first indication that differences existed between olive oil and other oils sprung from a Landmark Seven Countries study, started in 1958. Researchers in Japan, Yugoslavia, Finland, Italy, the Netherlands, Greece, and the United States looked at 16 groups of healthy middle aged men to learn just who might develop heart disease.

After ten years of observation, the men in Finland were found to be first with 628 fatal heart attacks per 10,000. Men in the United States came in second with a rate of 424 per 10,000. The other countries fell somewhere between 317 and 50 fatal heart attacks per 10,000 that is, except for Crete (an island off the coast of and belonging to Greece). Out of 655 Cretans, not a single male gendered human died of heart disease.

The usual contributing risk factors, like, smoking, obesity, high blood pressure, and blood cholesterol levels, were thought to be the explanation for the healthy hearts. Only until years later did another study come along and raise the possibility that the islanders' abundant use of olive oil could have some meaning to their unfamiliarity with heart attacks.

Individual scientists and those in the universities are learning and making progress in the study of the dietary aspects of olive oil, an oil high in monounsaturates, which apparently has value.

Studies between the years 1950 and 1974 caused a closer look at the Eskimos of Greenland. Only 3 heart attacks occurred among a population of 1,800. Was it the fish oils? Researchers found low blood cholesterol levels in the Eskimos, however, as with the Cretans, the levels were not low enough to explain the populations near nonexistent heart disease circumstance.

Later in the 1970s, scientists discovered that the Eskimos had fewer blood platelets, the blood cell fragments that initiate the clotting process. That means their blood takes longer to clot. Scientists believe this caused the reduction in heart attacks among the Eskimo population.

Yes' we now know that it is sensible to use a low fat diet, and if you are going to use an oil, olive oil is considered to be a good choice, however, none of the hard evidence suggests that we douse everything in oil. Also, prudence dictates we substitute some fish for meat as an entree in the healthy diet.

Cardiovascular (heart) Disease and diet

Physicians generally accept that a number of factors have some relationship to heart and cardiovascular disease. Most frequently mentioned factors include; HYPERTENSION (High blood pressure), CIGARETTE SMOKING, OBESITY, DIABETES, AGING, STRESS, INADEQUATE PHYSICAL ACTIVITY,BEING OF THE MALE GENDER, INHERITED TENDENCY AND HIGH SERUM CHOLESTEROL LEVELS. The more of these factors one human has, the higher the risk of having a heart attack, stroke or other cardiovascular disease.

A number of studies pertaining to other potential contributors of heart disease are being conducted. Included in these studies are individual oils such as, corn oil, meat fats and others of variable chemical compositions (saturated, monounsaturated, polyunsaturated, hydrogenated, etc). Varying and seemingly contradictory study results have been reported, consequently many physicians decline to make severe restrictive dietary recommendations to their patients.

Another area receiving substantial attention is that of CHOLESTEROL. Foods which contain cholesterol include; all meats, meat fats, fish, poultry, dairy products and shellfish (shrimp,lobster, oysters, etc). The role of cholesterol in cardiovascular disease is not totally understood, but in some way it contributes to blockage of blood vessels which can lead to strokes or arteriosclerosis.

What is known is that some people with high serum cholesterol levels have cardiovascular problems and and some do not. Some people with normal levels of cholesterol have the disease, and some do not. Some people have high cholesterol levels when ingesting only low levels. Others have low cholesterol levels no matter how much they ingest. Furthermore, It is not confirmed whether reducing cholesterol by dietary means will reduce a persons chances of having a heart attack or cardiovascular disease.

It would appear as though each individual has his or her special chemistry makeup that does not always fit a pattern or trend which may be the result of testing other people.

Cancer and diet

Cancers apparently occur when the body cells begin to multiply without the usual internal restraints. Each type of Cancer has it's own rate of occurrence and often tends to affect certain population groups sharing particular characteristics. Risk factors identified as potential contributors to Cancer development include: CIGAR-ETTE SMOKING, RADIATION, SUNLIGHT, OCCUPATION-AL HAZARDS, WATER & AIR POLLUTANTS, HEREDITY, PREDISPOSING MEDICAL CONDITIONS and CERTAIN DIETARY PATTERNS.

While the number of cancer victims in the U.S. has increased dramatically during the past 40 years, much of that increase is due to population growth. When changes in the size and age of the U.S. population are taken into account, the Cancer death rate has been shown to have increased 2-1/2% (between 1968 & 1978).

The suggestion has been advanced that much of the increase in respiratory Cancer mortality has been associated with smoking. On the other hand, trends in age adjusted mortality rates for virtually all other types of Cancer have remained essentially unchanged for the past 40 years. These include:

> **Colon, rectum, breast, prostate, and bladder Cancers with which dietary fat and other factors have been associated. Stomach Cancer mortality has fallen dramatically since 1930 for both men and women.**

In humans, proposed relationships between fat and Cancer are based on epidemiological data. Data for breast Cancer indicate that mortality in different countries is correlated with total caloric intake but not with intake of animal fat or vegetable fat. Recent data from animal studies indicates that the relationship between cancer development and diet may more likely be a function of total calories consumed than from any one dietary component.

Some studies suggest that high levels of dietary fat may act as a promoter of carcinogenesis rather than an initiator of tumors. A promoter is a compound that by itself is not carcinogenic but which enhances the ability of a carcinogen to produce Cancer. The existence, however, of a direct relationship between caloric content, fat unsaturation and carcinogenesis is unproven and very controversial.

CONCLUSIONS FOR EDIBLE OILS AND HEALTH

Scientists are in agreement on the positive roles of fats and oils in good nutrition and body well being. They are divided however, concerning the roles of various foods (including fats and oils) in regards to disease.

Industry leaders such as the McDonalds corporation (the largest single company as a source of fast food), do not make moves unless they are checked out thoroughly. A spokes person for that company says,"We use the highest quality of beef and vegetable shortening, and the reason we use that shortening is because it produces the highest quality finished product and best tasting one". Certainly a company with all that resource can ill afford mistakes, plus it seems clear that McDonalds demonstrates genuine concern for it's customers, the public.

The recommendations by the UNITED STATES Department of Agriculture and the UNITED STATES Department of Health and Human Services suggest the following six dietary guidelines;

1 EAT A VARIETY OF FOODS

2 MAINTAIN A DESIRABLE WEIGHT

3 AVOID TOO MUCH FAT, SATURATED FAT & CHOLESTEROL

4 AVOID TOO MUCH SUGAR

5 AVOID TOO MUCH SODIUM

6 IF YOU DRINK ALCOHOLIC BEVERAGES, DO SO IN MODERATION

Again' **Common sense** appears to be the winner, as most of the scientific community, and authorities concerned with nutrition and diet, indicate that MODERATION and variety are the best weapons in the prevention of disease and advocate of good health.

Primary Source:
The Economic Research Service, U. S. Department of Agriculture.
The Institute of Shortening and Edible Oils, Inc.

Foodborne Diseases

No matter if we hear about it or read about it, the thought of disease in relationship to the food prepared in your restaurant, is terrifying. When you hear the word Botulism or food poisoning you cringe inside, if only slightly. Do you know why you do that? Yes, that is right, out of fear. Underneath all that self confidence and the experience you have piled up so far, lurks a quiet little nagging element which periodically asks; What if someone gets sick in my restaurant?

Even though you have insurance coverage, and try to maintain a clean operation, there maybe a chance that undetected contamination or some particular bacteria has started a chain of events which you really can't see, unless of course your handy microscope (which you carry in a holster) spends 24 hours a day with your educated (Chemistry degree) eyes, looking for and examining foods, employees hands, surfaces which come in contact with employees and food items, cartons, cans, and hundreds of other things. Somehow, the microscope idea is not what you had in mind, however, you still have wishes that the fear of foodborne illness would disappear.

The best way to eradicate the fear, is to learn what the diseases are, how they multiply, methods of transport and contact, and finally, what you can do that will reduce or eliminate the chances of these events from happening. When the restaurant owner has accomplished these tasks, he or she will wisely devise and implement a restaurant health program of their own, which will arrest the fear.

Even after the owners fear is replaced with peace of mind, he or she must always be concerned, for there are always changes, additions and scientific findings which the world of chemistry will forever produce.

Salmonellosis

A group of bacteria called Salmonella was first identified in the year 1885 by Salmon and Smith. There are now 2000 antigenic types of Salmonella, with more being catalogued all the time.

Examples of foods involved:

Poultry, red meats, eggs, dried foods and dairy products.

What is the cause?

Salmonellae bacteria widespread in nature, live and grow in the intestinal tracts of human beings and animals.

What are the symptoms?

Severe headache, followed by vomiting, diarrhea, abdominal cramps, and fever. Infants, the elderly, and persons with low resistance are the most susceptible. Severe infections cause high fever and may lead to death.

Characteristics

Transmitted by eating contaminated food, or by contact with infected persons or carriers of the infection. Also is transmitted by insects, rodents and pets. Takes effect within 12 to 36 hours. The duration is between 2 to 7 days.

Preventive Measures

The bacteria is destroyed by heating the food to 140 degrees Fahrenheit and holding for 10 minutes. If you were to bring the food to a higher temperature, the holding time decreases rapidly. 155 degrees requires just a few seconds holding time. Refrigeration at 40 degrees Fahrenheit inhibits the growth (increase) of Salmonellae, but they remain alive in foods in the refrigerator or freezer, and in dried foods.

Botulism (Clostridium Botulinum)

There are basically two types: 1. Conventional Botulism 2. Infant Botulism. The following considers all forms of botulism, regardless of definitive titles, names or labels.

Examples of foods involved:

Canned low-acid foods, smoked fish, potato salad, seasoned cooked onions, garlic with soybean oil (the basic ingredient to a garlic butter), pickled Jalapeno peppers and more.

What is the cause?

Clostridium Botulism spores, forming organisms that grow and produce toxin in the absence of oxygen, such as a sealed container.

What are the symptoms?

Double vision, inability to swallow, speech difficulty, progressive respiratory paralysis.

Fatality rate in the United States is high, at about 65 percent.

Characteristics of the illness

Transmitted by eating food containing the toxin.
Takes affect within 12 to 36 hours or longer. Duration is 3 to 6 days.

Preventive measures

Once an opened can is sited and suspicion of botulism is confirmed, the food container and evidence are reported to proper authorities (usually the health and environmental department and the Center for Disease Control CDC). The destruction of the bacteria can be performed in the following manner, however unnecessary and unwanted in the restaurant environment;

The bacterial spores in food are destroyed by high temperature obtained only in the pressure canner. More than 6 hours is needed to kill the spores at boiling temperature (212 degrees Fahrenheit). The toxin is destroyed by boiling for 10 to 20 minutes, depending on the kind of food.

Staph (Staphylococcal Poisoning)

Examples of foods involved

Custards, egg salad, potato salad, chicken salad, macaroni salad, ham, salami, and cheese.

What is the cause?

Staphylococcus Aureus. Bacteria growing in food produces a toxin that is extremely resistant to heat.

What are the symptoms?

Vomiting, diarrhea, prostration, abdominal cramps. Generally mild and often attributed to other causes.

Characteristics of the illness

Transmitted by food handlers who carry the bacteria and by eating food containing the bacteria. Takes affect within 3 to 8 hours. Duration from 1 to 2 days.

Preventive measures

Growth of bacteria that produces the toxin is inhibited by keeping hot foods above 140 degrees Fahrenheit and cold foods at or below 40 degrees Fahrenheit. The toxin is destroyed by boiling for several hours or heating food in a pressure cooker at 240 degrees Fahrenheit for 30 minutes.

Perfringens poisoning (Clostridium Perfringens)

Examples of foods involved

Stews, soups, or gravies made from poultry or red meat.

What is the cause?

Spore forming bacteria that grow in the absence of oxygen. Cooking procedures which reach average high temperatures are generally sufficient to destroy vegetative cells, however, heat resistant spores can survive.

What are the symptoms?

Nausea with out vomiting, diarrhea, acute inflammation of the stomach and intestines.

Characteristics of the illness

Transmitted by eating food contaminated with abnormally high large numbers of the bacteria.

Takes affect within 8 to 20 hours. Duration will persist for 24 hours.

Preventive measures

To prevent growth of surviving bacteria in cooked meats,gravies, and meat casseroles, cool foods rapidly by refrigeration (40 degrees Fahrenheit or below) or hold them above 140 degrees Fahrenheit.

Other Concerns

The foodborne illness series that has been indicated, are the main concerns to the restaurant owner and most can be curtailed by temperature control. The methods of bacteria transmission which also bear extreme importance are declined personal hygiene plus insect and rodent (pest control) infestation. Both of these (human and animal) carriers can move the germs and make for bacteria multiplication and transmission of disease. The importance of hygienic food production procedures and eradication of insects and rodents cannot be over blown (see the Production/Operations and Maintenance sections for more information).

Foodborne Illness conclusions

To the average human being, restaurant owners are not average in every sense of the word, it is normal to consider unseen microscopic events with less consideration than the big car smash up outside, in front of the restaurant. It is very easy to forget the health inspectors visit two days ago. What everyone in the health business means to say to the restaurant owner is, "Please don't be average". They expect the restaurant owner to be well above average and grasp the appropriate procedures and seriousness of foodborne illness prevention. This message appears to be similar to the concerns most Americans exclaim when told that drinking and driving do not mix. Do you suppose it is because the responsibility of driving a 4,000 pound vehicle is being associated with feeding human kind from our restaurants?

The need for the education of food handlers (like restaurant employees) is clear, and the owner is the only person today, who can make it happen. Obtaining more reading and training material for employees is a step in the right direction. Why? Because it will help protect the customers, the industry and our restaurant business too.

Sources: U. S. Department of Health and Human Services,
Public Health Service, Food and Drug Administration,
Center for Disease Control and the Center for Food Safety and
Applied Nutrition.

FOOD-PROTECTION CERTIFICATION PROGRAM
(Foodborne Illness)

Why is there concern about Foodborne Illness to the degree that government authorities and leaders among the private sector feel the need for a testing program?

In 1980 alone, the CDC (Center for Disease Control) reported 612 outbreaks of Foodborne Illness with 13,791 cases nationwide. The leading culprits were Salmonella, Staphyloccocus aureus and Clostrididium perfringens. 54% (Fifty four percent) of the outbreaks were caused by food eaten in restaurants. There are many more occurrences than what we read or hear about, and therefore restaurant owners should be aware and act accordingly.

This is not an area where owners should take the attitude that, "This won't happen to me, it will happen to some other owner who is sloppy". Every time a case of Foodborne Illness is established any where in the country, that means, "X" amount of potential customers will not be eating out as much or at all. Foodborne Illness is not healthy for the person or persons who are victims, and it is not good for the restaurant industry. A step in the right direction is the "Food Protection Certification Program".

A nationwide testing program was started in 1985 and offered by the Educational Testing Service (ETS), a non profit organization out of Princeton, New Jersey. Many states and other smaller jurisdictions have already adopted the certification program, some making it mandatory for a member or members (employees and/or employer) of a restaurant establishment to be tested and certified.

The program is offered in all states and is voluntary to applicants in those jurisdictions who do not require manager certification.

Purpose of the program: To test persons who have an on going responsibility in protecting the consumer from FOODBORNE ILLNESS and work in food preparation, serving, or dispensing food establishments. The standards set forth are those in the FDA Model Food Service Sanitation Ordinance dated 1976, the Model Sanitation Ordinance for Vending Food and Beverage dated 1978 and the Retail Food Store Sanitation Code dated 1982.

Development of the Test: In 1982, the Food and Drug Administration (FDA) contacted the Center for Occupational and Professional Assessment (COPA), a division of the Educational Testing Service (ETS) to determine the feasibility of producing a national program for testing food industry personnel which would be job related, valid, and reliable. In 1983 COPA officials met with food specialists, local and state regulatory agencies, representatives of the food industry, educators, and FDA officials. Meetings were conducted in Washington D.C. and Chicago, Illinois.

After a great deal of input from all concerned, the FDA concluded that most jurisdictions believed a national testing program would be helpful and appropriate.

Since the program has been established, 25% of the states have adopted the program (as of this writing). Some states or jurisdictions require only one member of an establishment to become certified, while other states and jurisdictions will stipulate two or more.

General areas covered by the test

Hazardous foods: Identification, Preventative action and control. Applicable standards, including approved sources, proper temperatures,and the need for record keeping.

Serving and Dispensing: Set up procedures and proper utensils.

Processing: Thawing, preparation times, control for salmonella / Trichinella and toxic container and utensils.

Recycling Leftovers: Storage times and temperatures, cooling/ reheating, freezing and refreezing.

Storage: Correct temperatures, proper conditions, stock rotation.

Facilities and Equipment: Water supply, sewage, refuse disposal, toilet facilities, detergents, sanitizers, pest control and adequacy of equipment.

Purchasing & Receiving: Record keeping, sign of infestation, contamination and spoilage.

Employees: Health and hygiene, illness, infection, burns, and control of diseases causing foodborne illness.

Holding and Displaying: Safe / unsafe containers, holding times & temperatures, and protection from contamination.

Test program Information

The test is given at many locations throughout the U.S. (call or write for specific locations: See contact information).

The test takes two hours and is the multiple choice format.

Test schedule: The test is given on the second Monday of each month except December. The test is conducted at 4:00P.M. in every time zone in the U.S.

You may prepare for the test by sending for a booklet (see address at the end of this text), although it is assumed that applicants have some training.

Ten good reasons why owners should feel positive about the certification program?

1. It enhances public health and safety.

2. Establishes uniform standards of certification.

3. Increases professionalism in the retail food industry.

4. Transfers the burden of test administration, scoring, reporting, and record keeping to a highly qualified national testing service.

5. Offers a standard against which to measure employee knowledge for the protection of the public.

6. Provides better qualified personnel, reducing the risk of causing Foodborne Illness and exposure to shutdown and/or costly litigation.

7. Strengthens in-house training programs.

8. The more eating establishments which operate higher in health consciousness, cause more of the public to eat out.

9. The U.S. government agency wisely turned this program over to a specialized non profit organization. Red tape is not involved, making for simplification.

10. A certificate indicating your establishment is certified in the food protection program shows customers your genuine concern for their welfare.

Contact information

The Environmental Health Department in your jurisdiction, or contact directly:

**The Educational Testing Service
CN 6515
Princeton, N.J. 08541**

Phone: (area code 609) 921-9000

C P R (Cardiopulmonary Resuscitation)

CPR provides artificial circulation and breathing to a person whose heart and lungs have stopped functioning because of heart attack, shock, drowning, or other serious cause.

External cardiac compressions (see figure **8-two**) administered manually are alternated with mouth to mouth resuscitation (see figure **8-three**) to stimulate the natural functions of the heart and lungs, and often times, to save a life.

If a customer or employee shows evidence of need for CPR, it is good to know you can help save a life, although the odds are slim that you will ever need to do so.

Several booklets and information are available through your local Red Cross chapter. Why not call them and learn what types of materials and training programs they offer?

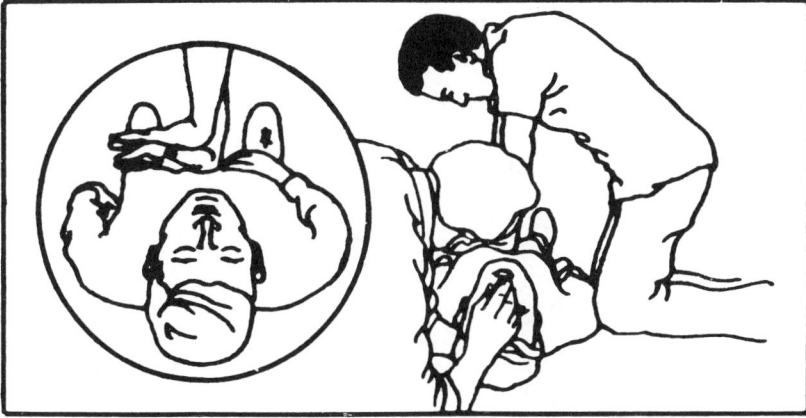

Figure 8-two

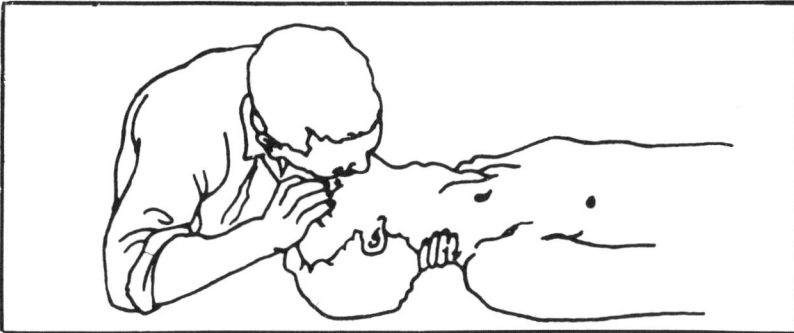

Figure 8-three
Courtesy of The American Red Cross

HEIMLICH MANEUVER (Abdominal Thrust)

When a customer or employee is choking it is usually something (food or other obstruction) caught in the wind pipe. Often times a simple thump (heavy pat) on the back will help relieve the problem.

Then there are those occasions when the Heimlich Maneuver (see figure **8-four**) may be needed. Contact your local American Red Cross office for posters, and training information. It's important.

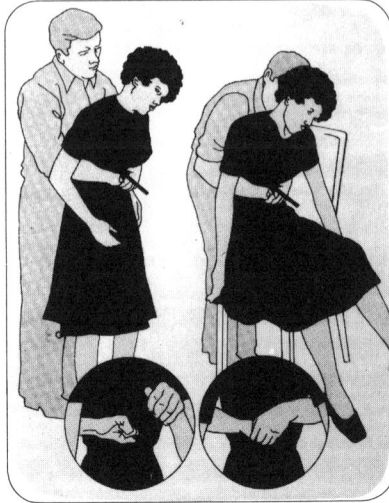

Figure 8-four
Courtesy of The American Red Cross

EPILEPSY

A nervous disorder marked by convulsive attacks with loss of consciousness, that is the brief description of Epilepsy. Should a customer or employee produce attacks of this kind, be sure that they do not swallow their tongue, apply cold wet compress to the forehead and keep the person calm. If after two or three minutes, the person afflicted does not revive, then you should call the paramedics or other emergency medical care.

BEYOND FIRST AID

Fire department, Police department, Paramedics, Hospital emergency, doctors office, and other emergency phone numbers are a must for the owner to have posted at strategic points in his or her restaurant.

There are three points which emphasize what to be aware of if you are not fully conversant with First Aid treatment and have feelings of apprehensiveness. In other words; if you do not do anything else, follow these points:

1.

When you see serious health problems or events which are beyond your capabilities, do not waste time wondering what to do. Call for professional help.

2.

When you are able to give First Aid to any degree, be sure that the afflicted or injured person receives professional attention, in any case. This relieves your liability, plus your insurance company would rather pay a doctors call or hospital emergency care bill, as opposed to legal defence in a law suit. In addition, Professional treatment demonstrates that your restaurant cares about it's customers and employees, which always works to your advantage.

3.

The Heimlich Maneuver, CPR and Epileptic seizure assistance are instances where time may be a simple matter of life or death. If you feel less than comfortable and confident in handling such events, CALL FOR PROFESSIONAL HELP.

AIDS:
(Acquired Immune Deficiency Syndrome)

The Restaurant is not a place where this virus is to be contracted.

How is it spread?

AIDS is spread by the sharing of body fluids. The evidence provided indicates that **sexual contact, the sharing of needles
by I.V. drug users, or transfusions of blood or blood
products,** that have become contaminated with the virus, are the
methods of contracting the disease.

What AIDS isn't

The virus, AIDS isn't contracted by **casual contact.** This simply
means that the virus cannot be transmitted from;

> a drinking glass,
> a toilet seat,
> a hand shake,...............or anything else considered to be
> **casual contact.**
> Food items are not known to transmit the virus either.

Education

It is said that blindness and Cancer are the two biggest fears where
illness, disease, bodily injury and affliction are concerned. Now
AIDS has joined the ranks. The reason is fear of what is not completely understood or known. As medical progress is inevitable we
can best serve the restaurant industry, hence our private enterprise, by keeping in touch with developments as they unfold.

Officials & industry authorities say

Several State Restaurant association leaders, officials representing various task force units and institutes which do research, all agree on at least two points which affect the restaurant industry;

1.   AIDS cannot be caught in a restaurant.

2.   Public concern about getting AIDS in a restaurant is virtually nonexistent.

You Can't Get AIDS—

By Shaking Hands   **Or By Hugging**

In Restaurants   **Or In Restrooms**

**AIDS doesn't spread through casual contact.
Don't let fear get in the way of facts.
Take the time to learn about AIDS.**

American Red Cross

Figure 8-five
Courtesy of The American Red Cross

There is a poster which is produced by the AMERICAN RED CROSS (see figure **8-five, previous page**) which points out,"You Can't Get AIDS", in restaurants, by shaking hands, hugging, or in rest rooms. Many restaurants have already obtained this poster to help educate both employees and customers alike.

For more information:

Contact: The American Red Cross
      National Headquarters
      Communication Services
      17th and D Streets, N.W.
      Washington, DC 20006

Or......... contact your local American Red Cross chapter.

Sources: The American Red Cross
Dr. A.A. Gonzales, Albuquerque, New Mexico.
New Mexico AIDS Services,Inc.

Food Additives:
(Facts & Consequences)

Overview

The restaurant kitchen is home to ingredients that make foods last longer and stay fresher, just as the cook stove or a walk-in refrigerator. Humankind have always endeavored to find ways to make food last longer and still be edible. Salt, sugar, acids, and smoke have been used in the past to preserve food (primarily fish and meat). Uses of this kind were usually performed on the farm or the kitchen at home.

Today, chemical additives used in foods are done so for several reasons; some are intended to improve the nutritional value, while others give color, enhance flavor, extend the food's shelf life and stability.

There are also those which keep food from spoiling, becoming rancid and bad tasting. ......The last three items are the ones which can have consequences that are of greater concern to the restaurant owner.

About Preservatives

Preservatives perform two functions; As microbial agents, they keep food from spoiling; And as antioxidants, they keep foods from becoming rancid or developing off-colors and flavors.

Antimicrobial agents are added to food to inhibit or prevent growth of molds, yeasts and bacteria. Antioxidants are used in a wide variety of foods, most of which contain fats and oils to prevent them from becoming rancid.

Antimicrobial & Antioxidant Findings, Rulings & Information

The Food & Drug Administration (FDA) has broad authority since the 1938 Food, Drug and Cosmetic Act, which allows for moves against responsible parties where chemicals in food are unsafe for human consumption. This authority was strengthened in 1958 with the passage of the Food Additives Amendment, which required proof of an additives safety.

Of at least twenty seven GRAS (**Generally Recognized as Safe**) antimicrobial and antioxidant agents, FDA has reaffirmed that six may continue to be safely used. These are:

1. Benzoic acid
2. Methylparaben
3. Propyl gallate
4. Propylparaben
5. Sodium Benzoate
6. Stannous Chloride

Several GRAS agent additives have not as yet been acted upon by reaffirming their safety, which means that the FDA is generally evaluating data before taking action. FDA has proposed (no action yet) that the following agent additives be reaffirmed as GRAS (Generally Recognized as Safe) ;

7. Ascorbic Acid
8. Ascorbyl Palmitate
9. Erythorbic Acid
10. Sodium Ascorbate
11. Sodium Erythorbate

Calcium Ascorbate was proposed for exclusion as GRAS, however, as mentioned for the above items 7 - 11, there has been no final reaffirmation to these agent additives as yet. The agent additives 7 - 11 are generally used in small concentrations to inhibit enzymatic browning and/or as preservatives in foods and beverages, such as; Concentrated milk products, meat products, pickling brine for pork, and beef cuts, baked goods, soft and hard candies, fats, oils, gravies, breakfast cereals, and processed fruits and vegetables.

Tocopherols: The Vitamin "E"Antioxidant

There are eight known forms of Tocopherols that occur naturally in animal tissues and in vegetable oils, cereals, nuts, and leafy vegetables. Six other Tocopherol derivatives are prepared commercially for use as antioxidants in foods. Alpha Tocopherol is the most potent vitamin E compound. All forms of Tocopherols contribute varying amounts of vitamin E to the diet. Mixed concentrates have been used as antioxidants in food since 1949. These include baked goods, breakfast cereals, milk products, gelatins, puddings, fillings, soups, snack goods, nonalcoholic beverages, seasonings, flavorings, and infant formulas.

Antioxidants not to be used;

Potassium Bisulfite

Potassium Metabisulfite

Sodium Bisulfite

Sodium Metabisulfite

Sodium Sulfite

Sulfur Dioxide

Sulfiting agents such as Sodium Metabisulfite, marketed as "vegetable fresheners" or "potato whitening" agents, were used by the food service and the restaurant industry. This is what many restaurant owners, operators, managers, chefs, cooks, etc, used in the kitchen to keep the lettuce fresh and crisp, plus the fruits and vegetables from discoloration.

In March 1983 after receiving reports of adverse reactions to sulfites among certain segments of the population, particularly asthmatics, FDA advised the state agencies responsible for overseeing the food service and restaurant industry that consumers should be informed when sulfiting agents are used through display of "conspicuous and easily readable labels, signs, placards, menu statements, or by other means".

FDA added that foods treated with sulfiting agents would not be considered safe unless consumers were properly informed of their use. Since that time many restaurant owners have stopped using sulfiting agents.

Sulfur dioxide is a colorless gas that has been used for many years to sanitize food containers and fermentation equipment, to inhibit microbial spoilage, and as a antioxidant. Sulfur dioxide is not to be used in meats or other foods that are substantial sources of thiamine (vitamin B), because of it's adverse effects on this vitamin.

The FDA concludes final action on Sulfiting Agents.

As of Wednesday, July 9th, 1986, the action of **Final Rule** was made law regarding Sulfiting Agents. This ruling is published in the Federal Register and should be found in most public library systems in each state. As the rulings text is quite extensive we will keep to the highlights.

The FDA concluded it's findings in early 1986 and submitted the appropriate proposal, which has a thirty day limit for appeal. Appeals come from private citizens, professionals (scientific, technical and medical), business, industry and political positions.

There were 553 comments in response to the proposal. Individual consumers accounted for 497 of these comments. The remaining were received from medical professional, scientists, health departments (state & local), government officials, medical associations, food manufacturers, trade associations, a consumer group, and a member of congress. Almost all of the comments agreed with the FDA. The conclusion of the FDA indicated that the use of Sulfites as a preservative on fruits and vegetables intended to be served raw or sold to consumers is not GRAS (generally recognized as safe).

More than half (306) of the consumers reported that either they or a close relative or friend is sensitive to sulfite treated foods.

In any case, the following is the heart of the written ruling affecting the six (6) Sulfiting agents (listed on page 157);

*Limitations, restrictions, or explanation. These substances (the six Listed) are generally recognized as safe when used in accordance with good **manufacturing** practice, except that it is not used in meats or in food recognized as a source of vitamin Bl, and that it is **not** used on **Fruits or vegetables** intended to be served raw to consumers or sold raw to consumers or to be presented to consumers as fresh.*

Even the lemon juice you use in various recipes is technically an antioxidant, however wonderfully safe.

Vitamin additives

A misconception among many is that the addition of vitamins and minerals always makes a food superior to unfortified foods. Adding nutrients already abundant in a diet provides no extra benefit, because the body uses only what it needs.

There can also be too much of a good thing. Excessive amounts of some nutrients, such as vitamins A and D, or even traces of copper, zinc, molybdenum and selenium, can be toxic.

Fortifying by nature or laboratory?

Some critics say that fortifying food is tampering with nature. They maintain that nutrients synthesized in the laboratory and then added during processing are inferior to those naturally present in food.

Actually, each vitamin, mineral or amino acid has a specific molecular structure that is the same whatever the origin of the compound. The body cannot distinguish between a vitamin that occurs naturally in a plant or animal product and the same compound created in the laboratory.

Additives for appeal (looks)

Coloring agents contribute nothing to nutrition, taste, safety or ease of processing. Some consumer advocates say that food is often made to look more appetizing at the risk of increasing health hazards.

Today, food colors are used in virtually all processed foods. While their use is not restricted, per se, they cannot be used in unnecessary amounts or to cover up unwholesome products. Artificial colors must be listed as ingredients in all foods excepting butter, ice cream, and cheese.

There are thirty three colors currently permitted for use in food. Nearly half of them are synthetic colors, which are created in laboratories. The man made colors are used the most because they are the strongest, and therefore can be used by manufacturers in smaller quantities at less cost.

The most widely used food colors are Red number 40 and Yellow number 5, and both are under close scrutiny because of possible health risks. Red number 40 is suspected of causing premature malignant lymph tumors when fed in large amounts to mice. In 1977 the Health Research Group petitioned FDA to prohibit it's use along with several other colors. FDA denied the petition, but tabled a final decision on Red number 40 pending further study. Since that time a scientific group reported (October 1981) to FDA, that the Red number 40 color was safe for use in food and drugs.

Yellow number 5 causes allergic reactions (mainly rashes and sniffles) in an estimated 50,000 to 90,000 Americans. The reactions are usually minor but in some instances can be life threatening. Because of it's relatively narrow effect, FDA has required manufacturers to list Yellow number 5 on labels that apply to foods which contain the food coloring.

Additives for flavor

Over one thousand seven hundred (1700) natural and synthetic substances are used to flavor foods. This makes flavor additives the largest single category of food additives.

Flavor additives have come under less criticism than colors or antioxidants, perhaps it is because they have a more direct purpose in foods. Still, some consumer groups question the necessity of using artificial flavors. FDA scientists maintain that anyone sensitive to artificial flavors are likely to react to natural flavors as well, due to the chemical similarities.

Flavor enhancers magnify or modify the flavor of foods, although they do not contribute any flavor of their own. Some of them work by temporarily deadening certain nerves, which are those responsible for perception of bitterness, thereby increasing other tastes.

MSG; The best known enhancer.

The amino acid, MONOSODIUM GLUTAMATE (MSG) is the best known and most widely used flavor enhancer. Scientists still are not sure exactly how it works, however, all indications seem to point to, increasing the nerve impulses responsible for perception of flavors. Some years ago , public pressure persuaded manufacturers to stop using MSG in baby foods, after studies showed that large amounts destroyed brain cells in young mice.

Other Additives: Emulsifiers (mixers)

_Stabilizers and thickeners

_pH Control agents

_Leavening agents

_Maturing and Bleaching agents

_Anti-caking agents

_Humectants

Emulsifiers(mixers)

Some liquids do not mix well unless there is an emulsifier. In salad dressing, oil and vinegar separate as soon as the mixing stops. When an emulsifier is added, the ingredients stay mixed longer.

Many emulsifiers come from natural sources. Lecithin, naturally present in milk, keeps fat and water together. Egg yolks, which also contain lecithin, improve the texture of ice cream and mayonnaise. The mono- and diglycerides come from vegetables or animal tallow and make bread soft, improve the stability of margarine, and prevent oil and peanuts in peanut butter from separating.

Stabilizers and thickeners

These compounds improve the appearance and the way foods feel in the mouth through uniform texture. They work by absorbing water. Without stabilizers and thickeners, ice crystals would form in ice cream and other frozen desserts, plus particles of chocolate would settle out of chocolate milk.

Stabilizers are also used to prevent evaporation and deterioration of volatile flavor oils used in cakes, puddings and gelatin mixes.

Most stabilizers and thickeners are natural carbohydrates. Gelatin, made from animal bones, hooves, and other parts, and pectin from citrus rind, are used in food processing.

pH Control agents

These affect the texture, taste and safety of foods by controlling the acidity or alkalinity. Acids, give a tart taste to such foods as soft drinks, sherbets and cheese spreads. They are also used to insure the safety of low-acid canned foods, such as beets.

Alkalizers alter the texture and flavor of many foods, including chocolate. After cocoa beans are picked, they are allowed to dry and ferment before they are made into chocolate. During processing, alkalizers are sometimes added to neutralize the acids produced during fermentation and to provide a darker,richer color, plus a milder flavor.

Leavening agents

Although air and steam help to create a light texture in bread and cake, carbon dioxide is the key to making baked goods rise properly. Without leavening agents that produce or stimulate production of carbon dioxide, we would not have light, soft baked goods.

Maturing and Bleaching agents

These are used primarily to get flour ready for baking because of natural pigments that give milled flour a yellowish color. Flour lacks the qualities necessary to make stable, elastic dough. When aged for several months, it gradually whitens and matures to become useful for baking.

Anti-caking agents

Compounds like calcium silicate, iron ammonium citrate and silicon dioxide are used to keep table salt, baking powder, powdered sugar and other powdered food items free flowing without sticking together. By absorbing moisture, these chemicals prevent caking, lumping and clustering that otherwise makes powdered or crystalline products difficult to use.

Humectants

These are substances that retain moisture in shredded coconut, marshmallows, soft candies, and other confections. One of the most common is glycerine. The sweetener sorbitol is also used for this purpose.

Source: Department of Health and Human Services,
U.S. Food and Drug Administration

EQUIPMENT

IX

A General View

As the established owner knows, there are literally thousands of pieces of equipment (tools of the trade) to be utilized effectively and efficiently in the restaurant business. Each year the various types of equipment expand, mature, offering new controls, features, and add-on devices, with a means to accomplish the productivity needs of the restaurant industry.

Many new types of equipment are effective in all areas of foodservice, while others may be limited. Cooking devices have experienced advances in construction, controls, insulation materials, heating elements, and designed air-flows that are still, or move in predictable patterns. Natural gas and electricity are still the primary sources of power for heat exchangers, microwaves, infrared beams, steam and those combination units. The sizes are also available which produce small amounts for minimum requirements, up to the Goliath tanks which cook stews and soups, etc, enough for a small army.

Quality and Service a MUST

The importance of quality cannot be over-stressed. The owner needs to look at construction, safety-features, and productivity, each time he or she makes a buying decision. In addition to these three primary ingredients to an equipment purchase, the owner needs to be reassured that the service and parts will be there when needed.

Oddly enough to most owners, the initial cost of a piece of equipment should be the last consideration. Unfortunately for many owners in the restaurant business, the reverse is true. Many times however, owners will purchase the least expensive piece of equipment which may be the wise choice. When the need for productivity calls for a no-frills (bells and whistles) item like a standard six burner stove and oven, then the reasoning for a lower cost piece of equipment may be appropriate.

When the owner purchases an inexpensive household toaster or microwave oven, it is a mistake to believe that the productivity and cost effectiveness are equal trade-offs for heavy duty, commercial units. In choosing equipment between manufacturers or within a line of equipment which essentially does the same thing, the focus should be on productivity, safety, service and finally cost.

Who is the NSF?

That little 1-1/4 inch blue seal with the letters NSF affixed to various cooking, refrigeration and dish-washing equipment means that the equipment manufacturer has had the NATIONAL SANITATION FOUNDATION complete a number of tests to that same model of equipment with identical manufacturing specifications. NSF's standards are consensus documents. Evaluation, testing, and listing are objective, third party certification procedures analogous to those provided by Underwriters Laboratories (UL); however, NSF focuses on the public health or the environment.

NSF is a "Not for Profit" corporation chartered in 1944 under the laws of the state of Michigan. Although they are a non-official organization, the testing of products, systems, and services are compared against government regulations, in addition to consensus standards and the NSF's own rigorous standards.

There is no official mandate for the use of NSF listing, Certification or assessment services. Manufacturers submit their products on a voluntary basis and pay for the tests and evaluation services. More than 150,000 products, made by 1400 U.S. and foreign manufacturers are currently listed. Annually, 1.6 million products are delivered with the NSF mark of approval.

The general equipment groups which pertain to the restaurant owner are:

RANGES, REFRIGERATORS, FREEZERS, COFFEE MAKERS, MILK AND SOFT ICE CREAM DISPENSERS, DRINKING WATER FILTERS, DISH-WASHING EQUIPMENT, GARBAGE DISPOSALS, HOT FOOD TABLES, AND OTHER COOKING EQUIPMENT WHICH REQUIRES TEMPERATURE CONTROLLING DEVICES AND MECHANISMS.

Equipment Problem and the NSF?

If you have a consistent problem with your NSF labeled equipment, be sure you contact the equipment manufacturer or dealer before jumping the gun. Sometimes replacement parts like thermostatic controls, are problematic or appear faulty. If the dealer or manufacturer is unable to come up with a solution or an acknowledgement that there is indeed a glitch in the making, it may be appropriate to ask the NSF to investigate.

The NSF is interested only if the equipment in question has their seal of approval on it, and if the problem is related to the test standards which they originally approved. Normally, the dealers and manufacturers take care of any equipment problem, however it is always good to know there are alternatives.

Contact regional offices at NSF:
Ann Arbor, Michigan
Upland, California
Chalfont, Pennsylvania
Atlanta, Georgia
Chelsea, Michigan
Brussels, Belgium

Source: National Sanitation Foundation, Ann Arbor, Michigan

NOTE: Equipment with the NSF seal on it is a primary concern, as it's value is diminished if manufacturers do not consistently produce the identical equipment which originally passed the NSF standards. NSF is may be additionally interested because they want to be positive they did not make a mistake. Nothing very serious can, in all probability ever come from an NSF investigation pertaining to their standards, although a report will receive attention.

Choosing Equipment

The first priority you should establish is based around PRODUC-
TIVITY. If you are not interested in producing enough to keep up
with demand, then you are a true elitist who probably would not
benefit from increased output. Most restaurants are very much
concerned with productivity, as they react to the emotional ups and
downs with the rush hour or hectic pace of an event, which stems
from a high level of activity through putting out food and drink.

CHOOSING BY PRIORITY:

First; Productivity. If you sell more, your revenues and profit
will increase. This basic rule of business over shadows all other
considerations as you are in business to answer the demands of
both the now-customer, and the prospective customer. If you do
not provide the quality of product and the service which accompanies the product, someone else will. Consequently the ability to
produce foodservice products to meet the demand is more important than the cost differential between two pieces of equipment,
one (the expensive model) of which increases productivity by 50
percent or more. This aspect can pay for the cost differential between the higher priced model and the lower priced model.

Second; Quality. The quality of a piece of equipment denotes
the workmanship and materials which provides for longevity. You
want a piece of equipment that is going to be in use for many years
therefore adding to it's cost effectiveness. SAFETY considerations
are a part of this second category and should be addressed when
questioning the quality.

Third; Service. Sooner or later equipment of all kinds needs
maintenance and/or repair and/or replacement parts. Being assured
of dependable service is an important consideration given the alternative of equipment down-time.

Fourth; Efficiency. Greater productivity produces a greater amount of energy. This is another reason why productivity is a first consideration. If the equipment you are shopping for is able to maintain the desired productivity level and afford energy savings over and above another model, then it will be truly efficient.

Fifth; COST. An important consideration? Yes. However not as important as the other four. Don't make the mistake of spending $500.00 for a piece of equipment that does not produce as much (25% or more) as the $1200.00 model which is built to last ten years longer. Even at a 25 percent increase in productivity, you will have paid for the $700.00 difference in less than a year.

BELLS AND WHISTLES

The nice to have features which allow for effective use of labor time are generally helpful. There are many electronic controlling devices which provide convenience and less thought for attention to the equipment. The points which you must deal with concern repair, replacement parts and down-time. If the convenience features deliver real productivity and safety benefits, they are probably worth the extra cost. If however, you're restaurant is located far from service and maintenance people, which can cause serious down-time problems, then you will be better off with the more basic and standard features.

Manufacturers and the Restaurant

Today there are many equipment manufacturers to choose from. Most are very quality conscious and offer equipment which gives the owner many years of use. Since competition among the equipment manufacturers is strong, it appears that the producers of the lesser quality equipment will either upgrade their product or go out of business.

Equipment manufacturers are eager to serve the foodservice industry because they recognize eminent growth. It is also true that equipment companies, by in large, are a major source of support to the restaurant industry. Who do you think purchases a great amount of advertising which appears in at least three restaurant trade journals, which are free to restaurant owners? Yes, that is correct, the equipment companies combined with the food producing companies probably account for at least 90% of those magazines income.

The paid advertising space which you see in these trade journals that comes from independent restaurants is usually in the form of classified ads. The information which owners provide to trade journals is generally used to learn what the restaurants needs are. That information helps the manufacturers and in turn helps the restaurant owner. The point is that; YOUR INTEREST WITH THE RESTAURANT IS ALSO THE EQUIPMENT MANUFACTURERS CONCERN, so when they say something about the foodservice industry, it is generally wise to listen.

Pictures of equipment providing identity and descriptions.

The following pages of pictures (figures 9-1 through 9-57) show the owner various pieces of equipment which are considered basic and important to most restaurants.

When you hold meetings with your cooks, chefs, culinary professionals, lenders, consultants, dealers, manufacturers, or other interested and concerned people, this section should provide some basis for reference in order to help determine your equipment (Production) needs.

REFRIGERATION EQUIPMENT:

Although all types of foodservice equipment are important to the specific need, refrigeration (including freezers) equipment should be considered **first**. Since spoiled food is impossible to prepare for consumption and an egg which is over-cooked can be easily replaced by cooking another egg, it seems clear that the quality and concern for refrigeration equipment should be given extra attention.

WALK-IN REFRIGERATORS

A walk-in refrigerator or freezer is much the same as other storage units which keep food cold. While various types of foodservice equipment (ovens, dishwashers, ranges, microwave units, etc) generally offer stock sizes, walk-ins can be constructed to most any size. Sizes range from 4 feet by 5 feet, to refrigerated warehouses with thousands of square feet. Walk-ins are also available in combination units (part freezer, part refrigerator, with multicompartments).

Of great importance to any refrigeration storage unit is the insulation. Polystyrene is less expensive than urethane, but does not offer the insulation value. Accordingly, urethane should be used in a freezer where polystyrene is adequate for the walk-in refrigerator. Thicknesses of insulation in varying dimensions are usually offered by higher quality manufacturers in order to satisfy different needs.

FIGURE 9-1. A Combination Walk-In Refrigerator and Freezer. One complete unit like this one is suitable for most medium size restaurants.

FIGURE 9-2. An Upright Refrigerator (Can also be purchased as a freezer). The quality of a high torque compressor gives faster temperature recovery. Full height solid doors.

FIGURE 9-3. Medium Temperature Storage Bases are similar to the reach-in sandwich cooler configuration except the better quality units are made for constant use. That is why there are drawers instead of doors which usually wear-out faster.

Figure 9-1
Courtesy of Arctic Industries, Inc.

Figure 9-2
Courtesy of The Hobart Corporation.

Figure 9-3
Courtesy of The Hobart Corporation

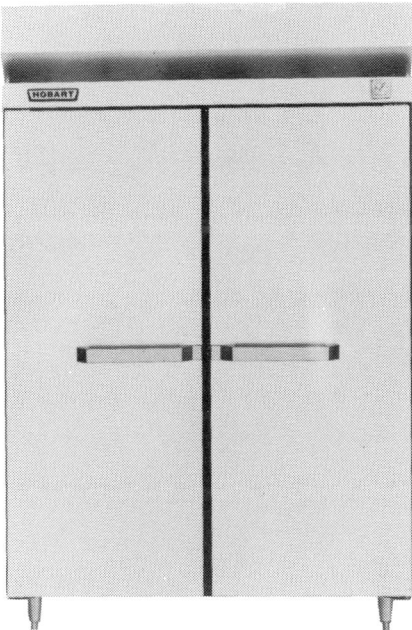

FIGURE 9-4. A Standard Slicer. Slicers are available with automatic features which can be time savers, particularly when employees are spread thin. It is important that the automatic features are not taken for granted by leaving the equipment unattended for long periods of time.

FIGURE 9-5. A 20 quart Bench-Type Mixer. This type has attachments which do such things as; Dicing, vegetable slicing, and food chopping. This is a 3 speed model.

FIGURE 9-6. A Tall Column Floor model Mixer. This model has an 80 quart capacity and operates in four speeds. Mixers range in size from 5 to 140 quart capacities.

FIGURE 9-7. The Cutter/Mixer. Many restaurants are finding this tool flexible for several production operations including; Mixing bread dough, batter, and pizza dough, to chopped meat, salads, crushed ice and more. This model has a 45 quart capacity.

Figure 9-4

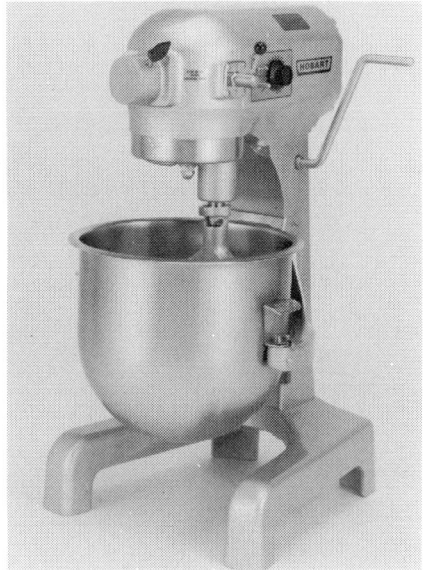

Figure 9-5

Figure 9-6

Figure 9-7

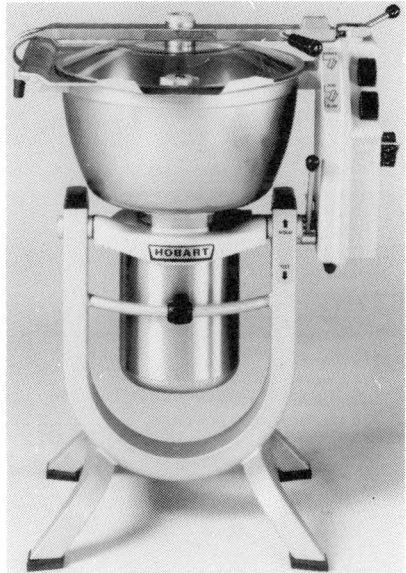

Courtesy of the Hobart Corporation.

FIGURE 9-8. This 14 inch Deep Fryer has an instant recovery feature which increases productivity particularly during peak business hours. Fryers have different types of control features which are designed to save time and utility power. If you are located in a metropolitan area, these extra features are usually beneficial to the higher volume restaurant. If you are located out in the boondocks, it is wise to stay with a more basic and less complicated unit because of the possibility of extended down-time when service is required.

FIGURE 9-9. The commercial Microwave Oven. Some smaller restaurants still use the household type and do not realize the benefits of rugged construction, faster cooking times and a more even distribution of heating which the majority of all restaurants have.

FIGURE 9-10. A standard Six Burner 36 inch model Stove with a full width conventional oven is the type many restaurants use. Natural gas is still the preferred utility.

FIGURE 9-11. The single Stock-Pot Range can be used in tandem with other single units. Used for slow cooking stews, soups, stocks and chili, etc, this unit is a favorite in the industry. The reason being; It is extremely cost effective for all size restaurants.

Figure 9-8
Courtesy of Keating of Chicago, Inc.

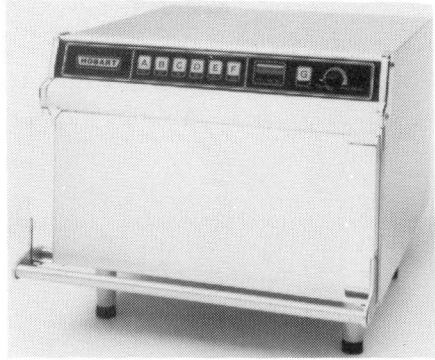

Figure 9-9
Courtesy of The Hobart Corporation

Figure 9-10
Courtesy of the Vulcan-Hart Corporation.

Figure 9-11
Courtesy of the Vulcan-Hart Corporation

FIGURE 9-12. A Combination Stove with 3 open burners and 3 EVEN-HEAT burner spaces. Full with oven is beneath the burners.

FIGURE 9-13. A heavy duty Six Open Burner Stove unit in combination with a Salamander-Broiler mounted above. There is a full width conventional oven below the stove top.

FIGURE 9-14. A heavy duty EVEN-HEAT Stove Top unit with a double deck high shelf. Full width oven beneath the burners.

FIGURE 9-15. A Six Open Burner Stove Combination with Extended Top (Hot-top or grill). There are two ovens, the conventional oven and a forced air convection type.

NOTE: Combinations, sizes and designed configurations of ranges, ovens, grill-tops, broilers, cheese melters and other equipment, are available from several excellent manufacturers. Over and above the many combinations offered as regular models, many of the manufacturers will put together special configurations to suit your particular needs. Heavy duty means the construction and materials used to build these ranges are beefed up to accommodate constant use. Standard commercial construction is usually more than satisfactory for most restaurants. Stainless steel is easier to keep clean, however, baked enamel surfaces will work just as well if you clean them once a day.

Figure 9-12   **Figure 9-13**

Figure 9-14   **Figure 9-15**

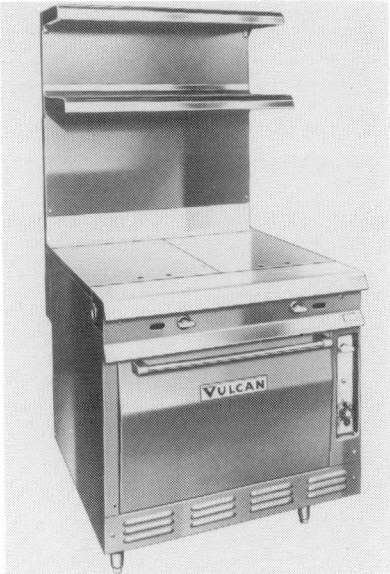

Courtesy of the Vulcan-Hart Corporation.

FIGURE 9-16. A 36 inch by 30 inch Gas Griddle. This cleans without the use of grill bricks. Using a scraper, cool water, a special brush and the companies special formulated cleanser is supposed to do the job. There are also energy saving controls which complement the metal of the cooking surface.

FIGURE 9-17. The Conventional Gas Griddle with a smooth surface. Griddles usually come in sizes ranging from 2 to 6 feet in width. Griddles are also available in varying thicknesses of the cooking surface metal. The extra thick griddles are most often used by hotels and institutions which is due to their heavy volume of production.

FIGURE 9-18. A Combination Griddle (flat surface) and Two Burner (open-flame) Range Top is handy when frying omelet contents.

FIGURE 9-19. A Grooved Griddle is used for steaks and chops when broilers are not appropriate. Cleaning should be accomplished as often as possible to prevent a buildup of food residual material.

Figure 9-16
Courtesy of Keating of Chicago, Inc.

Figure 9-17
Courtesy of U.S. Range/ALCO.

Figure 9-18
Courtesy of U.S. Range/ALCO.

Figure 9-19
Courtesy of U.S. Range/ALCO.

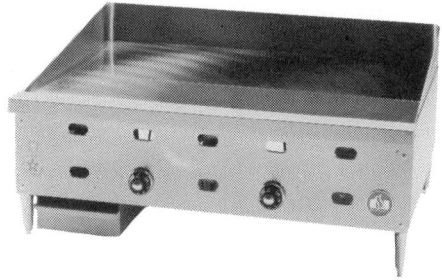

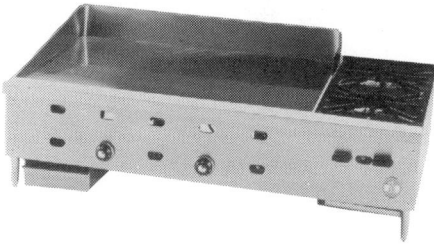

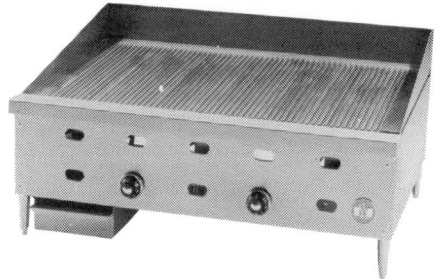

FIGURE 9-20. The Gas "PIZZA" Oven accomplishes it's task with a one inch thick core-plate, extra insulation, two thermostats, and two burners which put out 100,000 BTU'S. The 56 inch by 37 inch cavity permits six each 18 inch pizzas to be cooked simultaneously. Pizza ovens can also be stacked two high. There are also pizza ovens which are conveyor driven, maintaining constant productivity, although energy intensive.

FIGURE 9-21. This is a Bake and Roast Standard Two Pan Sectional Oven. The hearths are 14 gauge steel plate, which is different from the pizza oven. The BTU output is 50,000 compared to twice that number with the pizza oven. The standard bake oven offers more flexibility in preparing a greater selection of menu items compared to the pizza oven. Even though they look very similar, do not make the mistake of using the pizza oven for a bake and roast oven or vice- versa.

FIGURE 9-22. This Charbroiler is 34 inches wide with six burners using 96,000 BTU'S an hour. Other widths are available as well as combination units. All broilers with open flame burners need extra consideration regarding venting and exhaust systems.

Figure 9-20

Figure 9-21

Figure 9-22

Courtesy of the Vulcan-Hart Corporation.

FIGURE 9-23. A Salamander-Broiler. Broiling is accomplished by gas flame. Raising and lowering the shelving system controls the distance between the flame and the food item, which in turn simplifies cooking procedures. Salamanders should not be used as cheese-melters unless you pay strict attention to the operation while in progress as the heat is considerably greater.

FIGURE 9-24. This is a regular size Gas Convection Oven. 50 percent more efficient than a conventional oven, this model takes 13 inch by 18 inch pans, with up to nine racks.

FIGURE 9-25. This is the electrically powered version of the Convection Oven in figure 24. Many ranges, griddles and other cooking equipment are made to do their heating by natural gas energy. The demand for electrically powered cooking units is rapidly increasing due to the cost of utilities in particular locations, ease of hookup and the results of the cooking process. Convection ovens should be considered for purchase because of their versatility and effective cooking process.

NOTE: The ovens which we indicate as "CONVECTION", are dissimilar to the conventional oven because the convecting air flow process is stimulated by powered blowers, thereby creating a more rapid and uniform heating-cooking system. In addition, the insulation in the convection oven is usually increased as compared to the conventional oven system making it more energy efficient.

FIGURE 9-26. The Electric Steam Injection Convection Oven. Steam injection provides excellent baking of European style crusty breads, delicate pastries and meringues, etc.

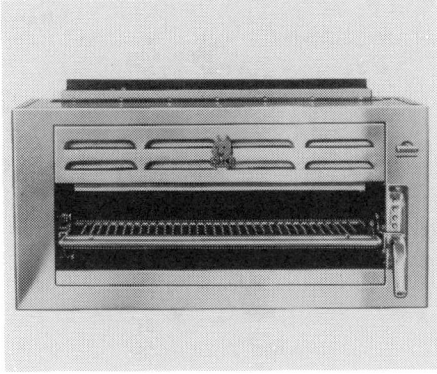

Figure 9-23
Courtesy of The Wolf Range Corporation.

Figure 9-24
Courtesy of the Hobart Corporation.

Figure 9-25

Figure 9-26

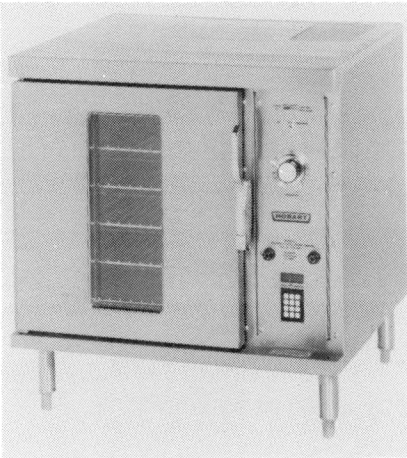

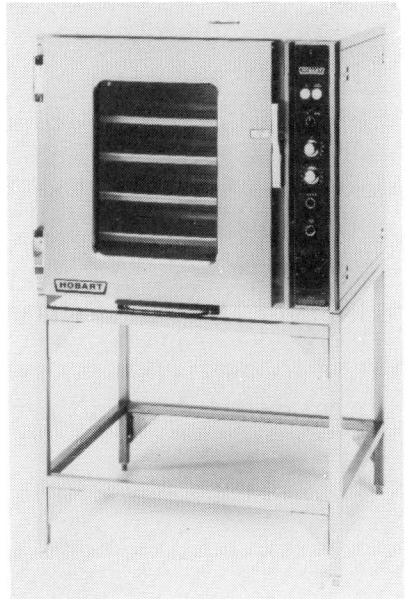

Courtesy of the Hobart Corporation.

FIGURE 9-27.   The Electric Combination Oven. This type of oven has a convection cooking process and allows for steam injection with or without convection heating. Versatility gives the chef; baking, roasting, braising, and steaming abilities.

FIGURE 9-28. A Counter Top Steam-Quick Convection Pressureless Steamer. This model can be obtained in either natural gas or electric power. Gas produces 170,000 BTU'S, where the electrically powered model produces a 24KW input. It has a capacity to hold six each one inch high trays measuring 12 inches by 20 inches. Steam-Quick refers to the higher number of BTU'S per compartment, allowing for faster heating levels attained, compared to super steamers.

FIGURE 9-29. A Two Compartment Steam Regenerating Pressureless Oven, available in gas or electric models. This compartment steam process is pre-vented, which reduces cooking time as excess moisture is removed from the surface of the food. Up to ten, one inch high trays, measuring 12 inches by 20 inches will fit into the oven cavity.

FIGURE 9-30.   A large capacity Gas Convection Oven with two compartments. Each compartment has eleven guides, allowing for as many trays. The depth is 21 inches. Baking and roasting is similar to figure 24, located on the previous page.

NOTE: Convection and steam-type cooking equipment is available through several manufacturers, there are numbers of controlling devices, capacities and design features which need to be taken into account before purchasing. This is important as there are many different needs by a great many kinds of restaurants.

Figure 9-27
Courtesy of the Hobart Corporation.

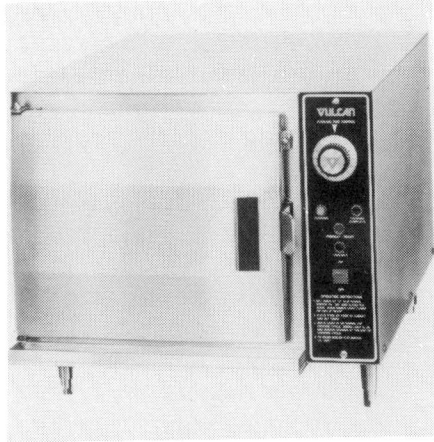

Figure 9-28
Courtesy of the Vulcan-Hart Corporation.

Figure 9-29

Figure 9-30

Courtesy of the Vulcan-Hart Corporation.

FIGURE 9-31. Tilt-Braising Pan. Can be purchased in gas or electric powered models. Available in 20 to 40 gallon capacities. This unit is made to saute, simmer, fry, grill, stew, boil, thaw, warm-up, steam (direct-steam), and braise. The tilting feature is unique to this equipment and helps the pouring of cooked foods into serving or storage containers.

FIGURE 9-32. This is a "BLAST-CHILLER" which is the cooling portion of a special process. This model has an ability to produce 1680 twelve ounce meals per day. For large restaurants and large catering events, this unit is part of a process called "COOK and CHILL" which was originally designed for hospitals and institutions. The unit shown here is a medium size, there are smaller and larger models available. Cooking is accomplished by way of any standard volume method, then meals are portioned out into serving trays, the trays are put onto special movable rack-units, then put into the "Blast-Chiller". The "Blast-Chiller" does not freeze, but obtains a 34 to 37 degree temperature. The contents of the loaded chiller is completely cooled within 90 minutes. Promptly after blast chilling, foods are stored in a regular walk-in refrigerator where they can be kept for up to five days prior to serving. When ready to serve, re-heat food using steam or convection ovens. This process allows for very efficient use of labor and serving.

FIGURE 9-33. A Two Compartment Convection Pressureless Quick-Steamer. Except for the larger capacity, this unit is identical to the unit in figure 28. This type of cooking equipment is ideal for rethermalization (reheating), when used with the "COOK and CHILL" system.

FIGURE 9-34. A Direct-Steam (fully jacketed) Kettle Cooker. These units are available in gas or electric powered models. This type of cooker comes in 13 to 150 gallon capacities. A tilting feature is available on particular models and have a capacity range from 20 to 80 gallons. Steam kettles are used for fish, meat, stew, soups, vegetables, sauces and other menu items.

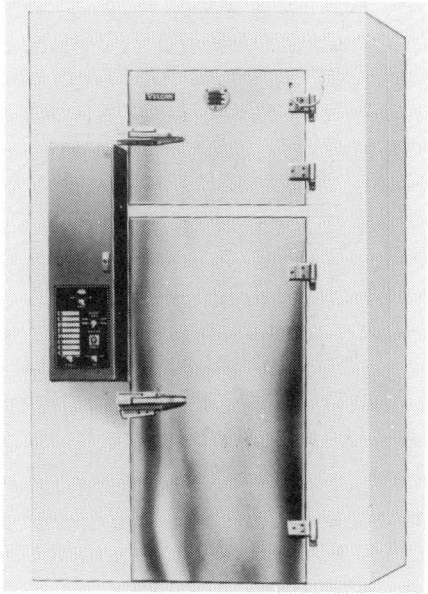

Figure 9-31   Figure 9-32

Figure 9-33   Figure 9-34

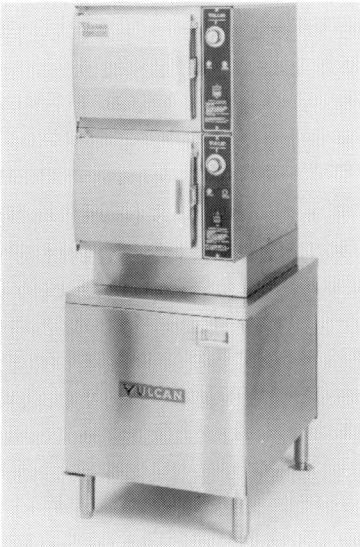

Courtesy of the Vulcan-Hart Corporation.

FIGURE 9-35. The "HALO" Heat Banquet Cart. Sizes range from 72, 96 and 160 plate capacities. This patented process of heating, keeps food from 60 to 200 degrees Fahrenheit. Thermo-statically controlled and electrically powered.

FIGURE 9-36. Electronic Cooking and Holding Oven. The patented thermal cable "HALO HEAT" process is based on a low density thermo-cable which uniformly distributes heat. This cook and hold oven is most popular with slow cooking meats because of the minimum loss (a 46 pound steamship-round cooked over eight hours, on hold for six hours @ 250 and 140 degrees respectively) of ten percent or less in shrinkage. The oven is also used for all types of meats, poultry, fish, vegetables, and the reconstituting of frozen foods. The cooking thermostat is maintained between 100 and 350 degrees Fahrenheit. The holding thermostat maintains a 60 to 200 degree temperature. The Halo process is an energy efficient process because of extra insulation and the controlled, even heating method. This model will handle 10 each, 12 inch by 20 inch pans.

FIGURE 9-37. Electronic Cooking and Holding Oven. This two unit (stacked) model is basically the same as the one in figure 36. There are two cavities, each capable of handling 8 each, 18 inch by 26 inch pans.

Figure 9-35

Figure 9-36   Figure 9-37

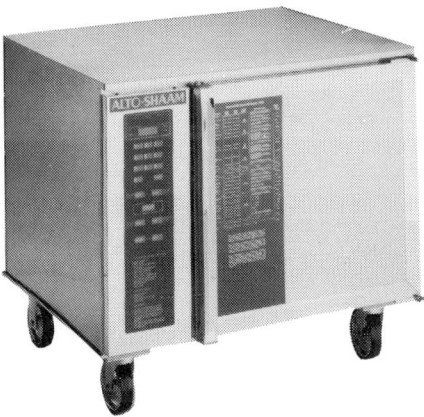

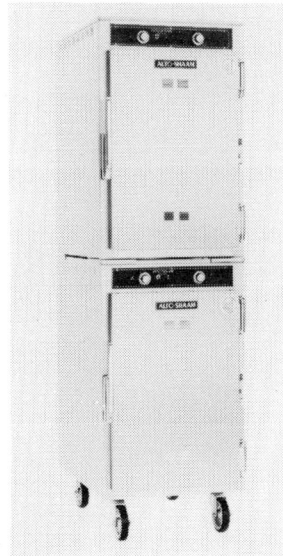

Courtesy of Alto-Shaam, Inc.

FIGURE 9-38. The Electric Hot Food Table. This model has an enclosed base. Adaptable for wet application using spillage pans, at five feet three and one half inches long, it accommodates several compartments and a partial roll-top cover. It is controlled by four thermostats providing variable heating.

FIGURE 9-39. An "Aeroshot" Hot Food Table. This hot food table is offered either electric or gas powered. With sizes ranging from 30-1/2 inches to 72-1/2 inches in length. There are optional features such as serving shelves, with or without glass panels, adapter plates for round insets, telescope covers, spillage pans, soup tureen, stainless steel carving boards, and an assortment of pans and shelving combinations.

NOTE: Restaurant owners always agree that preparation of food items is an important step to satisfied customers and they generally cook the soups, stews, vegetables and thousands of other menu items with pride and attention to the cooking process.

What many restaurants owners are becoming aware of is the importance of holding and serving equipment and the fact that heated water tables without regard for individual compartment temperature control, can cost them in waste through the deterioration of the products flavor and consistency. More emphasis needs to be placed on the holding and serving equipment that compliments the product, can help energy savings, and less food spoilage. The manufacturers shown are the leaders in producing the highest quality units.

Figure 9-38
Courtesy of Metal Masters Foodservice Equipment Co., Inc.

Figure 9-39

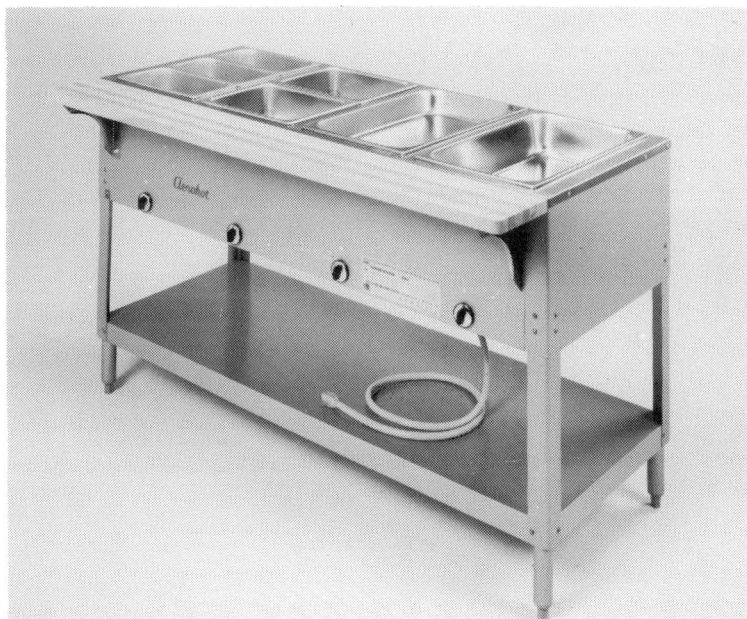

Courtesy of Duke Manufacturing Co.

FIGURE 9-40. A Portable Electric Hot Food Table. This model is 63-1/2 inches in length with four individually controlled openings. With sneeze guard, this unit is used for banquet and special set up. There are also heat lamps for additional heating and visual requirements.

FIGURE 9-41. A Portable Electric (Dry) Hot Food Table. This one has a cutting board running the length(5-1/2 feet) of the unit, and four individually controlled compartments. Larger models have five compartments.

FIGURE 9-42. A "HALO HEAT" Portable Hot Food and Carving Table. Electrically powered, this unit holds heat without water, using the patented thermal cable method. There is a thermostatically controlled base and adjustable heat lamps with on/off switch control. It is versatile in that combinations of carving stations and hot food table units can be arranged.

FIGURE 9-43. A Gas Water Bath Steam Table. This one is a three opening, eight setting temperature control, four foot model. The unit is also available with electric power.

NOTE: When owners select this type of unit which has one temperature control, it is important that he or she is aware that all menu items will be held at the same temperature setting. Since some foods have better flavor and maintain greater longevity at different temperatures than other foods, this awareness becomes an important consideration. Ask your dealer or the manufacturer for specific data of holding temperatures on various foods.

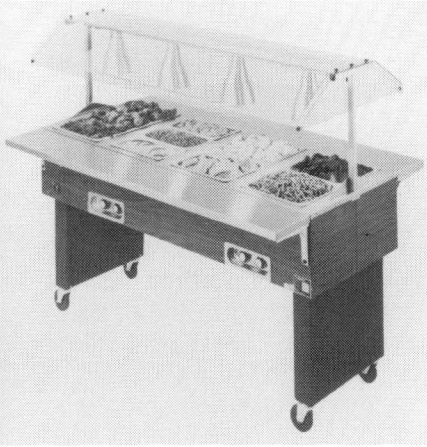

Figure 9-40   **Figure 9-41**
Courtesy of Metal Masters Foodservice Equipment Co., Inc.

Figure 9-42   **Figure 9-43**

Courtesy of Alto-Shaam, Inc.

Courtesy of Metal Masters
Foodservice Equipment Co., Inc.

FIGURE 9-44. A Table Top Electric Hot Food Unit. Operates on 120 volts compared to most electric hot tables which use 220 voltage. This smaller two opening model has individual temperature controls for each opening and each has eight temperature settings.

FIGURE 9-45. A Portable Electric (dry) Heat Table. This smaller version of figure 41, is a two opening type with 120 volt requirements.

NOTE: Cold pan units are not being shown because they are basically the same type of unit less the heating elements and in many cases have refrigeration capabilities. When you are considering a salad bar which will be in use for a limited period of time, then the cold pan unit (adding your own ice) is appropriate.

FIGURE 9-46. The ice maker and storage bin. This model has a 1260 pound production capacity. You can select from regular, diced or half diced (similar to shaved) sizes when purchasing this particular piece of equipment. Capacities range from 200 pounds to over 1700 pounds of ice produced in a 24 hour period. There are also models which are water cooled.

NOTE: When considering as ice machine, you should build in the anticipated growth of your business and allow an appropriate amount of capacity. Leasing ice machines is also a prudent thought given the fact that the lease payments include complete maintenance, repair, and same day replacement, should the machine have mechanical trouble. Leasing is also totally deductible as a business expense, where purchasing the equipment is depreciated over a predictable length of time.

FIGURE 9-47. A Hot Water Machine. This one produces 15 gallons of near boiling water in one hour. Sizes range from 2 gallons to 15 gallons. This unit is electrically powered.

Figure 9-44   **Figure 9-45**

Courtesy of Metal Masters Foodservice Equipment,. Inc.

Figure 9-46   **Figure 9-47**

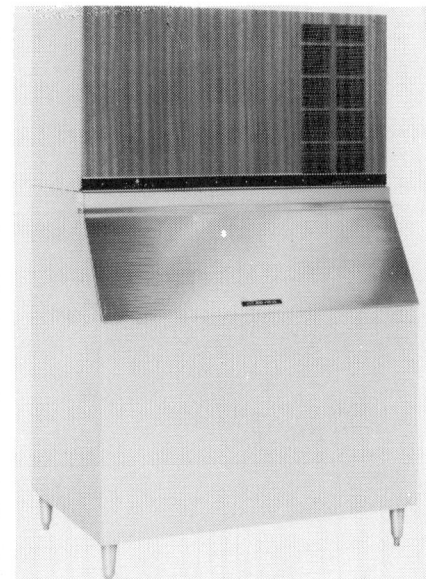

Courtesy of
The Manitowoc Company, Inc.

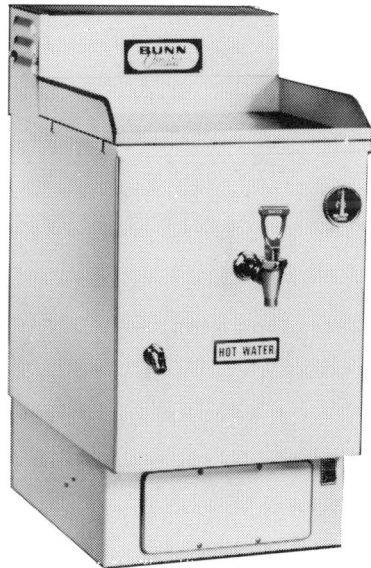

Courtesy of
the Bunn-O-Matic Corporation.

FIGURE 9-48. Automatic Coffee Brewers. One unit has two warmers and the other has five. Most restaurant owners find these two pieces of equipment a familiar sight. The smaller unit makes up to 140 cups per hour, while the larger five spot warmer makes 200 cups. Productivity also depends on the various electrical configurations.

FIGURE 9-49. A Portable Coffee Brewing/Serving System. The portable server is a two gallon size which will not spill even if dropped during transport. The brewer produces up to 2 gallons in ten minutes. There is also a hot water tap on this unit. This unit was designed for the restaurant that also does catering or has banquet facilities.

FIGURE 9-50. The Coffee Server One Gallon Portable Unit. This server works with any brewer made by this manufacturer and some others. The size is half of it's larger brother seen in figure 49. There are also portable warming stations available for this equipment.

Figure 9-48

Figure 9-49   Figure 9-50

Courtesy of the Bunn-O-Matic Corporation.

FIGURE 9-51. A Double (3 gallon twin) Coffee Urn System. This unit produces 25 gallons of coffee per hour @ 8.5 brewing cycles. With a 20 gallon water capacity, this unit will do the work of coffee urns two to three times larger. There are other service designed model variations of this equipment. A hot water tap is included.

FIGURE 9-52. A Dual Hopper Coffee Grinder. Produces 1.5 to 24 ounces of ground coffee on demand.

FIGURE 9-53. An Ice Tea Brewer with Portable Server. From fresh tea leaves, the brewer produces either 3 or 1.5 gallons in a few minutes, on demand. The server unit has a 4 gallon capacity. Paper filters are used. Larger stationary models are also available.

NOTE: A good cup of coffee is an indication of quality to many restaurant customers. Keeping equipment clean, using fresh (pure as possible) water, fresh quality coffee, plus maintenance of temperature controls (water temperature between 185 and 190 degrees Fahrenheit after brewing, and maintaining 200 to 205 degrees Fahrenheit during brewing) are the most important steps in achieving consistently high quality coffee.

Figure 9-51

Figure 9-52   Figure 9-53

Courtesy of the Bunn-O-Matic Corporation.

FIGURE 9-54. Single Rack High or Low Temperature Dishwasher. Production is 21 each 16 by 18 inch racks per hour. This unit is available in under-the-counter or freestanding models. Either high temperature (equipped with booster providing 185 degrees) or low temperature models (maintaining 140 degrees Fahrenheit). The low temperature type is equipped with a sanitizing pump system.

FIGURE 9-55. Single Rack High or Low Temperature Dishwasher. This unit cleans 80 racks per hour and is available in either the high-temp or low-temp (Chemical sanitizing) type. Choice of electric, gas, or steam injecting heating.

FIGURE 9-56. A Convertible (High or Low) Conveyor Dishwasher. The conveyor moves racks (19-3/4 inches by 19-3/4 inches) automatically through the wash and rinse sections and onto a dish-table at the rate of 203 racks per hour. Converts to either high-temp or low-temp. Choice of electric, gas, or steam injectors or coils.

FIGURE 9-57. The High Performance Two-Tank Conveyor Dishwasher. Cleans up to 6000 dishes per hour. High or low-temp methods available. These high production units usually used in hospitals, institutions and mess-halls, are being considered by shopping mall designers as a separate business, servicing many cooperative restaurants, thereby eliminating separate dish-washing facilities for each restaurant.

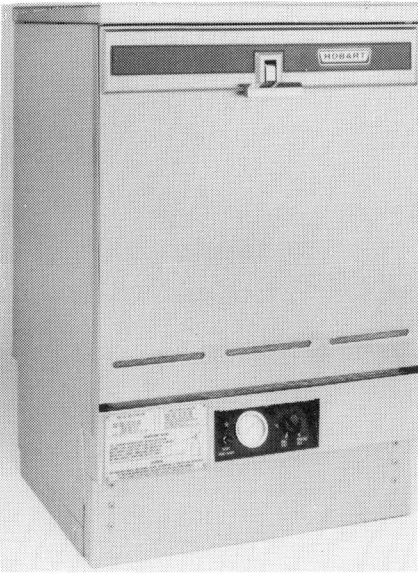
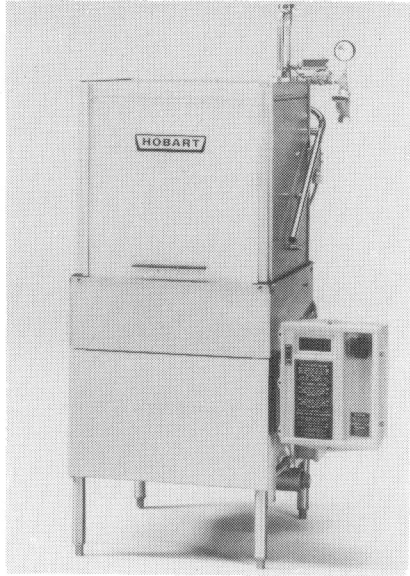

Figure 9-54   **Figure 9-55**
Courtesy of the Hobart Corporation.

Figure 9-56   **Figure 9-57**

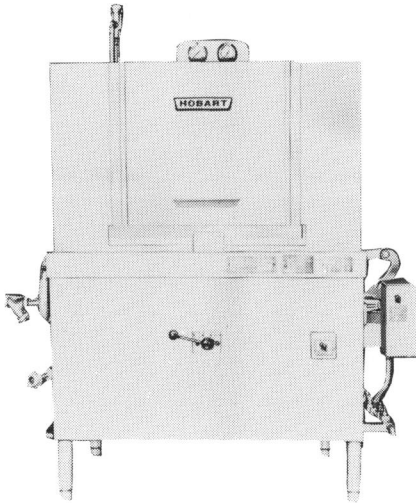
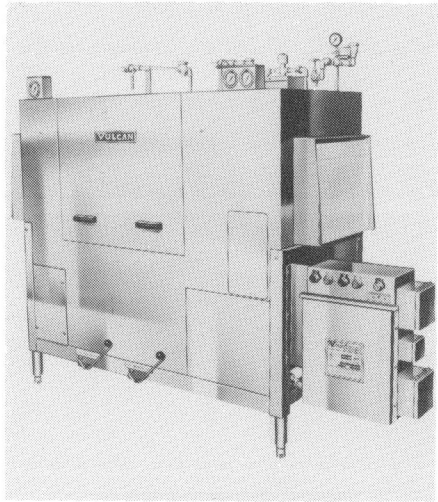

Courtesy of
the Hobart Corporation.

Courtesy of
the Vulcan-Hart Corporation.

Equipment so right..
I cannot fight..
The price is so dear..
I fear, I fear..
My customers yearn..
For more of the same..
Well I made the decision ..
So it's back in the game..
Equipment so right..
Don't fail me tonight..
Not breakdown nor problem can stop me you see..
For in my hands..
Is the makers guarantee..

MAINTENANCE

X

THE SITUATION

While the restaurant is in the midst of lucrative productivity (normally the rush hour), you find that the unthinking and inconsiderate heating system fails and your customers are beginning to identify with the freezing outside temperatures.

This typifies many restaurant owners experiences, most of which are not necessary, if a routine maintenance program was in place.

The cost of implementing a maintenance program for your restaurant is not twenty percent of what you will ultimately lose to repair and replacement service. Even though it may not appear to happen that often, the hourly charge, plus parts and inconvenience can add up to hundreds, or even thousands of dollars per year, most of which was probably preventable. This does not include that equipment which causes restaurant down-time, that in turn relieves you of sales dollars which will never be seen at your address again.

HEATING AND COOLING SYSTEMS

1. Change furnace filters each month (where possible) during use.

2. Check all the fan belts for wear. If you notice frayed edges, change the belt. This step alone can save you a great deal if you consider the alternatives

3. Oil moving parts as indicated by the manufacturer. If you telephone the manufacturer, have the model and/or serial number handy.

4. The refrigerated cooling system is usually integrated through the same duct work as the heating system, which may or may not share the same return-air filters. Change these filters once a month during use. If the filtering system is other than the conventional fiberglass replaceable type, then

consult the equipment manual or contact the manufacturer for cleaning instructions. If you find that your cooling system does not have a return air filtering system, have one put in.

Contaminated air from outside restaurants located in cities or near poor air quality areas can affect the taste and healthfulness of the food.

5. Refrigerated cooling systems have evaporators and condenser grilles similar to automotive radiators. They need to be cleaned at least twice a year. Doing so, keeps the compressor's head pressure down, causing better cooling and less wear on the compressor itself. Cleaning these grilles should be accomplished with care. Do not bend the grille blades. Use a 4 inch paint brush and a mild chemical degreaser, or a water hose if there is ample drainage for water run off.

6. Grease the fan (blower) bearings once a year. These bearings usually have grease fittings, if not, contact the manufacturer and ask them if it is appropriate to do so. Putting grease fittings in is not difficult, however, if you have not done so before, pay a service man to get the job done. This practice can save the life of the bearings, hence costly repairs and down-time. If you have sealed bearings, don't touch them.

KITCHEN EXHAUST SYSTEM

Clean the grease filters in the kitchen area (exhaust system) as often as needed. This process varies with the amount and types of cooking being done. Some restaurants that do little frying and operate during the breakfast and lunch hours, may need to clean the filters every other week.

Restaurants that produce a great amount of cooking and frying, plus are open around the clock, may need to clean filters as often as every 48 hours.

Usually the restaurants with heavy frying have two sets of filters which makes the process of cleaning more effective.

Keeping the grease filters clean has the benefit of better exhausting hot air which helps keep the kitchen cooler, while it removes smoke and greasy air.

VINYL COVERINGS

Besides the usual cleaning, vinyl will last much longer if cleaned with a commercial vinyl cleaner, followed by proper use of a vinyl dressing. This extra maintenance will help insure the vinyls flexibility and softness which helps prevent cracking and deterioration. It also beautifies your booths and/or chair coverings. This should be accomplished at least every three to four months.

PLUMBING

1. Keeping drains clean and clear is necessary in keeping expenses low and down-time at a minimum.

2 . Floor drains should have a wire mesh screen over them to prevent paper, mop strings and clogging debris from getting into the drain system. This measure applies to the sinks as well; A simple wooden frame with a screen (larger mesh than a window screen) fastened to it can save clogging and keep the grease trap from being cleaned as often.

3. Water faucets in restaurants, particularly the kitchen sink unit, have problems with washers, 'O' Rings, and other parts wearing out. The kitchen sink faucet complex is an item which should have a spare unit. After you replace the faucet unit, which is usually no more than cutting the water off and uncoupling the threaded joints at the wall, removing the faucet, then replace the spare unit in the same, however reverse manner.This way your faucet is back in running order, usually within ten minutes, and you can take the faulty faucet apart in your spare time, replacing the worn out parts.

WATER MAINTENANCE

Water maintenance begins with the knowledge of your tap water, whether by city or private well. Your equipment (pots, pans, dishwasher unit, steamers, pressure cookers, steam tables, etc), is made of metal (aluminum magnesium alloys, iron, stainless steel, etc), and there is a chemical reaction of varying degrees to the substances found in water. Primarily "Alkali" deposits cause the most problems.

Having your water tested is a good start. The water authority or nearby (private sector) chemist can supply this service.

FOR HEALTH REASONS:

Each state has an environmental improvement board (although the name may vary in some states). Public drinking water falls under the same regulations in each state.

Public drinking water must be checked for bacteria once a month. Since the city water authority does this, restaurant owners in the city usually do not hear anything about it. Restaurants in rural areas who obtain water from private wells need to comply with state operated services that check the water for bacteria once a month. If this is not being done, then report it to your state environmental board or water authority.

Drinking water is also checked for Nitrates every four years. Again, whether it is the city water works who manages the water or if water is obtained through the use of private wells, water used for consumption by the public must be checked for Nitrates.

Water testing for bacteria, Nitrates and hardness are usually relatively low in cost. Special tests for specific minerals and other elements are usually accomplished by private sector chemists. The special testing of water can be expensive.

DEPOSITS FROM WATER AFFECTING EQUIPMENT

There should be concerns about water and the deposits water is responsible for. The effect of alkali and other mineral deposits on equipment which uses steam in the cooking process (like a direct steam kettle cooker), can be serious enough to hamper the equipments operational continuance. Mineral (like alkali) deposits can affect valve performance.

EXAMPLE: When a kettle type steamer is shut down because of alkali deposits clogging valves, the immediate reaction is to call the serviceman (justifiably so), who will do some cleaning and possibly replace parts, which are needed, however costly and probably avoidable with the implementation of water maintenance.

The annual practice of having your water analyzed for strengths of metallic contents (specific hardness), should be routine when cooking equipment such as direct steam cookers are used. Water softening equipment, chemical additives and special filtering, etc, should be considered where appropriate. Further, it is beneficial for restaurant owners to check with equipment manufacturers (directly) regarding any cooking equipment which uses water and can be affected by water deposits.

CLEANING EQUIPMENT

Sweeping, mopping floors, vacuuming, and scrubbing porcelain fixtures in the rest-rooms, etc, is something that established restaurant owners know is essential. Therefore it should be easily recognizable that a CLEANING-PROGRAM that includes equipment and tools of the trade, is one that can only benefit the owner.

NEAR 90 PERCENT OF ALL EQUIPMENT FAILURE IS DUE TO A LACK OF PROPER AND REGULAR CLEANING.

To set up a Cleaning Program for your equipment requires the following simple steps:

1. List all of your equipment, from cooking to dish-washing, plus refrigeration, electrical and all else which will cost you money in the event of a breakdown.

2. Separate this master list into groups based on time cleaning should take place (daily, weekly, monthly, etc).

3. Indicate next to each piece of equipment; The tools, cleaning implements, and a brief description of just what needs to be accomplished and when it was last completed.

You can add to this basic starter program as the need arises. The attention you pay to this kind of maintenance, can save you hundreds or even thousands of dollars. When equipment has past it's average life span, the percentage of savings is increased dramatically.

Prideful Chef "Clean" couldn't stand for anyone else touching his heavy duty pressure cooker, that's the one with the six tie-down plastic wing nuts, and no rubber grommet. One day a new dishwasher employee by the name of "Joe Fast", had Chef Clean's cooker and was in the midst of scrubbing it to a " fare-thee-well", Hold it right there' Clean exclaimed, what do you think you are doing? Chef Clean took the cooker away and started cleaning the threaded clamp-bolts with a small wire brush. Joe Fast looked on in amazement , both because he had never seen a chef do much cleaning and he wanted to know why this attention to threaded bolts was so important.

Chef Clean noticed the dishwashers interest and explained the reasoning; Look here Joe, at the ALKALI deposits on these threaded bolts, by cleaning the collecting Alkali deposits off, we prevent the threads from being crushed by the wing-nut when tightening the pressure cookers lid down.

This example of Chef "Cleans" attention to equipment is probably selfish on his part, because of the accolades he gets from his boss and the customers, when they slurp down his home made chicken soup. In any event the owner (Mr. Know) is happy because he hasn't had to service the pressure cooker since it was purchased three years ago.

ERADICATION OF INSECTS AND OTHER DISEASE CARRYING PESTS

You can pray that it will never happen to you, however, it is much safer and surer to have the professional insect eradicator (Bug spray person), do their job once a month.

If you have ever experienced the "German Brown Roach", you know exactly how bad an infestation can be. Other types of roaches like the "American" type, although much larger, do not reproduce at the racing speed of the German Brown. It is as if they were all experiencing free sex in a "Sodom and Gomorrah" community, without preventative measures concerning reproduction. Since a restaurant is a prime target for many kinds of insects and other pests, it makes good sense to be prepared through a professional maintenance program.

All insects , including the common housefly, carry forms of bacteria. If you stop to think; "Where have these insects been in the last 24 hours?" You could hardly keep from understanding why medical scientists at the FDA show concern about these matters, for the good of the public.

Many pest control companies will take care of the rodent population as well. Just be certain that they guarantee their work.

Someday, probably in the next ten years, the government will maintain a stronger program designed to better assure the public that restaurants and other foodservice establishments and institutions, are free from specific levels of bacteria contamination.

Although health inspection programs are in-place in most jurisdictions, they lack the sensitive bacteriological equipment which has yet to be invented. Until that time comes, the best cleaning, and insect-rodent eradication maintenance programs restaurants can implement, will provide the public (customers) with increased confidence. That will benefit all restaurant owners.

MARKETING

XI

Marketing, What is it?

If there was ever a misused term affecting any and all business and industry types, it is Marketing. In this respect, the least the Restaurant Owners can do as representatives of the largest employee based industry is to know just what it is.

The reason being to give credibility and respect to the restaurant owner and the business acumen they posess.

The simple answer is: Marketing is a function which determines the future effects of business. As is often the case, many people, professional and layperson alike, associate sales with marketing, when in fact that is only a fraction of the responsibility. Marketing affects FINANCE, PRODUCTION, EMPLOYEE JOBS, SERVICE and SALES. Many companies have used the term marketing when the people involved are doing only a portion of what marketing encompasses. On the other hand there are those companies with the ability to utilize the full scope of all that marketing entails.

Sales in a Restaurant business, is the same as in manufacturing or the big oil company. All are dependent upon marketing analysis, due to the fact, this function determines where the sales are, and how best to access a specific group of buyers. These findings relate to a predetermined need. Filling that need is also an exercise for marketing. Now you should understand the difference between those companies using the full potential of marketing and those stopping at the sales determination point.

Since all other departments, including the kitchen, it's equipment, staff, and facilities, the bath rooms, storage area, garbage disposal plus the procedures which govern and operate the restaurant effectively, etc,.....are all affected when sales go appreciably up or down: Doesn't it then seem appropriate that the marketing job should determine what it's sales result will have on the entire operation?

In learning of an advertising promotion that will double his or her business (sales), does the owner stop at this point and drool over the prospect of cash in abundance? No. That owner better make preparation for the onslaught with equipment evaluation and the overall productivity ability, to include waitress/waiter needs, kitchen help and the hours of possible preparation and stocking of inventory, etc. If these considerations in addition to sales ideas, are not thought about and filled according to probable need, then the service and quality of that restaurant will be in serious jeopardy, like the following questioning examples;

If the customer isn't served as he or she is used to, will the customer return?

If you run out of certain menu items when some customers were looking forward to your zucchini stuffed with crab meat, will they be back? If so, when?

When the kitchen is running nuts on wheels and two kitchen people leave because they are not use to this level of pressure or activity, who will replace them to continue proper service?

If your biggest seller on the menu is broiled fish and your equipment is geared to produce 60 orders of this item per hour and orders are coming into the kitchen at a rate of 120 (broiled fish) per hour, do you now wonder about the affects of marketing schemes?

It's too late for today, that is for sure, so now you will scramble to get your thoughts organized and try to come up with some answers that will solve your over sales problem, which you thought you might never see happen in the first place. Is there any peace of mind in this business? Yes, there is when you think in complete terms where marketing is concerned.

When the owner comes up with a sales promotion, it is a partial marketing function, and being aware of that fact, means that the owner will make a check list that indicates the possible affects;

MARKETING AFFECTS CHECK LIST

I. What additional kitchen help (how many people) will I need to produce 25% more orders_____
50% more orders_____
75% more orders_____
__% more orders_____

2. Will the amount of increased kitchen production require additional labor hours, or shift changes?_____
_____

3. Are there any menu items which cannot be produced according to the anticipated increase due to equipment limitations? If so, name them;
_____
_____
_____

If there is equipment which will not be able to keep up with anticipated production, you should identify the space where another piece of equipment could fit (along with utility hook up) and see if there is other equipment which (with the chefs genius) could produce the same menu item. If you find that you must have either an additional or higher production replacement piece of equipment, then call your dealer for loaner (short lease) equipment, or if confident, purchase the equipment and proceed.

4. How will the extra sales affect your server element, whether waitress, waiter, buffet style, cafeteria, pay and seat yourself, kitchen counter service (like the fast food chains) etc?

How many additional servers if:
25% more orders _____
50% more orders_____
75% more orders_____
Other_____

5. How will you accommodate other considerations;

Bath rooms_____
Cashier _____
Extra seating_____
Coat & hat rack_____
Food & Beverage supply_____
Parking_____
Waiting area_____

Now that some deeper understanding to marketing is made, and you know that real marketing is more than clocking traffic counts at the shopping plaza, you may ask yourself what growth ideas can expand your restaurant?

MARKETING:
QUALITY, SERVICE AND PRICE

To the customer, quality, service and price are the ingredients they are looking for, and wouldn't you know, these are the basic business elements for all of business and industry (any kind, any type). The correct amounts of each one of these elements, spell out value to the shopping customer. The attraction of one establishment maybe the decor and the manner in which he or she is treated, or to another, it could mean that New York strip steak and vintage wine, still another can translate value as the, "all you can eat salad bar", which affords a great deal of food for the money. A few other reasons that customers choose one place over the other, may be:

Reasonable priced specials at lunch time.

Homemade cornbeef hash for breakfast that the customer can't locate anywhere else.

Romantic atmosphere that offers views of the mountains or water front.

Special treatment by waiters or waitresses,who call customers by name.

Fast service, which gives the customer the time to have the excellent home cooked meal at lunch time,which they otherwise would not have.

The best full service family dinner at the most reasonable price.

There are thousands of individual reasons for eating out at particular restaurants and they all revolve around those three business elements, **Quality, Service** and **Price.** With some people, it's the low price for the amount of food, and the atmosphere just doesn't matter. Others want the highest quality in elegant foods and atmosphere and the cost is not of concern. Generally, or so it seems, the expensive dinner is often payed for by the same person who budgets lunch for less than the price of a hot dog.

Value has come to mean the highest possible quality for the lowest possible price, and the trend toward this meaning of value keeps increasing.To be sure, there is always a balance between the three elements (quality, service and price), which indicates that at least one of the three must suffer, regardless of the product or who offers it. Even the best in hamburgers may be the fresh 100% pure ground sirloin, prepared to exacting requirements, but it can not be produced at a price which could compete with the big burger chains. Price must suffer in this instance.

After all that has been said about value and the quality, service and price elements, it must be noted that QUALITY in the restaurant business is the second most important element to the consuming public, and this trend will continue for many years. Why', you ask? Because the marketplace keeps coming up with new methods, old recipes, ways of obtaining fresher and more varied kinds of food stuffs for preparation.

The television commercials of today as compared to yesteryear indicate that the consumer is much smarter and knows more about what looks real and what doesn't make sense, and that is proven by the products which were once seen in the marketplace, but not bought, and are no longer there. The public today is not so easily fooled, consequently, they demand value, and that means, a higher quality of prepared food in the restaurant business.

SERVICE is the most important concern to the customer who is complaining about it's decline over the past twenty years. In fact most customers would place service over and above quality, as an element of value.

HAROLD'S PLACE: The exception for service

Oil and water do not mix, or so the adage indicates. Customers will find and feel comfortable in certain surroundings, and that means you cannot please everyone, however, it's a good idea to shoot for the majority of tastes and moods, unless of course you are daring, and have an off beat idea that just may be the next craze. There will naturally be those who are even extreme to the off beat originator, and here we present an example which purely demonstrates the extreme. The purpose is either to give you a feeling of just how far your own ideas might go, or leave you wondering, how the guy gets away with it.

Years ago in Chicago, there was a small out of the way lunch spot which we will call, "Harolds Place". At the time I wondered why so many three piece suit executive types would line up to eat lunch at this poorly located establishment which served bratwurst and sour kraut, plus many other delicatessen items.

One day, after being coerced to go, my cohort and print buyer associate and I went to Harold's Place for lunch. We walked in a little before noon and lined up in front of the meat and cheese cooler only to hear profanity at it's best coming from the owner, Harold. Standing there with my mouth open no doubt, Harold announced to the world and some celestial beings I'am sure, that the customer who was not prompt in giving his lunch order, should get out of his restaurant and never think of coming back, plus many choice words about the customers looks and religious affiliations.

Everyone at the tables were munching on their cold cuts or drinking in the chicken soup, they turned and laughed, so that the man being insulted was sure to show an emotional release, but before he had a chance, Harold came around the counter, took the man by the arm and showed him the door. This was going on as Harold was telling the customer that he needed to know what he wanted, that his slowness was holding up his business. I couldn't believe my ears, my face must have been scarlet from embarrassment for that poor fellow, plus I was slightly apprehensive about giving my lunch order to the same crazy idiot.

When it was my turn, I gave Harold my order so fast I could barely understand it myself, He smiled a little (very little) to himself and it was all over, I could now sit down and eat my lunch. Now that smart rear-end buddy of mine broke into gales of laughter and added, what do you think, different hah?

Yes, you could say different, and you could say undignified and rude, however, the survivors of Harold's Place did learn to adjust and to control themselves under duress. Actually, I benefited by getting out the anxieties and found myself going to Harold's Place at least three or four times a year for five years.

With all the insults plus offensive service, Harold's was always packed, something must have clicked with the customers wants. Not many daredevils would try this service technique to the restaurant business, however, it is an example of the extreme in service. If you decide to try something like this, please have a battery of attorneys on your side.

SERVICE BY ITSELF

The most important part of marketing to the restaurant business is service. No matter how many great ideas you or anyone else comes up with regarding an ability to attract the customers, nothing means as much as service. This is a true statement based on the premise that a quality product invoking value, is already inherent.

Personal contact (verbal and visual) by all employees representing your business is the biggest marketing tool a restaurant can have. The other aspects are generally adaptable and have financial considerations which the owner will do or not do as the customers in the market demand.

The "Please" and "Thank-you" together with a pleasant, however, natural smile should be basic mandatory fare. It is personal attention which spells tips for the employees and repeat business for the owner. The behavior at the table, booth or counter, is as important as the cashiers friendly manner when money changes hands.

When the owner, manager, operator or employee in charge greets and recognizes customers it provides the human patronage with a feeling of belonging. When first time customers are greeted warmly and are treated with care and respect, people will feel comfortable. Even when a food mistake occurs, and they do in every restaurant, customers who are made to feel welcome and even special, will overlook a mistake. This kind of attention brings true "word of mouth" advertising and increased business.

How do you implement these personal attention practices? By making time to train employees. Sending an employee to a seminar is not an answer. Conducting your own training program is.

Menu Pricing

Overview

Most restaurant owners seem to use the "Times Factor", in calculating menu prices. When you multiply the per serving food cost times a factor of 3, 4, 5, etc, you have established a set price which has been used by the industry for a very long time. The factor however, should be dependent on the type of restaurant, it's service, dollar volume and quality of food relative to the decor (atmosphere) and overhead. Another consideration is whether the menu item is offered for breakfast, lunch or dinner.

Some restaurants will cater to customers that spend higher amounts of money for attention, fanciful cuisines, prepared by ranking chefs and culinary elitists. Whether the customer is aware of it or not, these restaurants of high status, offer it's clientele self-image.

Because most of the high-classed establishments offer so much quality, service, atmosphere, plus this added element we call, "self image", the menu price is almost inconsequential. This type of restaurant can and should look at the menu price formula from the traditional business view, much like a manufacturer considers the retail price of a product.

The average wage earner dines in a surrounding less opulent, however, comfortable, with meals prepared in systematic orchestration, so designed to move the hungry in and out of the establishment. The annual dollar volume which the various types of independent restaurants brings in, ranges from small (100 thousand) to very large (over 24 million).

Overhead: A true pricing consideration

When the large restaurant chains consider menu pricing they include all aspects including overhead. Except for those times when deviations in the economic climate and competitive dueling prevails, menu pricing considers overhead first. The payments on the land, building, equipment, illuminating sign, and a percentage of the annual advertising budget, are all part of the fixed overhead factor. This is one time when advertising is not a part of the operating expense.

The secondary points are labor and operating expenses, including; utilities, insurance, maintenance, repairs, uniforms and miscellaneous.

The third concern is one which most independent owners place first, and that is food and beverage cost. Since most large chains control the cost of food and beverage through the corporate headquarters and portion control is exercised in a thorough manner, it is not their daily priority as is the case with the independent. Further evidence of this third point consideration, is the fact that most, if not all of the large chains are privileged to a "National Price List". The "National Price List", which may be referred to as a "Contract Price" allows for volume purchases of food stuffs and beverages over various periods of time. Independents will usually have a difficult time attempting to get within 5 percent of the "National Price List".

Ideally, all menu pricing should start with the overhead factor, except independent restaurant owners are usually faced with a much different set of rules.

Competition and Value

The average wage earner segment of the market concerns itself with something called value. It is the element of value which brings to menu pricing a major consideration called competition. If the market you are in, caters to the average income group, then the prices of similar restaurants in your general geographical location should be analyzed. If you do not make this critical observation, you may price yourself out of business, meaning too high or too low.

Comparing the likeness of other restaurants begins with these points;

I.
Check the table seating capacity.

2.
Check the decor. Is it fancier, or less than the gilding you have?

3.
See if the atmosphere is in some way attracting a volume market or merely concerned with offering food and beverage.

4.
Is the service above or below what you offer?
Service is represented by the manner of the
servers, hostess and other employees who come
in verbal and sight contact with the customer.
Check for the reaction of customers to the service element.

5.
Is the selection of menu items up-to-date with
what the media indicates?

6.
Are there menu items which you offer and they
do not and vice versa?

7.
Are the prices above, below or competitive to
your own?

8.
Check the advertising and image projection aspects. Is there a sign or other outstanding feature
which draws attention to the street traffic market?
Does this restaurant use advertising methods to
obtain customers?

9.
Does the restaurant have parking facilities for it's
customers?

10.
Is the quality of the menu item above or below
your restaurant?

Setting a Menu Price

Using the "Times Factor", adjusting for "Customer Value" through competitive analytical observation, and your appraisal of what the "Traffic will bear", are the three fundamental parts in menu pricing for most types of independent restaurant businesses.

In this following method, we assume you know how to arrive at the per serving food and beverage cost, which takes into consideration all the food which is represented by each items price.

Find your own "Times Factor" by multiplying a number (between 2 and 5) times the per serving food cost of your most popular Item.

Now compare that result (test price), to as many competitive, similar restaurants in your area. That means comparing your test price to the other restaurants, like-menu-item prices.

Then adjust your "times factor" up or down to bring the menu price in line with the competition.

Once you have established your "Times Factor", which maybe 3.5 or 2.8 etc, for all of your entree items, dessert items, salads, beverages and other item groups, you should use the same application to each mealtime (Breakfast, lunch and dinner). This means you will end up with several "Times Factors", not just one or two.

When you use your own developed "Times Factors" in application to a perspective menu item it should be used to multiply times the per serving food cost, and then adjusted up or down considering the competitive value differentials.

EXAMPLE: **Menu item: Hamburger Deluxe**

Food cost: .28 cents= ground beef
             .12 cents= pickles, lettuce,tomato, onions
             .13 cents= French fries
             .08 cents= Bun
             .61 cents TOTAL PER SERVING COST

Times Factor: Through the mentioned process you have determined that 4.0 is this items "Times Factor".

Primary result: 4.0 X .6l cents = **$2.44** (rounded off to the
                                              next highest cent)

Competitive Value: Three restaurants in the area have been determined as somewhat similar after analyzing. Because their deluxe hamburger is priced between $2.25 and $3.60 you know your competitive value adjustment is probably going to be upward. The restaurant whose menu price is $3.60 offers parking, advertises more than you do, does more volume business, and has a little higher overhead. All other aspects appear to be on a par level with your restaurant. The two other restaurants show similar quality, however their service is less than what your restaurant produces.

The price: The deluxe hamburger should be less than the $3.60 and more than your "Times Factor" has indicated. Your judgement will now prevail and your menu price will probably be between $3.00 and $3.50 depending on what you believe your clientele will tolerate.

Final Comment

For most restaurants today, the menu price needs to be viewed from the customers eyes. Considering what value you bring to the restaurant business marketplace, is primary. Using the "Times Factor" method is usually the best alternative because traditional "costing and pricing" formulas can cause market price distortions.

The central elements to arriving at <u>all</u> menu
price determinations;

1. Overhead

2. Operating expense

3. **Competition**

4. **Value to the customer**

5. **Food and Beverage cost**

Note: The three items in bold print (numbers 3,4 &5) are central
to the "Times Factor" method.

If you establish the method described herein, it is important that
you keep revising and reviewing the entire menu at least twice a
year, more often where applicable. Once you have kept a good
record of all your items and factors, plus notes concerning value
and competition, it will not be difficult to update these records.

Forecasting

The balancing act

Management in the restaurant business is just what you probably
suspected all along; A juggling act in the circus of life. No matter
how long you have owned or operated a restaurant, by now you
realize that keeping a balance between purchases, working employees, cash flow, amounts of food to prepare, and the unexpected deliveries, is a real circus you actually ran away from home to
join. Balance in the universe is common and yet not totally understood by the astronomers, so how can a restaurant owner be ex-

pected to understand and use balance in business? The answer to that question is simply, any owner of a restaurant for two or more years knows the importance of keeping some balance, otherwise they are most likely not going to see the third year.

"Order more produce, frozen shrimp and 2-1/2 lb (maximum weight) chickens, get some full time help on the second shift server line, and you better prepare the tables in room "B" (extension room, normally used for banquets), don't forget we need help in the dish washing department".

These edicts indicate a familiar feeling of panic when inaccuracies occur, because information between all the necessary contributing factors did not present itself appropriately, thereby making forecasting through crystal ball gazing and other guesstimating techniques, unprofitable. This is why "Forecasting" with professional methods is so important, and once you have that down pat,the balancing act becomes second nature.

Overview of forecasting

If you have or are about to commit to computerized assistance, that will be of immense help to your business management, however, there are those owners who like to do things from memory, some even possess a remarkable mathematical aptitude, which in certain instances, can make the computer seem inconsequential. The problem with the latter type individual is not that he or she can do mathematical tasks necessary to many applications in the restaurant business, but rather; Who else in the organization can follow the same practices with the same talents when you are not available?

Is the extra time wisely spent doing such mathematical work, when a computerized assisted system would allow you the owner more time for other important matters? In any case, **Forecasting,** can be accomplished by hand or by computer assisted systems.

Forecasting business is simply gathering information, formulating it, indicating predetermined percentages which were arrived at by performance establishing restaurant standards. Established restaurant standards means, data that each particular restaurant has recorded over time. Taking standards relates to the function of making a record of information, such as;

The number of guests in a shift, hour, day etc.

The number and type of meals served during a particular hour, day, etc.

The number of dollars taken in over a particular hour, shift, day etc.

The number of employees working on certain shifts, on particular days, and described by job title.

With basic data (information) collected each day, you can plainly see how the process works. It is an accumulation of particular information which is totaled and averaged out, plus, you naturally make allowances for changes in events, time of year (if seasonal business aspects apply) and other deviations from the norm.

The exception to forecasting is the business which does the same (within 5% or so) amount of business (dollars and food and beverage items), each identified day, week, month, etc, and maintains little or no variances.

Fortunately for the independent restaurant owner there are rarely any occurrences of the same type of day twice in any year. What's that you say, "MacDonalds does the same tremendous business each day".

As independent restaurant owners, anything we can learn from MacDonalds is information worth learning and having. They are not the biggest restaurant chain in the world because some fellow in Desplains Illinois got lucky. The marketing abilities of that golden arched organization is so extensive, that other industries like the automotive one should ask them to do market analysis. The fact of the matter is, when large successful food operations (out of the independents realm) do something, there is generally a good reason for it, so, it is better to listen and learn, than shoot from the hip and criticize. We might not always agree with everything being done by others in business, however, they have the same rights, and that is good for you and your business and great for this country.

NOW BACK TO FORECASTING

If Friday and Saturday nights are at a high level in the winter and spring seasons, and the summer and fall show considerable changes, then you should compare appropriate seasons, or at least make allowances. It is always best to make comparisons of likenesses, such as, apples to apples etc. If there are particular days as holidays, convention days, weddings and other events, then you need to make allowances for those too.

There are several forms of forecasting and equally as many methods, however, it is fitting that a complete forecasting method be demonstrated. Because restaurant operations can vary in detail and scope to a small and sometimes great extent, there will be some owners who may not find the following totally applicable to their operations. It is true that all owners will find the Brian Sill forecasting method interesting and beneficial if you translate job descriptions and appropriate functions etc.

FORECASTING:
THE PRACTICE

Restaurant : Dining Room

Period/One Year: August 1987

Meal Period: Dinner

Note: In this example we are Forecasting for the coming week which is Monday August 3rd through Sunday August 9th. You will obviously substitute your own appropriate data including dates, and guest counts etc.

FORECASTING   CHART

Day #	1	2	3	4	5	6	7
Day	M	T	W	TH	F	S	SN
Date	8/3	8/4	8/5	8/6	8/7	8/8	8/9
Occ#1	201	167	260	245	322	297	(391)
Occ#2	229	182	245	199	359	340	200
Occ#3	242	219	223	214	350	333	210
Occ#4	195	211	241	240	312	316	231
Total	867	779	969	898	1343	1286	641
Average	217	195	242	225	336	322	214
SPC Occ	-20	+40	---------------------------------------				
Forecast	197	235	242	225	336	322	214
Act Gsts	211	242	212	222	330	359	236
FC Acc%	-7	-3	+12	+1	+4	-9	-10

Last Year

Guests	286	313	259	293	368	331	227
Date	8/4	8/5	8/6	8/7	8/8	8/9	8/10

Source: Brian Sill Associates, Seattle, Washington.

Steps to Take,
Implementing the Forecasting Chart;

Step 1. Enter the name of the restaurant or outlet where it says "Restaurant:Dining Room".

Step 2. Enter the current period and year you will be forecasting just below the restaurant name.

Step 3. Enter the meal time period as we have, in the case of this example:"Dinner". Volume of business will vary from day to day and shift (Breakfast, lunch & dinner) to shift, so accuracy and detail are important.

Step 4. Enter the correct day of the week and corresponding date for the current period. Note: If you are using a Julian Calendar period accounting system-January, February, etc, the day number, will be the same as the date. The format presented here will work for the latter, a 4-4-5 week, or 13 period accounting cycles.

Step 5. Enter the corresponding date and guest count from last year. Example: Monday August 3rd (this year), corresponds with Monday August 4th (last year). 286 guests were served on this day last year.

Step 6. The last 4 occurrences (Occ#1 through Occ#4), Correspond to the previous recent 4 weeks of guest count by day of week. Enter these counts by week as indicated. Occ#1 is one week ago with Occ#2,3 & 4 following in sequence so that Occ#4 is the oldest week.

Step 7. Enter the total of each of the four occurrences (Occ#1-Occ#4) for each days happening. Example: In the Monday column you should have 867 as a total.

Special Note; If one or more of the previous occurrences is particularly high or low as is the case for Occ#1 (391) on Sunday, circle it and do not include it in your averaged total. When these previous occurrence days are either too high or low, they weight the average number. As you can see by the total average for Sunday, we did not include the 391 guest count for Occ#1. This is where those unusually heavy or slow days, for whatever the reason, need to be noted, but not counted in averaging.

Step 8. Divide the total of 4 days of each weeks data, by 4 to arrive at an average for that particular day. Example: Monday has 4 each Occ (Occasions) ; 201+229+242+195 = a 867 total which you divide by 4 to come up with an average of 217. If you can only use 3 days data (as in the case of Sunday), then you total the 3 days and divide by 3 to arrive at the average.

Step 9. In the "SPC Occ" row you see a -20 and a +40 under the Monday and Tuesday column, respectively. Enter your management decision for a plus, minus, or a no change factor for each day, just as Brian has done in the forecasting chart.

The plus, minus, or no change factor, in this step is the most important because it requires judgement rather than mathematical routine. Once you get a handle on the judgement portion of the forecasting system, the entire system will be routine. The decision that management makes at this point is how to justify a substantial increase or decrease between last years (see step 5) corresponding days guest count compared to the average (see step 8) days guest count, which was calculated from the previous four weeks.

Example: In the case of Tuesday, the chart has indicated a +40 factor which falls between the 195 guest count average taken from the previous four weeks, and the 313 guest count of last years Tuesday reading. What actually happened was a reserved wedding party that established additional above average guest count for that day a year ago, plus the more recent Tuesdays have been slower due to a change in hours for Tuesdays, which is now back to regular shift hours. The judgement here is that business will be up in guest count, however not to the level of 313 as it was a year ago.

Some other reasons for substantial changes from year to year are:

1. The restaurant is now larger than it was.

2. Because an activity (ball game, parade, holiday event) located far from your restaurant caused a decrease in guest count, or, the reverse meant a booming business that day.

3. Renovations cause obvious guest count differences.

4. The weather was three feet of snow that day.

And; **thousands of other reasons, known only to you and the management of your restaurant.**

Step 10. Add or subtract the special occurrence number (SPC Occ) as appropriate. The total is the forecasted guest count to be used for labor planning, food production planning, purchasing, Etc.

Step 11. In the row identified "ACT GSTS", enter the actual guest count for that day.

Step 12. Make a note of any unusual occurrences if any for that day, such as holidays etc, which will assist in future forecasting accuracy.

An Example of a simple "Unusual Occurrences list "which can be
a part of your forecasting chart, or kept in a separate note book,
depending on how you like to organize things:

Unusual Occurrences List (daily notes)

Day no.
1 _____
2 _____
3 _____
4 _____
5 _____
6 _____
7 _____

*Just continue through to 31 days so you will have a complete
monthly record.*

Step 13. Compute the accuracy of your forecast and enter where
the row heading is "FC ACC%". You arrive at a plus or minus
percentage number as in the case of: Monday and the -7% reading. 197 subtracted from 211 equals 14, which is then divided by
197, that equals -7%(negative 7%). This means that you under-
forecasted by seven percent.

The purpose of this step is to evaluate the forecasting accuracy,
not to show business success or failure. The mark you should
shoot to be within is a plus or minus 15 percent. If you fall outside
this limit then it is necessary to investigate and learn why. When
you practice this system, there is no reason that you shouldn't be
able to hit within 5 percent. At least the challenge of doing so is
personally satisfying, not to mention profitable to the restaurant.

Research source: Brian Sill Associates
Seattle, Washington

Final Comment: The Guest Forecast System is a viable tool for restaurant owners when projecting weekly staffing needs, whether used by hand or computer. Increased accuracy in forecasting instills greater confidence in the labor scheduler which removes the tendency to flat-staff or over staff departments. The fact that the system is based on guest count rewards the owner in quality of execution and a higher level of profits.

Note: There are several personal computers and the necessary software which can accommodate this type of forecasting system.

ADVERTISING

XII

Image Principles

Advertising is making people aware. The kind of awareness and the marketing concept you are looking for depends on the image you want the chosen advertising-audience to receive. Therefore image includes the message plus an expectation of what the potential customer will get for his or her patronage. An honest representation of what is advertised will more often than not, harness a re-peat customer. Repeat customers return because they feel they can depend on CONSISTENCY. Consequently advertising must include some indication of PRICE, QUALITY & SERVICE which converts to VALUE, and that is what customers are CONSISTENTLY looking for.

Image is the way your business appears to your clientele. From the manner of the employees, to the candle lit tables. The sign out front and decor of it's interior are also important. And of course the quality level of the menu items which your kitchen produces ranks uppermost in the minds of the majority.

There are a varying number of elements which constitute image, however, your restaurants image is what the majority of other people believe it to be. By this we mean; If your customers believe that the wine (from a nearby domestic source) you serve is better than the high priced, world class, imported, gold medal winner, then that taste becomes apart of the image in that customer market segment. It doesn't matter what the aristocracy of wine palates indicates, only what the majority of your customers demand because they like it. Image is what the consumer believes is fact, at least until something happens to change that image. If you change the wine which so many enjoy, you must consider your image appeal to another segment of the overall market. This image principle applies to all of the good selling menu items, and sometimes to those slower moving choices.

Are you an advertising expert also?

In doing creative advertising to your restaurant business as you already have, with your menu, sign and probably some other forms of general advertising, you are no doubt looking for approval from one or more people. Good', that is as it should be. Knowing the image you wish to reflect to the customer- audience is certainly part of being an owner.

To some extent you are an expert about your restaurant, at least you know what goes on inside. Assuming this is true, you want to be as creative as possible where advertising is concerned. Your participation may be total, or you are advocating the ideas of others with your eventual approval. In any case, you are involved with your creative opinion. If you are not artistic enough to be comfortable in doing the graphics part of a menu, newspaper ad or other forms of advertising the restaurants image and message, you will have someone (preferably a professional) else do the task.

Hiring and working with a graphics designer to do your prepared finished artwork ready for reproduction can be inexpensive or expensive depending on who does the work and the involvement of the reproductive treatment. The fact is, almost any kind of advertising which gets the message to the prospective customer is better than nothing at all. Although, excellent graphics and high level message-copy will produce the best results, provided it finds the correct audience. The decision regarding cost and designers, is best answered through your own testing.

A few points which can help;

Start with something simple like a menu or an ad which will appear in the local newspaper or shoppers guide etc.

Locate a graphic designer through the yellow pages who is nearby and willing to meet with you at the restaurant.This way the designer will get a better feeling of the image to be projected and you will not have to leave the premises. Explain to the designer what you want in simple terms, do not elaborate, rather listen to the designers response.

Get some idea of the designers charges, most of which charge by an hourly rate. Some designers will give you a flat rate for small jobs.

COMMUNICATING AWARENESS

It is true today as it has been in the past, that WORD OF MOUTH advertising through the opinions of the consumer, is the most solid form of advertising. WORD OF MOUTH is more often than not, the result of other awareness forms which are designed to affect a large number of consumers through a preliminary advertising method. Methods such as NEWSPAPER ADS, RADIO ADS, TELEVISION ADS, DIRECT MAIL ADS, and other less demonstrative means which attract the prospective customer, will usually achieve a preliminary image awareness concerning your business. Once your business obtains effective preliminary advertising results, the customer will be left with a first time experience, hence impression that will provide positive or negative WORD OF MOUTH advertising. If the CONSISTENCY of the customers return-experience is positive (by majority of your market), then the compounding WORD OF MOUTH affect will develop successfully.

MEDIA METHODS: Newspaper, Magazines, Radio and Television.

An Advertising Agency or not?

It is not necessary for restaurant owners to go through an advertising agency to obtain space or time to advertise, although, given the owners limited time and the size of the project, it may become a real consideration. Yes indeed, the advertising agency will cost you considerably more than if you handle it yourself, however, their professional expertise may be required. If you believe an ad-agency is an alternative, then go to the yellow pages and contact a few. You should meet with them and discuss the project you have in mind, the worst of which can happen is that you will learn something from the meeting. If you decide that the cost of an agency handling your advertising project will benefit you because of their expertise and your lack of time to devote to the project, then some of the following advertising material concerning media contact will not be particularly important. If on the other hand, you can provide the time to oversee the advertising project, and you need the cost savings which circumventing an ad-agency usually provides, then a few simple points to follow are appropriate.

Some fundamental guidelines which the owner should consider when approaching communicative (radio, television, newspaper, and magazine, etc.) media companies are as follows:

I.
Stick to the realities of your business. Do not oversell what you cannot deliver.

2.
Contact radio, television, newspaper, magazines to obtain their RATE schedule information. Rate information should include a cost for time or space where applicable.

3.
Inquire when special rate offers will be in effect.

4.
Inquire about in-house production abilities and the costs for doing this work. When available the production abilities of media companies can prove cost effective while providing timely results. Check it out.

5.
Select the specific company (radio & TV station, newspaper, magazine, billboards, etc.) or the companies which reach your market, which is the market you wish to address.

What should a restaurant offer?

When advertising, a restaurant naturally allows the audience to know it's name and location, beyond that there are a few general considerations. The fact that you are offering "dinner fare" doesn't always require advertising the hours of operation, although deviations from normal dinner hours may. The same applies to "breakfast" and Lunch" times. Emphasis is commonly placed on offering your standard menu items, prices and special offerings.

What interests the majority of consumers is value, consequently as an example; The fresh salad bar which goes with your $7.99 Steak dinner, may be the value your market segment is looking for. If you point up the fact that this steak is graded U.S.D.A. Choice and your chef uses a marinading process which creates the "Flavor and Tenderness you've been searching for", you may have found the creative advertising message you need. Above all else, be truthful and accurate.

Customers today are intelligent and are therefore aware of receiving anything less than their interpretation of what the restaurant has offered. It is always a good idea to give something in addition to the offer which comes as a happy surprise (value-added) to the customer who took you up on your advertising offer. The "Value-added" feature may be in the form of extra service, a rose for the lady, a rice pudding dessert which comes free with the meal, personal attention by the owner, or a thousand other ideas.

The idea of offering something "FREE" seems to be somewhat popular among many consumers, although there are definitely potential problems. When you offer an extremely low priced, or even free item, will a large percentage of those customers who received the "too good to be true" menu item, be back if you do not repeat this kind of offer again?

You have witnessed large restaurant chains who periodically offer the consumer reduced prices on their standard fare and/or decorated glasses, hats, "T" shirts, games, dolls, and hundreds of other items which may or may not require some financial reciprocation on the part of the customer. Take a good look at what the large chain operations do and you may be able to expand on an advertising project of your own.

The fact is; MacDonalds, Burger-King, Pizza Hut, and the other restaurant giants have accomplished strong advertising programs which have been very successful, and since they have expended great amounts of time, expertise and money, it makes good sense that restaurants who do not possess the dollar volumes which allow for such marketing and advertising efforts, should pay some attention and learn that which may be applicable to their business.

Advertising Cooperatives

GROUP ADVERTISING is most beneficial where cost is concerned.

When there are events such as ball games, state fairs, and other seasonal attractions, you want to make the potential food lover aware of your restaurant, you should consider Group-Type advertising, especially if costs need to be kept down.

Whether you use the local newspaper, direct mail shoppers guide, printed posters indicating the event and your offer, or the cities magazine or other publication, all print media wants to sell advertising space (with very little exception). If a group of business people (including you and other businesses which could be other restaurants, etc) decide to share advertising then the cost of advertising is divided, creating great savings.

If for example you share the advertising expense with five other businesses, taking a full page ad in a newspaper or shoppers guide, the full page space can be keyed-in to the upcoming event (may be a football game) which includes the sales of each participating business, including the best service and salad bar in town (like your restaurant), etc.

GROUP ADVERTISING: A check list to get you started;

I.
Check out various upcoming events through the newspaper, Chamber of Commerce, local hotel calendars (meetings management office) and other known sources.

2.
Select an event which will benefit your restaurant and other types of businesses.

3.
Be sure you have plenty of time to prepare for the advertising and all the other involvements which will make a success of the entire advertising program.

4.
Select a media for the advertising, such as the local newspaper or your cities magazine,etc. It is always best to choose from three or more.

5.
Obtain rate cards or rate information from the communications media you have selected. This will give you the cost information on ads so that you can make comparisons.

6.
Call the various business owners or managers which you believe will benefit from your advertising scheme. Tell

them what your plan is and how several businesses who join together can save on advertising and obtain more business at this upcoming event.

7.

Prepare for a meeting (at your restaurant) with an agenda that each business owner can identify with.

Example: Information about the event, The time frame which will affect each business, Information about each business (Name, address, phone number, sales items) which they wish to sell (whether a special item or just the company name), graphics coordinator, etc.

8.

At the first meeting of the cooperative business owners upcoming event advertising campaign, you should find the person with the most graphics experience to coordinate the ad copy and work with the publisher or other appropriate media company. If no one is willing or able, you should look to the yellow pages for a graphic artist.

9.

If this is your first experience with GROUP advertising, then allow yourself plenty of time, lets say **three months** (from the first group meeting to delivery of the publication). After your first group-advertising effort, you will be able to put more complicated programs together in 3 or 4 weeks.

10.

Have the publisher or whatever media company is involved, bill each advertising business separately , however showing the total expense, in order that each cooperative advertising member knows he or she is being treated the same.

You should use your imagination to come up with thousands of good solid ideas which will bring you and the GROUP business advertiser's sales, plus a beneficial relationship.

These ten basic steps do not contain all the answers, but rather enough to get you involved in what can be a very effective advertising program, particularly when the GROUP is together time and time again.

CONGRUOUS
(TWO-TYPE) AD PROGRAM

This is a particular method of handling restaurant advertising that can only be used with different businesses which envision the benefits of two companies complementing each other.

The difference between the CONGRUOUS and the GROUP method is that the Group-type only shares advertising space, where the Congruous method works with advertising space and selling or representing it's products through either or both companies.

Example: The cola company helps sell the restaurant by combining both companies in an advertising program, and vice versa. The two companies share the advertising costs and both companies are promoted through the restaurant, and/or other media.

In addition, when each company has an established reputation of high standing, they will strengthen their image through a joint demonstration of complementary business activities.

As you can imagine the benefits can reach high levels if applied properly. The most difficult aspect is that of finding an appropriate and harmonious, congruous advertising partner. You must be aware and keep searching for the right situation.

During your search for the compatible advertising company, you must know that well known names will be attracted by more perspective customers than Ziggy Rangler, who has not as yet made the front page. The more popular the other company's name is, the more you must be willing to concede when you offer a deal. When you think about the many soft drink companies, bakeries, soup companies, makers of ice cream, wines, fisheries, meat companies, produce growers, hundreds of jams, coffee's, teas, and fresh fruit grown in the sunshine, you think of well known firms who would jump at the chance to be a congruous advertising partner, if you present a sensible and workable program.

When you come up with your own idea that you believe has the makings of success in this type of advertising, what's to keep you from approaching several companies? If you think you have a good ad-program idea, who's to say the Campbell Soup Company or the Häágen-dazs Ice Cream people won't believe in it also? The point is don't be afraid to contact other companies, as the worst thing that can happen is that you will learn something from the process.

Before you attempt this method of advertising, understand the following points;

1.

Make sure that the restaurant and your perspective congruous company partner will have mutual benefits. Without the benefits, a potential congruous advertising company partner is not interested.

2.

Prepare written plans showing all costs involved.

3.

If applicable, consider this idea as a localized marketing test for your intended congruous partner.

4.

Point up the customer service and the value added features that the consumer (prospective customer) will be attracted to.

5.

Be willing to take a smaller slice of the visual graphics presentation of your advertising idea.

6.

Do not test your idea out on friends or less interested parties first, try it out on a lesser known congruous partner instead. This is most important as it is amazing how your original idea can be pirated because of opening your mouth to people who can't help themselves from telling it as their own thought. Keep it to yourself, it is your creation, regardless of the level of acceptance.

7.

Be prepared for costs to be incurred mostly by you as many times the big name companies may feel their name will capture (pull) the sales. Sometimes well known companies push this thought as they have already paid for their well established prominence. On the other hand, many large companies may pay for all the costs because of the marketing information you will supply. Consider this aspect carefully.

8.

When you and your congruous company choice are enthusiastically in agreement on a program, have professional legal assistance (your attorney) prepare an appropriate document.

How much will this method of advertising cost? Some restaurants have incurred little or no cost, however, if you wish to share a billboard sign just off the expressway going into the big city, you may find more expense than you are ready for, which of course depends on your idea and the volume of business your restaurant already enjoys.

Final comment:

Congruous advertising is a method which can encompass all forms of media-communication, graphics, products and ideas which can be tremendously beneficial, particularly when both parties (companies) involved, share a thoughtful rapport and profess mutual success.

Business is off.....indicate positive. Competition treated with respect, silence, or both?

When business is slow and/or it just isn't up to the par-level you are more content with, do not take it out on the competition with slurs and fits of jealousy. Never run down your competition as it looks as if you are the one with the problem, and that isn't good for business. If you can't say anything good about the other guy, keep silent. Demonstrations of good character is very good advertising, plus you may need that competitor some day.

If business is off, do not reflect anything but positive feelings and indications to your customers. Advertising negative thoughts does not promote business. If you find yourself in that situation, remember the days when business was better, test yourself by getting the employees and customers in an up mood, and by doing so you will create warm positive thoughts which is the best form of advertising. It only costs you a little self control, which further enables you to create the idea that life in your restaurant is truly the Shangri-la on earth. "Now that's advertising".

Right or wrong we test the image..
To let the people know..
How good our plates are selling..
See that item glow..
Shouting out through ad and sign..
More business shall be mine..
Creative food keep moving..
For worried I shall be..
Until that day I cannot say..
More people in the nooks..
When bills are paid, I'am not afraid..
And see the balanced books..
Oh' Ad's you are a working..
Thank all that has been lent..
With pride alive, I race inside..
Because I can pay the rent...

CONSULTANTS / INFORMATION-ACCESS

XIII

Consultants and You

There are restaurant owners today that wouldn't consider hiring a food industry management or design consultant because they are not aware of what a consultant is and can do. There are others who wouldn't hire one because they have heard negative things about consultants. There are also owners who will not make a growth decision without the advice of the professional consultant. Often is the case when rumors can be traced to a source that is usually ignorant or jealous. The truth is simply that too many restaurant owners do not know enough about the consultant's role.

Consultants in the foodservice industry are people like we are, except they have been educated and trained to exercise their profession, just like a doctor, or a major league ball player.The bottom line is the same here as it is with anything in business life: "Choose the best for the value of the job to be performed". The fact that professional consultants who are excellent at what they do, and are proclaimed vital by their clients (mostly restaurant owners), leads us to the conclusion that something needs to be learned about the consultant's role.

When should an owner consider a consultant ?

When the volume of the project meets the serious intent of the owner, and he or she realizes that other professionals in the industry may have more specific knowledge appropriate to the project being contemplated.

After the owner has acquired the experience to confidently grow with change, and realize that the consultants educated perspective can benefit and add to the owners inside knowledge.

When an owner is concerned about the restaurant's future considering the economic, environmental, structural, organizational and productive aspects to his or her business, plus, the owner understands the declining risk factor when a professional contributes in areas in which the owner is not proficient.

Who can afford a consultant?

Consultants earnings may come by way of fees, retainers, by the hour, commissions, or flat amounts by project. Some consultants also earn income from speaking engagement honorariums.

Generally, consultants are more expensive than the restaurant employee who is your dishwasher and less expensive than building a space shuttle (this is a wide gap for an example , however it points out that consultants vary in the way they are remunerated). Again, the point is that consultants range in the amounts they charge because it depends on who the consultant is and what the proposed project or assignment is. There are also consultants who specialize in particular areas of foodservice and others who join together under one company to handle most every kind of need.

Example by parallel:

Mr. Know had a restaurant business for 5 years and his operation was doing well. He had two ideas. One, he wanted to expand to the west side of town where the new development was. Two, he saw potential in adding a membership lunch and dinner club to his existing establishment. Since Mr. Know had good credit, some real estate holdings, and a savings account that he felt was respectable, he saw no apparent reason for not finding a way to accomplish at least one of these ideas.

After careful thought and meeting with his banker, he decided to have a foodservice consultant take a look at his plan and learn of marketing data and strategies which he was not expert in developing, plus he could not spare the time, even if he possessed the ability. Mr. Know called the association which represents professional consultants, the local restaurant association and a few substantial restaurants in the area for recommended consultants who were specifically proficient on the subject of restaurant marketing.

He went over the list of names and chose three to contact. It wasn't long before he realized that the probable expense involved just to the point of marketing studies, in fact , analysis of the entire two point scheme, was going to cost as much as a fine attorney in a two month law case.

Finally, Mr. Know justified the cost of this preliminary work due to the fact that he would need it to confirm his ideas, assist in obtaining financing, serve as a basis for the follow- up work project itself, and the fact that all the findings would be confidential and his alone. He also reasoned that without the consultant's help, he may make financial decisions that could literally cause the professional's fee to look like a few grains of sand on a beach of chapter eleven's.

Mr. Know selected Mr.Wise who needed a portion of his total fee payment in advance.This did not seem unreasonable as Mr. Know checked the consultant's work through six clients who indicated satisfaction. Mr. Know also visited the site where two of Mr. Wise's clients finished projects were seen and proudly shown.

The complete study was finished and the results showed that Mr. Know could add a restaurant location to the west side of town, however closer to the Interstate highway system than he had originally envisioned.

He also learned the size the restaurant should be, three suitable property choices available, the days and hours business would best provide customer traffic, general cost approaches to full construction through to opening day, and some financial information including expected ranges of revenue and advice about financing the project. The idea about the membership lunch and dinner club was ruled out for a number of reasons; one was a cost effective comparison which showed no reasonable return on investment for 3 years, due to the number of executives in the area, plus their proximity to the downtown restaurant itself.

Mr. Know followed the consultant's reports and findings, and has a second location closer to the Interstate which is highly successful. He also kept the first location and made only a few kitchen production changes which the consultant recommended, and this unit is also doing very well.

Who are clients of consultants?

Some consultants are hired by far-sighted equipment manufacturers to assist in marketing analysis or evaluations, however, the majority of clients are owners and corporate leaders of both independent and chain restaurants. To be included among the consultants clients are the institutional foodservice cafeterias, hotels, restaurants, clubs, schools of all types, prisons, hospitals, company in-house food service, and most any place where people are fed outside the home.

What kinds of consultants are there?

Consultants range from individuals who specialize in a particular aspect like design and architecture, to large consulting firms which have many specialists covering all aspects of a project up to and including turn-key (opening day) complete contracts.

A major share of projects which the professional consultant is involved in surrounds the new restaurant, the restaurant renovation and the additional restaurant location. In addition: Consultants will also do specialized studies for independent and chain restaurants.

The consultant helps in areas of uncertainty, and during the consultant's project involvement particular problems may surface. The consultant confronts the client with data and a solution, and sometimes the findings can be unexpected. Whatever the style of the consultant (personality wise), the fact is confrontation with real issues, unearthing honest data and showing the sometimes tough alternatives will surface, illustrating to the owner those things which he or she cannot see from the inside. The owner must know that change is needed, that is why he or she feels the need for serious professional work.

Consultant Project Areas

DESIGN	MANAGEMENT	MARKETING
Architecture	Management Systems	Research
Engineering	Employee Training	Feasibility-Studies
Equipment	Menu Planning	Concept Planning
Specifications	Recipe Formulation	Programming
Facility Layout	Food Specification	Studies
Decor	Nutrition	
Energy	Portioning & Packaging	
	Cooking Methods	
	Operations Review	
	Trouble Shooting	

The above listing covers the majority of foodservice consultants' project expertise. There are other areas which are offshoots or outgrowths of the listed categories, however, they are not frequently found.

How to find a consultant

You can call the local restaurant association in your area and ask for recommended consultants, most local associations keep a list.

Contacting restaurant owners you know, who have used consultants or you suspect have used consultants. Or contact the foodservice Consultants Society International (**FCSI**). Their address is;

Foodservice Consultants Society International
Suite H (Consultants Information)
12345 30th Avenue N.E.
Seattle, Washington 98125

The FCSI is an association which does not admit membership by simply paying a fee. In order to qualify for professional membership status (the highest level of expertise) an applicant must have ten years experience as a consultant, five years of project director responsibilities, must be qualified to design or implement foodservice programs, must be employed as a professional consultant by an organization which provides consulting services to the foodservice industry, must submit a 2,000 (minimum) word article for publication in the official Society publication. Relevant college experience may count as part of the ten years. All of these requirements are reviewed by a special committee, after which a board of directors pass approval, unless there is a question raised, and then that question usually requires an investigation.

If you believe these requirements are rigid it is only because they are, and there are more.

In either instance of contacting people for recommended consultants, be sure you indicate the type of project that involves a consultants help.

How do you know if the consultant can do the job?

I.
Ask the consultant for client references where similar services have been performed. Contact those references and ask the following questions;

> a. Were you satisfied with the services performed?
> b. If not, why not?
> c. Would you hire this consultant again?
> d. If not, why not?
> e. Was the work performed on time according to agreement?
> f. If required; Did the consultant coordinate services with other specialists on the project? (like architects, contractors, zoning authorities and equipment manufacturers, etc).

2.
Visit the locations of some referenced projects, if reasonably convenient. Talk to the owners or operator and learn of any praises or dissatisfactions.

3.
Ask the consultant to generally and briefly outline how he or she intends to perform the task. You are not asking for details, after all that is what you are hiring the consultant for. In other words, ask to see the steps that are to be taken and why. This lets the consultant know that you are serious about your project and it will give you a better understanding of the consultant's expertise as it may apply to your project and his or her profession.

Your part in this consultant determination is centered around the well-defined need which you have provided.

In Summation:

Consultants may not be for every restaurant owner. It largely depends on the owners needs.

If addressed properly, and for the right reasons, consultants fill an important and specific niche in the restaurant world. Knowing how to find the consultant who will work with you, the owner, to produce the desirable result will be as important as the owner being able to outline specific and general goals. Exactly How, Where, Why and When these goals are to be implemented, plus the actual construction and form of the project, is the responsibility of the consultant.

Finally; it is the owner's responsibility to learn and understand what the consultant's role is, when and how to participate in the project, and to protect his or her interest by working with the consultant, from the project's beginning, to its happy and successful conclusion.

Source: C. Russell Nickel, FCSI, Seattle, Washington
Bert Marshall Jr, professional consultant, FCSI Professional member, Mesa, Arizona.
Brian Sill, Associate FCSI member, Seattle , Washington.

Information Access

Becoming Aware

The real secret of accessing information is and always has been right there in front of us. Our problem is in not recognizing it. Or, do we have too much pride to admit how lazy we are?

Awareness through access holds no deep dark secret or innovative method that you should pay for, through the nose.

Stimulating your mind to a point of developing new ideas and becoming aware of what is out there, happens only when we get off our beam and seek it out.

How does all of this come about? By acquiring INFORMATION. Think about this word; Our whole life is built upon it. Where do I go? How do I find it in relation to the restaurant business? The same answers apply, no matter what business you are in.

1.
Start with your telephone; Talk to informed people.

2.
Go to the public library. Seek out business information.

3.
Trade associations have a wealth of information, much of which is free for the asking.

4.
Government agencies and offices have more information than you can imagine and most of it is free for the asking.

5.
Companies relating to the foodservice industry, such as food producers, suppliers, and equipment manufacturers. Contact them, they all have people who need your questions, just as much as you need the answers.

6.
Authors that have written on subjects relating to your situation. Contact them, they need your input and can help you.

7.
Read newspapers and trade journals to keep abreast of current events. Remember; rules, regulations and economics are ever changing in the restaurant business.

8.
Both in and out-of-state telephone directories contain many sources of information.

9.
Most universities today have a computer library hook up for research requests.

I0.
Information from your U.S. government pertaining to loans, grants (such as research grants), etc.

Most importantly, keep a SOURCE FILE. This tells you where to obtain information. Also included should be; The date of the material, which helps identify information that needs to be updated. You will find that a source file is like money in the bank drawing interest over the years. The source file pyramids over time, compounding into opportunities which spring from your ingenious mind.

Some have a fear

Certainly, one of the greatest stumbling blocks to the quest for information is fear. Fear of what? The fear most people have is that of rejection, being told; No, or; Who do you think you are calling here? Many restaurant owners feel free to tell the vendor who supplies the food stuffs what is wrong with the order they received, however that is because they know the person they are talking to and they feel in charge as they are paying for something which has a flaw. Many owners have difficulty making a cold call to a strange source. If you are an owner with this type of fear, you must learn to take charge of the situation and realize that you have a perfect right to access most kinds of information that the world develops. This type of fear is generally put to rest after you are aware of it, and put it to the test by looking up a source, calling on the telephone and asking questions.

Accessing information solves problems

Solving business worries and turning that feeling of failing around. When you find a key and it opens doors, all of a sudden there is an attitude change and the ideas bloom.

Example: Take the case of Mrs. Latebloomer, a woman , who at age 50 , is the owner of a small restaurant. The restaurant provided a living for 15 years, but never grew to the size she had originally expected. Frustrated and ready to throw in the towel, she started to read more about business in general, and attended some evening classes at the university. She soon realized that all business is basic, also through doing research for homework, she found the library was much more than a place to read "Shakespeare" or "Dickens". There were directories that located industries, companies, trade associations, and a multitude of information sources for research and to build a source file.

Although Mrs. Latebloomer was a rather quiet person, she began to pose and answer questions which led to solving her own business dilemmas. She became involved in the "Teaching people to read" program and held classes in her restaurant, thereby, giving herself notoriety which resulted in great advertisement for the restaurant.

Today, her new restaurant is twice the size and the dinner fare requires a serious reservation. Why did all of this happen? Simply because her renewed enthusiasm was brought about by self education through accessing information. When you actively access information, one thing leads to another, and if you are not afraid to get involved, your knowledge will pyramid.

There is also another benefit from accessing information and that is developing talents. After a period of time (it naturally differs from one person to another), hidden interests you didn't necessarily know were there, become talents. As you may know, when a talent surfaces and is recognized, other profitable opportunities usually come into being.

The results produced by one person cannot be entirely compared to another, however, the key here is in knowing how and where to locate information and following up by learning from it.

Where to locate information

The public and university libraries are the best two places to start.

The following sources are but a small sample of where to access business information:

TRADE DIRECTORIES OF THE WORLD This title lists 8,783 directories in the United States alone. Items like the " Directory of Top Computer Executives" and "State and County Officials", are among the thousands.

TRADE SHOWS AND PROFESSIONAL EXHIBITS DIREC-TORY This title is an international guide to scheduled events providing commercial display facilities, including conferences, conventions, meetings, congresses and councils, fairs and festivals, trade and industrial shows, merchandise marts, and expositions.

THE ENCYCLOPEDIA OF ASSOCIATIONS This title lists nearly 21,000 national organizations in the United States, plus thousands more throughout the world. Associations in all industries, law, science, medicine, education, sports, hobbies, labor, culture, religion, agriculture, public affairs, and much more, are thoroughly represented by non-profit associations. The information completely describes the associations intent, activities, computerized services, contact information, and lists the publications, etc..

NOTE: NON PROFIT TRADE ASSOCIATIONS MUST PROVIDE A CERTAIN AMOUNT OF INFORMATION TO THE PUBLIC IN ORDER TO MAINTAIN THEIR TAX EXEMPT STATUS.

This means that even though you are not a member of a particular trade association, you are entitled to some information. An example is the National Restaurant Association; The fact is, you do not need to be a member to purchase books, acquire free brochures which contain statistics and other information, attend seminars and many other services and events. You will probably have to pay a little more for most items and services, however, if the multitude of services meets your particular needs, you should consider becoming a member, as it may be financially justifiable.

THE STANDARD PERIODICAL DIRECTORY This is the most comprehensive directory of U.S. and Canadian periodicals available. Listings of over 65,000 periodicals (consumer magazines, trade journals, newsletters, government publications, house organs, social group publications and more). Listings include information about each publications circulation, number of pages, computer identification, contact people, including the publisher, address, telephone, frequency of the publication, etc.

STANDARD AND POOR'S REGISTER OF CORPORATIONS, DIRECTORS AND EXECUTIVES. This is a guide to basic information about American corporations.

DUN'S ACCOUNT IDENTIFICATION SERVICE
This title lists information about thousands of small businesses.

THOMAS REGISTER OF AMERICAN MANUFACTURERS
This title is a purchasing guide that tells you who makes the products you need.

SWEETS CATALOG FILE
A purchasing guide with the manufacturers of building materials.

BEST'S INSURANCE REPORTS
Gives financial information on all types of insurance companies and rates their excellence. Best's "Flintcraft Compend", gives information about premiums, cash value and dividends.

The STANDARD DIRECTORY OF ADVERTISERS and the TRADE NAMES DIRECTORY Both list hundreds of current trade names and the addresses of the companies behind these names.

THE EDITOR AND PUBLISHER MARKET GUIDE
Gives essential information on potential markets for your service or product.

DIRECTORY OF FRANCHISING OPPORTUNITIES
Covers all types of companies offering franchises.

MOODY'S INVESTORS SERVICE
Provides current financial data on corporations and government
agencies that offer bonds or other investment instruments.

VALUE LINE, STANDARD & POOR'S OUTLOOK, and
MOODY'S COMMON STOCK HANDBOOK All give expert
opinions on current stocks.

WEISENBERGER INVESTMENT COMPANIES SERVICE
This title is an encyclopedia of mutual funds with information you
need to know before you invest.

PRENTICE-HALL FEDERAL TAX GUIDE
For those who need a detailed explanation of the current IRS
code.

THE U.S. INDUSTRIAL OUTLOOK
Gives the future prospects for over 350 industries.

THE CATALOG OF FEDERAL DOMESTIC ASSISTANCE
Provides details about financial assistance programs of the federal
government to business.

THE OCCUPATIONAL OUTLOOK HANDBOOK
Describes the many career fields and their requirements and gives
a job market forecast for each occupation.

The United States Government publishes many compilations of
business and economic statistics. THE U.S. STATISTICAL AB-
STRACT, ECONOMIC REPORT OF THE PRESIDENT plus the
 HANDBOOK OF LABOR STATISTICS AND BUSINESS
STATISTICS.

These are but a few places to start obtaining information in addition to your "Yellow Pages" and all the Yellow Pages of the U.S.
cities usually located at the telephone companies business offices.

REMEMBER: Find information Through the public and university library nearest to you, the offices of government agencies, trade associations, corporate businesses, and thousands of organizations around the world.

Do not be afraid of using the telephone to ask questions.

Start and keep an updated source file.

Do not believe everything you hear third hand, **find out** first hand, for yourself. When you do this, you will cause a pyramiding effect that always starts more questions, hence more answers and more information. If you comprehend the information, you will create the knowledge you were seeking, and if you apply that knowledge correctly, you will have attained a degree of wisdom, understood by the most successful people.

NOTE: For information about books, trade magazines and schools, see the "Reference Section".

Afraid of growing I found..
Was not knowing, what is blowing,
        in the wind..
Picking the secrets while listening,
        in places they say..
Read that book, call that firm,
        it's OK..
A headache from searching,
        not knowing enough..
Can't find that listing..
Gee ain't that tough..
All this info is a source-file thrill..
Too bad it's depressing,
        with the telephone bill..

COMPUTER EVALUATION: S.P.E.

XIV

Selection, Proposal, & Evaluation (S.P.E.)

What should you know about a computer? It will be of immense help to you if you have some understanding of mathematical logic. More than that will increase your comprehension of the following material.

Logic is what computers are all about. It is not necessary to be a computer buff or hacker. Common sense through black and white or yes and no thinking is what a computer does, and it does so in the electrically controlled, powered, and operating sense. The computer speaks in positive or negative terms, no gray areas. The basis of computer electrical communications is the binary code which is much like the Morse code, one channel is opened by an electrical switch while another is closed. Combinations of these opened and closed channels, make other computer languages possible and usable for various programing requirements.

Operating a system requires some practice and training, also, software applications and hardware systems have manuals which contain training elements designed to get you up and running. Besides the self training materials, there are vendors who offer training programs, some are included with the purchase of a system. The training and practice we have mentioned is centered around a keyboard, much like a typewriter.

Some owners have had computer systems working for their business for years, and know that the computer is not only here to stay, but a necessary tool which helps make business competitive and profitable. Some owners are unsure about the computer because they are afraid they cannot handle the technological mysteries. There should be no feelings of fear about a computer, it is just like anything else, once you learn how to use it, you will wonder why you didn't do so earlier. There are also those owners who keep waiting for the cost of computer systems to go down, and while they are waiting, other restaurant owners are installing the systems, becoming more efficient and profitable. Procrastination in improving business abilities is not a cost effective measure when using future technological upgrades and the probable lower initial cost of computer systems, as an excuse.

Computer systems companies (the vendor)

When you work with vendors who sell the various systems, you should find them helpful in all areas of the the computer assisted systems, as they want your continuing business. Vendors know if your business grows, so will their sales and profits. Therefore, you can understand that the computer companies interest means more (or should) than the initial sale of a system. In any case, if you follow this evaluation process you should feel more comfortable and confident about dealing with the vendor, hence benefit. The vendor will also know that your well defined request for proposal is evidence that you are both serious and aware.

Purpose of S.P.E.

The main purpose is to afford the owner of a restaurant, an organized approach to determine the need for a computerized system, familiarize the owner with various terms and computer abilities, right on through to the order for a system which is picked (by the owner) to increase productive efficiency. This process is also appropriate to those restaurant owners who have computer assisted systems and want to increase it's present capabilities.

The amount of dollars, time and aggravation which can be spent on setting up a system is one that can cause you to have more ulcers than a room full of advertising account executives. In order that greater confusion does not occur, it is important that the owner be in control of the computer (S.P.E.) evaluation process from the start through to the installation and first months operations. If after that time, the owner wishes to appoint some other responsible employee the job of systems management, that would then be appropriate.

When the system is in and rolling along, and you see the reports, payroll, employee records, forecasting schedules, inventory, purchasing comparisons, plus hundreds of other possibilities, what ever your needs may be, you will certainly feel more confident about the future.

Note: Todays computer systems including software applications, are generally packaged for "Turn-Key" operations ("Turnkey"; Meaning, complete hardware, software and training, through to operational set up). If at any time you feel uncomfortable about your selection of features and/or needs, etc, the vendor should assist you. If you are still unsure you can contact a computer assisted systems consultant. When "Turnkey" type computer packages are not appropriate, it generally means that more than one vendor will be involved and that "Custom" hardware and/or software etc, will be necessary. True "Custom" computer systems usually require the expertise of a professional computer systems consultant. "Custom" computer systems are most often utilized when a restaurant has one or more units. Understanding the SPE process in the following pages of this section will increase your working knowledge, when and if a consultant becomes necessary.

How to be comfortable about S.P.E.

The length of this section on S.P.E. is relatively great, however, the majority of text is simply features and items for you to select where needed. If you remember the following basic points, you will find this process routine:

1. _____SELECTION; You are following the P.O.S. (Point of sale) systems features list, with definitions, only to select that which you need. Accounting functions follow a similar pattern.

2._____PROPOSAL; You are preparing information based on your POS selection and /or indicating Accounting functions, posing questions for the vendor to answer , for the purpose of providing vendors with data (request for proposal) in order that they will make appropriate proposals (quotations).

3._____EVALUATION; You are evaluating the vendors proposals in order to select the vendor or vendors who answer your needs and offer the appropriate balance of quality, service and price.

Important Information:

Due to the fact that technology in the field of computers is ever changing, and the number of variables so great, the material herein is relatively brief. it is not possible to list each and every identifiable item or combination of elements. In each of the following SELEC-TIONS, QUESTIONS to pose to the vendor, and your own identifiable requests, etc, you may find it necessary to add requirements which may not be contained herein. When you use this system for evaluation of your restaurant business, it will be of great help if the following two things are accomplished;

1. When you are serious about making a request for proposal, have your CPA or accountant go over the selection and specifications with you.

2. Make a copy of just those pages in this section which apply to S.P.E., to be used as a preliminary work sheet. This is an isolated exception to the publishers note (" No reproduction of this book is to be copied in whole or part without the publishers written permission"), however no resale of reproduced pages will be permitted.

P.O.S.Features for Selection
(with definitions)

Many P.O.S. (Point Of Sale) features may require custom adaptation which the vendor should address.

Point of sale (P.O.S.) systems can encompass a broad range of features from traditional accounting functions to automated beverage control systems. The success of point of sale system installation is dependent on how well a large number of these features work together as a complete system to support the style of operation. A successful point of sale system requires careful consideration of the many features in terms of fit, ease of use, speed of service, control and cost. Care should be taken that the, nice to have, high visibility features do not influence the purchase decision.

The POS selection information describes a number of features commonly found on restaurant point of sale systems. The features have been presented according to the following three categories;

I...Server/Cashier-work-stations:Covering keyboards, displays, and functions used to process orders and settle customer checks.

II...Remote-displays & printers: Covering hardware and features used to transmit orders and display them in kitchen service or bar areas.

III...Back office & management considerations : Covering system hardware such as the central processing unit and management functions such as reporting and maintenance of system controls.

Coding and Indicating Your Selections:

___(indicate)_____

Where you see this (above) line: Indicate with a "YES" to the left of the word "(indicate)", that will point to your selection. If you see items which you do not want under any circumstances, indicate by putting a "NO" , otherwise leave the space blank. The added line to the right is for your question, comment, or additional requirement. If you are unsure of a selection put "?" (the question mark), that will result in an appropriate response from the vendor.

Code "EX" :This Identifying code is to be used only by restaurant owners to indicate those elements (Hardware, software, features etc...) which exist in the present system. This code lets the prospective vendor know what you already have so that the vendor can configure software or hardware, utilizing your existing system where possible. If you do not have a functioning computer system in your business, ignore the "EX" coding procedure.

I...SERVER/CASHIER WORK-STATIONS
Hardware

Keyboards-Preset: Consists of a key arrangement with defined meanings, normally menu items. Committing a large menu to presets can result in an unworkable keyboard. Most systems designed to handle a large menu use a combination of preset and PLU keys.
___(indicate)_____

Keyboards-PLU: (Price Look Up) Consists of an amount of numeric keys (0-9). Orders are entered by code which identifies a menu item. PLU keyboards can be small, unobtrusive and very fast for the experienced operator.
___(indicate)_____

Keyboards- Touch Screen CRT: Similar in function to a preset keyboard, however, the video display (menu items and instructions) and preset keys can be changed rapidly in response to menu or transaction requirements. Touch screens can be programmed to prompt operators for required information, are easy to use and are flexible.
___(indicate)_____

Keyboards-Preset, Notebook Style: The notebook style keyboard is a variation on the preset keyboard allowing re-definition of the keys through a notebook style(hinged) keyboard overlay. This scheme is a little awkward, however, very useful as a solution for a large menu.
___(indicate)_____

Key Types-Plunger: Traditionally, keyboards have been based on an array of individual keys, when depressed, activate a mechanical switch. Plunger keys are still preferred by some restaurants, as they provide a positive tactile response when depressed.
___(indicate)_____

Key Types-Membrane: Membrane keyboards consist of a sealed number of sensors which are activated when touched. Membrane keyboards are very reliable and frequently have a removable overlay which can be easily changed for different menus or functions. Membrane keyboards are somewhat error prone since accurate finger positioning and correct key depression is more difficult.
___(indicate)_____

Security Keys: Consisting of magnetic badges, optical badges, or keys can be used to protect against unauthorized access. Systems requiring staff employees to carry a card or key are generally difficult to manage. Use of keys for management functions and changeable security codes (under management control) is probably the most workable solution.
___(indicate)_____

Printers: Customer receipts may be produced from a guest check or receipt (roll) printer. Some guest check printers include the ability to automatically read a check number to be used for retrieval of the prior balance. Guest check printers may also be used to validate employee time cards. The control provided by guest check printers (in conjunction with pre-numbered guest checks) can be achieved in other ways, making the receipt printer a more economical, reliable and simpler solution (in most cases). In addition, a clearly printed receipt with a complete item description, price and total is preferred by many customers.
___(indicate)_____

Displays-Character: Neon or LCD displays may be used for customer and operator. Character displays are often limited to 15 characters. Displays may be stand-alone or integrated into the cashiering unit. Customer display showing the amount due is an important control element in formats where check settlement is managed between the cashier and customer.
___(indicate)_____

Displays-Video: These are full screen television (like) displays. Video displays can present a great deal of data and can be programmed to display conditional operator prompts such as preparation instructions that are required for particular menu items. Video displays are normally programmed to display menu options, guest check information, or operator entered data for visual verification. Additional screens can then be displayed depending on the choices made on the primary screen. Touch screen CRT'S are essentially a video display with touch sensing capabilities. Video displays are flexible, easy to use and learn; They are also bulky and bright for dinning room placement. Video displays can also be slower for the experienced operator.
___(indicate)_____

Remote Entry Devices: These allow entry of customer orders at the table through a hand held data terminal. Once entered, the order is transmitted to the kitchen or service area. These are relatively new devices which can potentially speed up service and reduce labor costs. Unless they are used in a discrete manner, they may be disruptive to the server-customer communications relationship.
___(indicate)_____

Journal Audit Tapes: Reflecting all operator generated transactions. Journal tapes have been a key element in accounting control systems, some POS systems offer an "electronic journal tape", which can be printed as needed. Even without the electronic journal tape, the controls on most systems reduce the need for a dedicated journal tape printer.
___(indicate)_____

Cash Drawers: System controlled cash drawers should be used for cashiering functions.
___(Indicate)_____

Other Equipment: Depending on needs, point of sale systems can support a variety of other devices, including coin changes, code scanners and much more. If you have an idea for inclusion into your system, indicate so in the following space;_____

_____
___(indicate)_____

Function-Order-Processing

Multiple Menu Levels: Allows the same preset keyboard to be defined for different menus, such as, BREAKFAST/LUNCH/DINNER. Notebook style keyboards, and some membrane style keyboards are aware of this shift automatically. Other systems require operator action (under management control) to shift from one menu to another. In the case of a PLU system, a menu change usually establishes the price charged for and the availability of specific items.
___(indicate)_____

Menu Shift Levels: Allows preset keys to be defined differently depending on the use of an additional key (shift key). The shift key operates in much the same way that the typewriter shift key works. Example: The meaning of the "FRENCH FRY" key could be changed to mean "LARGE FRENCH FRY" when used in conjunction with a shift key. The shift levels are normally pre-printed on the key.
___(indicate)_____

Modifier Keys: These allow a preset key to be further defined through the use of an additional descriptive key or keys. Example: A key defined as "PIZZA SPECIAL" may require the use of a size modifier key such as "SMALL". Modifier keys can include the following capabilities:

    a. Entry of specific menu item forces operator entry on one of a pre defined list of modifier keys.
    b. Modifier key use allowed only in conjunction with specified menu item keys.
    c. Modifier key defined as + or - charge item.

Modifier keys are typically used for add-on's, preparation instructions, holds, partial orders or substitutions. Modifier and shift keys can be used to keep the number of preset keys down, however, use of these keys does complicate order entry, unless the operator is experienced.
___(indicate)_____

Order Recall: Used primarily in a pre-check environment allowing the display or reprint of an order by table or order number. Order recall is also useful in fast food for drive- through orders, home delivery, and pickup orders.
___(indicate)_____

Order Transfer: The ability to transfer orders between servers is a useful feature in a pre-check environment, providing that accountability can be maintained. Transfers should be handled by "Transfer to" server or the manager to avoid abuse.
___(indicate)_____

Operator Security Codes: Access control is essential at the system level, management function level, and at the operator accountability level. Properly managed code based systems for operators are normally the most workable.
___(indicate)_____

Conditional Prompts: Prompts may be tied to specific menu items (such as preparation instructions) or to function keys. Prompting enhances ease of use and facilitates learning, however, prompting can be slow unless the operator is experienced.
___(indicate)_____

Guest Identification: The ability to identify specific menu selections by table and seat designation. This capability can be a helpful service reminder and it also facilitates splitting checks when the customer requests separate checks.
___(indicate)_____

Designation Keys: Indicate when a particular order is either "EAT IN" or "TAKE OUT". This step can provide useful marketing information.
___(indicate)_____

Training Mode: Some systems support a separate training mode allowing entry of orders and transactions which are excluded from the systems accountability reporting. The training mode, while potentially useful, provides for easy abuse unless closely monitored.
___(indicate)_____

Buffered Keystrokes: Buffering normally allows the operator to continue with the next transaction prior to completion of system processing.
___(indicate)_____

Special Functions: Includes walkouts, server errors, free meals, complimentary items, etc... These indicate where food was prepared but no cash or payment received. This type of transaction needs close scrutiny by management.
___(indicate)_____

Function-Order-Settlement

Cash Drawer Accountability: Should provide clear accountability by the operator. Features include:

    a. Drawer activation for specified transaction types only.
    b. Separate drawers for each operator.
    c. Drawer activation only by the assigned operator.
    d. Transactions are tracked by by operator, for each server.

___(indicate)_____

Server Banking: Features should include (for each server) full reporting of sales, markdowns and establish clear accountability for all orders opened in the system.
___(indicate)_____

Settlement Methods: Including credit cards, cash, house charge accounts etc... The system should support entry and validation of customer charge account number or other appropriate number identification for charges.
___(indicate)_____

Cash Drop Alert: This can be a useful reminder to supervisory personnel when excess cash has accumulated. This alert should be capable of being changed by amount and time of day.
___(indicate)_____

Markdowns: Discounts, coupons, 2 for 1 specials, etc... Should be tracked by type and server/operator. Markdowns should show a reduction to full value sales. Generic discount keys are easily abused and should be avoided wherever possible.
___(indicate)_____

II...REMOTE DISPLAYS & PRINTERS
Hardware

Remote Printers: These are the remote devices paced in kitchens and bar areas, which print orders entered by service personnel.
___(indicate)_____

Remote Video Displays: Frequently used in fast food operations. Remote video displays normally show either:

1. Orders listed chronologically
2. The cumulative quantity required of specific menu items.

Video displays are typically equipped with a device to control the screen display (called: "Bump Bars"). Bump bars may be used to scroll the screen to view the next order or reduce the required number of a menu item following production.
___(indicate)_____

Function-Controlling
(Remote Displays)

Remote Display Location: Display location is very important to the overall usefulness of the remote display feature. Capabilities should include the ability to direct menu selections to a specific display based on the following criteria:

1. Menu items ; Always direct selected menu items to a specific remote display.
2. Entry location; Route selections to a specific remote display based on the point of entry.
3. Split; In some cases, a single menu selection may require information displayed in two separate locations.
___(indicate)_____

Sequence: Control of the print or display sequences of a specific order.
___(indicate)_____

Ingredient list: In some cases, remote display of menu selection accompanied by a list of particular ingredients and quantities can be helpful. This feature can be useful for pizza orders, and other menu items where the ingredients vary.
___(indicate)_____

Display Format: Video display should be capable of showing total production requirements (like 50 hamburgers) which can be decreased through a bump bar.
___(indicate)_____

III...BACK OFFICE & MGMT
Considerations

H a r d w a r e

System Architecture: All point of sale systems depend on one or more computer processors to control system operations. Decentralized systems consist of linked computer processors frequently located within a server/cashier work station. Decentralized systems offer some security against system failure since the failure of one computer processor generally does not affect the remaining processors. This redundancy can be more complicated and expensive. Centralized systems consist of a single computer processor (in some cases with a back-up) where all server/cashier work stations, remote displays and other equipment are attached. Centralized systems are more flexible and less expensive for increased configurations.
___(indicate)_____

Processor type: Increased numbers of systems are being designed to utilize powerful off-the-shelf personal computers and related equipment. The personal computer based systems have a number of advantages including; ease of maintenance, flexibility, and cost. However, the long term reliability of personal computers is not as yet firmly established. Because personal computers may not be able to facilitate all of the needs that you have, you may need to consider a custom mini computer system.
___(indicate custom or personal)_____

Printers: A standard 80 column matrix printer can make system generated reports far more readable and useful, than most any other kind except laser printers, which are very expensive.
___(indicate)_____

Management Terminal: A management terminal (a video display with keyboard) can ease the process of managing the system .
___(indicate)_____

Communications: The point of sale system should be capable of communicating with an on-site or remote computer. Hardware requirements consist of a communications port and modem for remote communications via the telephone lines. To facilitate the transfer of information from point of sale system to the computer, the POS system should support one of the commonly used personal computer protocols. Other methods of transferring data can be quite difficult and should be researched carefully.
___(indicate)_____

Backup: Every system should provide a way to copy program and data for safekeeping. Backups can be very important in case of a system failure.
___(indicate)_____

Function-Management

System Management: All systems provide utilities which support menu modification, price changes, tax changes, and other chores. In some cases, these functions require complicated keying sequences and allow only limited latitude in customizing the system to meet certain requirements. The ability to readily customize the system to fit your format and style of operation can have important implications in the area of speed of service, cost control and management reporting.

___(indicate)_____

Management Reporting: Point of sale systems are capable of producing a variety of management reports covering sales analysis, cash control, labor cost and food cost etc...

___(indicate)_____

Diagnostics: The most perplexing and costly point of sale problems are those which occur erratically without an apparent cause. To guard against this kind of problem, it is important that the point of sale system will include sophisticated error detection and diagnostic capabilities.

___(indicate)_____

Accounting Support: POS systems are capable of providing varying levels of general accounting support. Accounting applications such as accounts payable, general ledger, payroll and sales analysis may be run concurrently with restaurant operations. Some systems which can not support accounting applications directly, are frequently capable of providing time keeping and sales data in a compatible format for processing on another system. It seems appropriate that most restaurants would incorporate both POS and accounting applications into one system.

___(indicate)_____

Source: Business Computer Applications
Mr. Paul Malmo, consultant
Kirkland, Washington

Accounting Functions

Guidance information
to the accounting function portion of SPE.

The purpose of this section is to familiarize that restaurant owner who is mainly concerned with computerization of accounting functions.

This section of SPE indicates <u>only some</u>   (this is a sampling by reason of brevity) of the accounting elements **you and your CPA** may wish to include in your proposed computer system. Be sure that **you and your CPA** add the additional accounting features which you both agree are necessary.

Due to the fact that POS (Point Of Sale) features often include many or all of the accounting functions and features, there will be a tendency to overlap information when making a request for proposal to prospective vendors. In the case of overlapping specifications, the vendor should provide a list of accounting features and applications that are incorporated in the POS system.

If on the other hand, you are not interested in POS features and you wish to begin a computer system which is only concerned with the four basic accounting functions (General ledger, Accounts receivable/Sales journal, payroll and accounts payable), you would do well to seek out personal computer systems (hardware and software) at a personal computer business store, or check out vendors who offer these packages through the *"Directory of Computer Hardware and Software for the Foodservice Industry"*.   This title is authored by Mr. Joel

Chaban and is available through the National Restaurant Association (NRA) located at the following address;

NRA
311 First Street, N.W.
Washington, D.C.   20001

You can also use this accounting function portion of SPE to help identify those elements and features, etc, you want in a personal computer package.

Coding and indicating your needs.

In this following section you are indicating <u>amounts</u> and answering <u>yes or no</u>. There is also space which calls for additional options which you should stipulate when and where applicable.

ACCOUNTS PAYABLE (Function)

Accounts Payable: Indicate yes or no........ "<u>Yes/no</u>"
1. Automatic interface, appropriate entries are to be
   automatically generated.
2. To incorporate the General Ledger.   _____
3. Incorporate Inventory.   _____

Multiple Accounting distribution to:
1. Accounting periods.   _____
2. Cost centers.   _____
3. Banks.   _____
4. Account Numbers.   _____
5. OTHER_____   _____

Indicate yes or no........"Yes/No

**Entry for handwritten checks for distribution
and check reconciliation.**   _____

Editing for duplicate invoices.   _____

Checks for payment by;
   a. Date due   _____
   b. Vendor.   _____
   c. Individual invoices.   _____
   d. Discount rate.   _____
   e. OTHER_____   _____

**Automatically produced labels with
vendors names and addresses.**   _____

Automatic computation of discounts.   _____

**Multiple invoices to the same vendor are
to be on a single check.**   _____

Terminal inquiry into;
   a. All invoices for one vendor.   _____
   b. A single invoice.   _____
   c. All invoices by due date.   _____
   d. OTHER_____   _____

Invoice History report.   _____

Aging report by;
   a. Company name.   _____
   b. Due date.   _____
   c. Invoice number.   _____
   d. Discount rate.   _____
   e. Vendor.   _____
   f. OTHER_____   _____

Indicate yes or no....... "Yes/No

Check reconciliation report, showing
check number,dates,cleared checks
 and accounts payable checks.   ____

Check register report;
  a. check number.   ____
  b. Amount.   ____
  c. OTHER_____   ____

Editing for corrections to be automatically
generating recalculations.   ____

Additional options (reports, system
 requirements, etc)you to designate;

_____

_____

Processing Volumes: Indicate AMT: current&future   AMT

  a. Average number of checks written per month.   __|__
  b. Number of vendors.   __|__
  c. Number of GL accts involved in distribution
     of accts payable.   __|__
  d. Average number of entries per invoice.   __|__
  e. Average number of invoices/vouchers
     processed per month.   __|__
  f. OTHER_____   __|__

Note: The proposed system should be able to handle current and future volumes
with complete software compatibility. This should also be stipulated in your request for proposal.

Indicate the frequency of processing:
  a. Daily   _____
  b. Weekly   _____
  c. Monthly   _____
  d. Quarterly   _____
  e. Annually   _____

PAYROLL

Reports required: Indicate yes or no......... Yes/no

a. Transaction proof report.   _____
b. Payroll check with stub details.   _____
c. Employee master list.   _____
d. Payroll register.   _____
e. Earnings register   _____
f. Deduction register.   _____
g. GL distribution journal.   _____
h. State and Local tax reports.   _____
i Quarterly 941A's.   _____
j. W-2's.   _____
k. Check reconciliation reports.   _____
OTHER_____   _____

Types of pay:
a. Hourly.   _____
b. Salary.   _____
c. Commission.   _____
d. Other.   _____

Pay periods:
a. Weekly.   _____
b. Bi-weekly.   _____
c. Semi-monthly.   _____
d. Monthly.   _____

Overtime calculations:
a. Time & a half.   _____
b. Double time.   _____
c. OTHER_____   _____

Indicate yes or no.........."Yes/No

Types of earnings paid for;
    a. Vacation.   _____
    b. Regular.   _____
    c. Standby.   _____
    d. On-Call.   _____
    e. sick.   _____
    f. overtime.   _____
    g. OTHER_____   _____

Hourly rates;
    a. Whole cents only.   _____
    b. Multiple rates based on job code.   _____
    c. OTHER_____   _____

Other earnings;
    a. Meal allowance.(indicate percentage)_____%   _____
    b. Tips.   _____
    c. Reimbursed expenses.   _____
    d. Uniforms.   _____

State & local taxes;   _____

Standard deductions
(FICA, Federal income)   _____
a.OTHER deductions_____   _____

Automatic interface (appropriate entries
are to be generated to);
    a. General Ledger.   _____
    b. OTHER_____   _____

Manual check entry to GL.   _____

Employees may work multiple
job codes in same shift.   _____

Indicate yes or no........<u>Yes/No</u>

Employees may work multiple departments in same shift.   _____

Terminal inquiry into;
  a. Employee master information.   _____
  b. Current transactions by employee.   _____
  c. OTHER_____   _____

Medical insurance report;
  a. Employee name.   _____
  b. Job code.   _____
  c. Date hired.   _____
  d. Pay type and rate.   _____
  e. SSN.   _____
  f. Number of sick days.   _____
  g. OTHER. _____   _____

Additional options (reports, system requirements,etc) you to designate;

_____

_____

Processing Volumes;   Indicate current & future............. <u>AMTS</u>

  a. Active employees.   _|__
  b.Checks per pay period.   _|__
  c. Number of W-2's annually.   _|__
  d. Entries per pay period.   _|__
  e. Average number of
     states/localities per employee.   _|__
  f. Average number of departments
     per employee pay period.   _|__
  g.OTHER_____   _|__

Note: The proposed system should be able to handle current and future
      volumes with complete software compatibility.

ACCOUNTS RECEIVABLE / SALES/ ORDER ENTRY (Function)

Reports: Indicate yes or no......... <u>Yes/no</u>

a. Cash receipts journal   _____
b. Invoice register.   _____
c.Customer statements.   _____
d. Customer invoices.   _____
e. Sales tax report.   _____
f. Aged trial balance (accts receivable)   _____
g. Sales to date by customer.   _____
h. Sales to date by menu item.   _____
i. Gross profit by customer.   _____
j.. Gross profit by menu item.   _____
k. Inventory master list.   _____
l. Inventory transaction register.   _____
m. Stock level report.   _____
n. On-order report.   _____
o. Re-order report.   _____
p. Sales by sales person (cashier or other)   _____
q. Transaction proof report.   _____
r. OTHER_____   _____

Discounts on invoices:

a. $ only.   _____
b. % only.   _____
c. Auto discounts based on customer.   _____
d. Auto discounts based on menu item.   _____
e. OTHER_____   _____

Unit pricing required in mills.   _____

Indicate yes or no........Yes/No

Tax exempt sales based on;
a. Donated items. _____
b. Customers. _____
c. Other_____ _____

Selectively printed statements. _____

**Auto interface; Appropriate entries
to be generated to;**
a. GL _____
b. Inventory. _____
c. OTHER_____ _____

Terminal inquiry into;
a. Inventory level. _____
b. Back orders. _____
c. OTHER_____ _____

Processing Volumes;
Indicate current & Future..................AMTS

a. Sales transactions per register a week. __|__
b. Total sales transactions per shift. __|__
c. Total sales transactions per day. __|__
d. Total sales transactions per week. __|__
e. Total number of open items (average). __|__

**Additional options (reports,system
requirements,etc) you to designate;**_____

_____
_____
_____

GENERAL LEDGER (Function)

Reports required: Indicate yes or no.................Yes/no

a. Trial balance. _____
  With detail. _____
  Without detail. _____
b. Balance sheet. _____
c. Income statements. _____
d. Sources and applications of funds. _____
e. Proof list of manual journal entries. _____
f. Proof list of automatic entries. _____
g. Other_____ _____

Reporting requirements;

a. This year only. _____
b. Last year only. _____
c. This year and last year to date. _____
d. This month and this month last year. _____
e. This month and YTD (Year To Date) _____
f. This month and YTD last year. _____
g. OTHER._____ _____

Income statements;
a. MTD (Month To Date) _____
b. YTD only. _____
c. MTD and % _____
d. YTD and % _____
e. Month and YTD with % _____
f. This month and YTD and
    this month and YTD last year. _____
g. This month and YTD with % and
    this month and YTD last year with %. _____
h. Month with budget. _____
i. YTD with budget and %. _____
j. Month and YTD with budget and %. _____
k. Month and year with budget. _____
l. Budget allocations. _____
j. OTHER._____ _____

Indicate yes or no..........,Yes/No

Automated scheduled journal entries.   ____

Consolidated reports;
a. Balance sheet.   _____
b. Income statements.   _____

**User maintenance of
flexible chart of accts.**   ____

Terminal inquiry;
a. Current acct balances.   _____
b. Other_____   _____

Multiple chart of accts.   ____

Accounting periods;
a. 13 period.   _____
b. Calendar month.   _____
c. 4-4-5 Quarters.   _____

**Additional options (reports,system
requirements,etc) you to designate.**_____

Processing Volumes: Indicate current & Future.AMTS

a. Number of GL accts.   __|__
b. Number of journal entries per month,
   originating automatically from accts payable,
   accts receivable and payroll.   __|__
c. Number of departments/divisions, requiring
   financial statements (accountable entities).   __|__

Note: Your CPA or accountant should explain reasons for each accounting
requirement prior to constructing a resquest for proposal.

Source: Don Cream, Consultant for Business accounting systems,
Albuquerque, New Mexico

Request For **PROPOSAL**

Preparing a request for proposal is a compilation of all that you have selected and indicated, it will be a considerable number of pages, as you have probably assumed by now. Besides the POS selection and all of the accounting elements, much of the following material should also be included:

Ask the vendor to answer the following;

1. Describe upgrade options where possible.
2. Describe any mandatory or desirable environmental requirements.
3. Describe file backup procedures.
4. Is a service contract available?
5. Is a service contract recommended?
6. Estimated response time to services call?
7. Is the response time guaranteed?
8. Estimated time to fix a problem?
9. Is the estimated time to fix guaranteed?
10. What backup or replacement service is available when extended outages occur?
11. Do you provide on- site training?
12. Describe the training you do provide.
13. Do you provide operating manuals?

Software Service:

14. Is the service covered by contract?
15. Who provides the service?
16. Estimated response time for service calls?
17. Is the response time guaranteed?
18. Are manuals and training available?
19. Will the source code be provided?
20. Will programming services be provided?
21. Are periodic software updates provided?
22. What training is recommended?

General Questions to the vendor:

Describe vendor and customer responsibilities during implementation.
How are implementation services charged?
Is there a lease program available?
Please provide sample contracts and other agreements.
Describe warranties.
Describe the anticipated implementation plan.
Describe or furnish information about your company, (Products, age, number of employees, etc).
Provide a reference list. Customers using similar hardware and software.

The following hardware components should be described (where appropriate) **by the vendor in the proposal: Include the following;**

    Computer Processing unit (CPU)   Type:_____
      Main memory;   Capacity:_____
    Hard disk:
      Memory;   Capacity:_____
    Diskette:
      Memory;   Capacity:_____
    Tape(reel):
      Memory;   Capacity:_____
    Tape(cartridge):
      Memory;   Capacity:_____
    Tape(cassette):
      Memory;   Capacity:_____
    Terminals. (video)   Type:_____Number:_____
    Terminals.(Printing)   Type:_____Number:_____
    Printers.   Type:_____Number:_____
    System console.   Type:_____Number:_____
    Modem;
      (telephone communications link);   Type:_____
                                     Capacity:_____

The following software and operating requirements should be described by the vendor in the proposal;

Utilities:
a. Spooler.   Type:_____Capacity:_____
b. Sort.   Capability:_____
c. Editor.   Type:_____
d. Should the program have an import/export capability
    to move data to other types of software?
e. Vendor to indicate other utilities where appropriate.

Languages:
    Vendor to indicate suitable language such as;

a. Basic.
b. COBOL.
c. Fortran.
d. RPG.
e. Other_____

File mgmt:
    Vendor to indicate appropriateness of;

a. Indexed.
b. Sequential.
c. Multi-key, indexed.
d. Direct.
e. Database.
f. OTHER._____

General Requirements
Include any or all of the following in your proposal;

All input fields are to be tested for logic, including type, usage, and where possible, validated against a master file.

Capability to:

a. trace all transactions from their source to final reports.
b. Reconcile current transaction totals to current balance.
c. Reconcile beginning balances plus current balances based on dollar amounts and record counts as appropriate.

All reports containing dollar fields are to have grand total.

Understandable error or warning messages are to be produced where appropriate.

Access control codes such as operator number and passwords are required.

a. System level.
b. File level.

A convenient technique for periodic backup of critical files.

All application modules are to be menu driven.

Final system payment will be contingent on successful testing.

All applications are to be capable of concurrent operation.

Special Requirements:
In some cases special requirements may be necessary. This means that custom programming or hardware configurations may prevail. In most instances you will find that ready made software packages are available, however, you will need to obtain information which allows you to check hardware and operating systems compatibility.

Note: The 1987 Directory of Computer Hardware and Software for the Foodservice Industry. That is the title of a most comprehensive computer directory for the food service industry (hundreds of software applications and hardware types). Contact information is located in the fourth paragraph of the accounting functions beginning text, page 292.

Should you the owner find that your special requirements are too complicated for regular service in your area and you still wish to accomplish your computer assisted systems project, than you should probably seek out a good computer systems consultant who is familiar with the restaurant business and use this process to describe your needs. It will take less of the consultants time if you can be specific as possible.

Cost breakdown:
Vendor to indicate costs as follows;

Non-recurring;

Hardware	$_____
System Software	_____
Applications Software	_____
Training	_____
Installation	_____
Freight	_____
Taxes	_____
Other	_____
TOTAL	$_____

Recurring;

Hardware maintenance	_____
Software maintenance	_____
Communications service via modem	_____
Supplies	_____
Service Contract	_____
TOTAL	$_____

Now type up your request for proposal
and send it to a minimum of three vendors.

Special Note: Your proposal will certainly cause questions and dialogue between you and the vendors involved. This is as it should be, you will learn from them, and they will learn from you and your requirements. Remember that the probability of two restaurants having identical systems is remote, each one is special and should be treated as such.

EVAULATION
(of the vendors proposal)

Now that the request for proposal has been accomplished, you can evaluate the vendors proposals (quotations) .

In evaluating the vendors proposals you will consider these areas of concern first;

1. Minimum requirements. If the vendor does not meet your needs, then you must disqualify that vendor.

2.Support provided. What quality of support can be anticipated from this vendor? Hardware, software, maintenance, training and documentation are all included in this category.

3. Overall quality: The considerations are flexibility, ease of use and reliability. Flexibility should address the ability to expand; The ability to add new applications and availability of useful features beyond those which you now believe are needed.

4. Cost: Certainly a major consideration to most restaurant owners.

The point system in evaluation:

You have eliminated those vendors who do not meet your requirements. If you have eliminated too many vendors you may need to send more requests for quotation proposals.

The vendors who have made it to this stage of your evaluation are judged in three areas; Support provided, Overall quality, and Cost.

Support provided: Give the appropriate amount of points
to each vendor;

10 points = Less than desirable (less than you would like)

20 points = Adequate (Can do the job)

50 points = Better than required

Overall quality:

10 points = Less than desirable

20 points = Adequate

30 points = Better than required

Cost:

This is a slightly flexible consideration. There is also the need to obtain the highest levels of the first two considerations, otherwise the cost could be much greater with the passing of time. The average restaurant owner (if there is such a thing) considers cost to be worth half of his or her evaluation, therefore the following points are applicable;

30 points = Highest price (out of three vendors).

50 points = The price in between the highest and lowest.

70 points = The lowest price among all proposals.

The vendor with the highest number of points becomes a **candidate** for contract. You should consider two candidates if the total points are 10 points apart.

Candidates for sales presentation and demonstration;

Ask questions during the presentation that revolve around your selection of features and support.

If you are able to attend a **demonstration** of the same type of hardware and software, do so. During the demonstration, ask to see various methods of recovery from errors.

Check References: Check out the references which the candidate vendor (or vendors) have supplied.

Is the referred system comparable?

Has the vendor demonstrated the ability to meet commitments?

What is the overall satisfaction level?

Your decision, after checking the references will be narrowed to the vendor or vendors which will provide the best system for your business.

What ever you do, be C O N S I S T E N T.

Efficient is what I shall be..
Come heaven or high voltage you see..
If the organizers dream..
Is of disks and keys..
Can we please have some time..
To get on our knees..
Praying for profits to a T.V. screen?..
What has my eatery come to, so mean..
A computer they tell me..
Will fix all the ways..
But can I adjust..
To these orderly days?..
So I did it, I got it, I love it, it works..
Now others can lear..
As I laugh at those jerks...

THE FUTURE

XV

Since crystal ball gazing is a thing of the past, and Merlin the magician is unavailable, predicting the outcome of the future is left to logic and statistics, with an element of conceptual estimating. Looking into the future is only as difficult as the degree of hopeful accuracy. What we intend, is to use the best information, apply conceptual thinking to a series of natural responses involving social reactions which provide for guesstimated conclusions. A little common sense also applies to the process.

General Overview

The future years will bring about such concern for health and nutrition, that more changes will affect the food service industry than the AT&T breakup has had on the communications industry.

Technology will produce robotic servers, processing foods through conveyor cooking equipment, handling produce preparation, garbage removal and other tasks presently performed by employees. Since it is necessary to train people to operate and maintain these sophisticated devices and the fact that the cost will prohibit rapid acceptance for the next 30 years, there seems to be enough time for the food service industry to grow into these types of changes, however, those who prepare with knowledge of what to do, generally benefit the most.

Of great concern to the restaurant owner should be the public and the government sectors involvement with health and disease control. Many restaurants do not follow strict disease control regulations. The different jurisdictions (Federal, State and Local) involved in administering some control over restaurants and the food service industry, will obtain the amount of funding and enforcement procedures necessary to curb those diseases which threaten the public sector. To be sure, the trade associations representing the food service industry will lobby long and hard to prevent these legal happenings from occurring in the manner presented to Congress. This change will probably mean requisite testing and licensing for the established owner or representative and pre-certification for a new owner. So serious will this situation be, that owners and operators will be jailed for ignoring the new law. The probability this will happen in the next 10 to 15 years is very high.

Population patterns and trends are the basis of marketing. We will see shifts that true entrepreneurs will take advantage of.

EQUIPMENT WITH LASER HEAT

Technology will make advances in the kitchen that may cause chefs to change their traditional white tower hat to a white rimmed face mask. The range will change to "Laser injection". Laser technology has already been tested in the area of heat disbursing with wide beams. Scientists know how to control the strength of a laser device.

When metallurgists finally produce the metallic compound which is tough like Nickel, conducts with rigidity like Tungsten, is non sticking like Teflon except resists surface breakdown, and does not react to temperatures below 1200 degrees Fahrenheit and only slowly up to temperatures of 3000 degrees, then cooking will take seconds instead of hours. Cleaning the cooker will be a case of rinsing with cool water containing a sanitizing chemical. Injectors coming from above the range top will be lowered into the center of the pot containing soup, sauce, stew, chili, etc, with an appropriate lid fastened into place, and in 10 to 160 seconds the contents will be cooked evenly, thoroughly and with no evidence of ever burning.

This all sounds rather far fetched until you look at the last fifty years of all kinds of technological advances and discoveries. With the exception of the microwave process, no innovative cooking or cooling process has come along for quite awhile. The refrigerated system with it's compressor moving a coolant causing evaporation and heat removal, hasn't changed much.

General equipment view

The Solid state controls, insulation materials, fastening methods and design improvements have made the original invention much better, but the basic method, be it natural gas heat, electric cable or element, pressurized steam, or heat by lamp, hasn't changed a great deal. Sure the equipment has been improved upon so that a decided difference in production and longevity is and has been beneficial to the restaurant owner, however, innovations to the level of discovery will come by the year 2010, if not sooner.

Distributors

Competition among the larger food suppliers will force them to become more involved with the production of food stuffs. Because of consumer demand for quality and nutritional content, the distributor will gradually acquire a degree of vested interest in canning, agricultural growers, and other primary source companies.

Where detailed product specifications become less effective, distributors will find themselves working closer with manufacturers quality control personnel, and in some instances will maintain a staff, working full time to manage and assure the overall quality, consistency and the cost of raw ingredients.

This change which is already beginning, will see some price increases, however great improvements in the production of aqua-agricultural growth and harvesting will produce relatively lower cost fish and sea-vegetable food sources.

Due to discoveries in the field of water purification, agricultural products will be grown in areas never before considered. This will bring the distributor closer to the farmers land-harvest through support of cooperative groups and long range contractual commitments. Unions representing pickers and packers will be working closer with special government agencies designed to fill the need of both labor and agricultural companies or co-ops etc.

This effort will benefit the union representation, the worker, agricultural grower, the distributor, the governments tax burden, the restaurant owner and consumer.

Smaller distributors will find exclusive"specialization" a way of business life. Imported products, agricultural specialties, certain meats and poultry, and a variety of expensive organic food products will top the list.

The affects that will cause change to the distributor can only benefit the restaurant through higher quality, and consistent balance to year-round prices and availability.

REGIONAL AND NATIONAL POPULATION CHANGES

Between 1984 and the year 2010 (refer to figure 15-One), we will see the total work force increase close to 34 percent. That means there will be 40 million potential restaurant paying customers to consider. This is a constant growth factor, as the owner is already involved, though somewhat less than the shock of the immediate arrival of the year 2010.

If the number of independent restaurants were to stay leveled off at 470,000, that would mean each restaurant would have an increase of 85 customers eating and drinking at their establishment as often as maybe six times a week. Now when you consider the total population growth expectation of over 64 million by the year 2010, you can add the family members to the customer increase, as they accompany the paying worker to your restaurant.

This customer growth scenario will be somewhat diluted however, because the number of foodservice establishments will also increase. The question here is; Will your restaurant change with the needs of the future? Since the future really begins in less than one second from now, you can see why it is essential to accentuate the predictable future statistics of the year 2010. The owners who are aware of customer needs, hence opportunities, are the proprietors who will obtain the most success today and tomorrow.

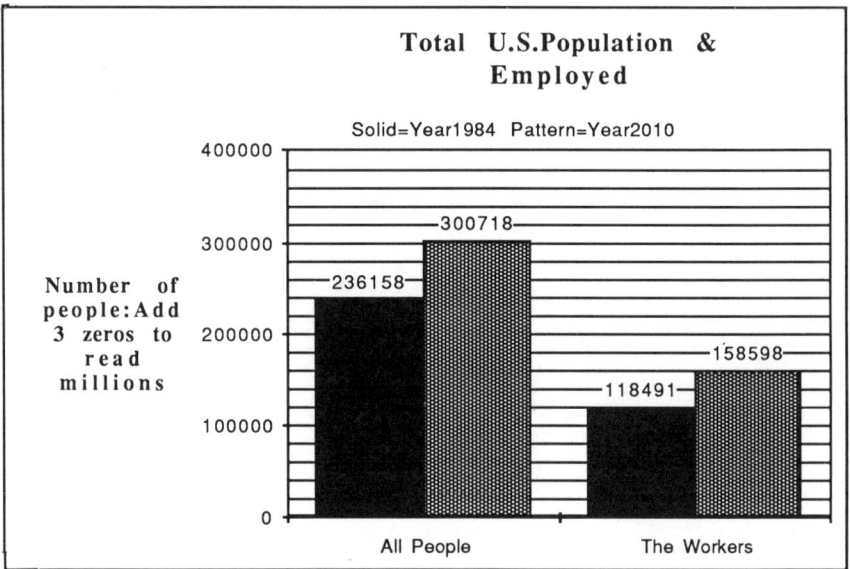

Total U.S.Population &
Employed

Solid=Year1984 Pattern=Year2010

Number of
people:Add
3 zeros to
read
millions

400000

300000 ──────────300718──────────

236158

200000 ──────────────────────158598──────────

──────────118491──────────

100000

0

All People   The Workers

Figure 15-One
Source: Woods&Poole Economics, Washington D.C.

8 Regions   The States in each Region

New England	Connecticut, Maine, Massachusetts, New Hampshire, Rhode Island, and Vermont.
Mideast	Delaware, Maryland, New Jersey, New York, Pennsylvania, and the District of Columbia.
Great Lakes	Illinois, Indiana, Michigan, Ohio, and Wisconsin.
Plains	Iowa, Kansas, Minnesota, Missouri, Nebraska, North and South Dakota.
Southeast	Alabama, Arkansas, Louisiana, Florida, Georgia, Kentucky, Mississippi, North Carolina, South Carolina, Tennessee,Virginia, and West Virginia.
Southwest	Arizona, New Mexico, Oklahoma, and Texas.
Rocky Mtn	Colorado, Idaho, Montana, Utah, and Wyoming.
Far West	Alaska, California, Nevada, Oregon, Washington and Hawaii.

This Regional breakdown by states should be used in conjunction with figures,15-two, three, four and six.

The information which is derived from these national and regional population projections can be used for long range planning, particularly when you consider selling your business and/or opening a restaurant in another region.

The population growth by 2010 shows that in numbers of population (Figure 15-two), the Southeast region will have the most with 19,473,000 more people. The fastest growth rate over and above present population (1.54% average per year) is the Far west re-gion, although they will achieve an increase of 17,097,000, a fig-ure less than the southeast.

The number of employed will grow most rapidly in the Far west region with an annual average increase of 1.57%. This region also commands the lead in it's rate of population growth.

These types of data are important to existing and forthcoming re-staurants. Shear numbers of population expectation will be gener-ally satisfied by existing establishments, where growth rates that are greater in particular regions often spell a more rapid restaurant business growth. Both situations are agreeable. However, the larger number of population expectation regions will usually re-quire a restaurant to be more established (seasoned) than the re-gion which maintains a more rapid population growth rate (per-centage of population increase).

Local Consideration

There is no question that localized area information concerning growth and rates of growth are vital to most any restaurants busi-ness. This information can be accessed through the marketing de-partments of large banks, utility companies, the local government planning commission, cable TV companies, and other companies and organizations logically collecting DATA about the public (consumer).

U.S. POPULATION GROWTH

Solid=year1984   Pattern=year2010

Number of people add 3 zeros to read millions

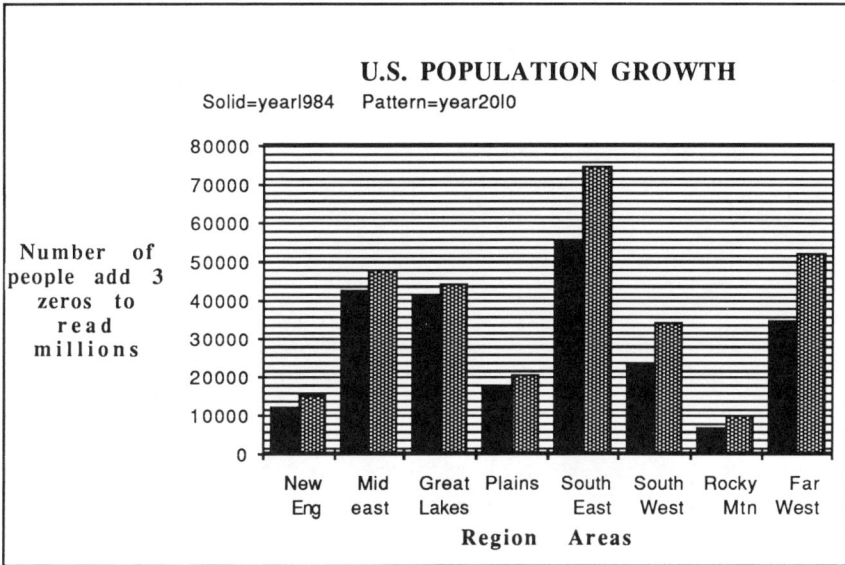

Figure 15-Two
Source: Woods&Poole Economics, Washington D.C.

Older and Healthier

In 1984 the percentage of people 65 years and older was 11.8% (see figure 15-Three). By the time the year 2010 rolls around that percentage will grow to 13.57% of the total population. People over 65 years of age will be much healthier and will require satisfaction when they eat out.

This older faction means that a cozy atmosphere serving a variety of nutritional menu items, to be served via cafeteria style and table service will still be in demand. This probability does not diminish the tremendous growth in both delivered and take-out restaurant service.

It is expected that the Plains region will still represent the greatest percentage of 65 and older members (16.34%) of the population in the year 2010. The New England region will follow with 15.26% and the Rocky Mountain region will have the smallest percentage of 65 plus age group, with 12.29%, however that is a considerable increase from a 9.0% figure in 1984.

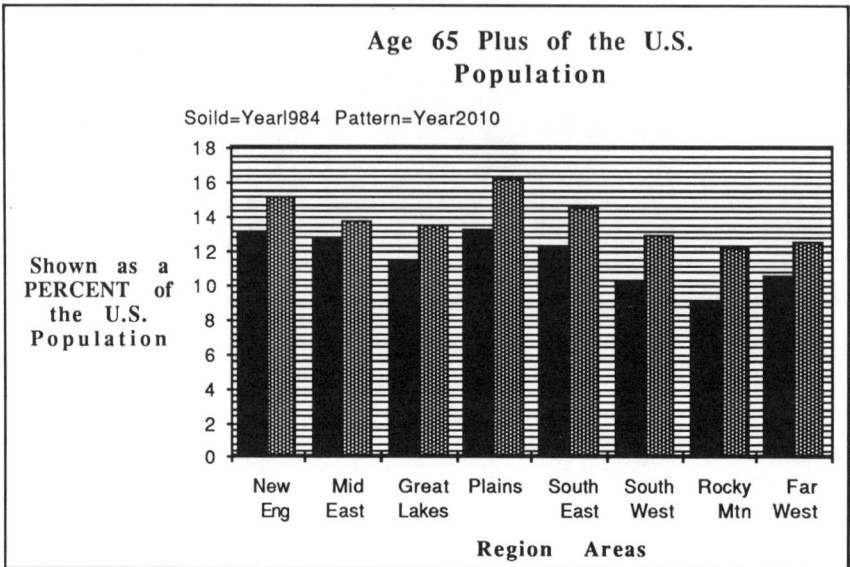

Figure 15-Three
Source: Woods&Poole Economics, Washington D.C.

Restaurant Service Additions

During all of this growth throughout the nation, women will be increasing their representation in the work-place by an estimated 52% (of the work force) in the year 2010. This will accelerate the need for take-out and home delivered dinners, in addition to an already increasing demand.

Due to medical advances and the need for individual nutritional diets, a simple method of determining a persons complete nutritional requirements will be discovered. From caloric intake to a breakdown of every fatty acid known, to vitamin requirements and more. Medical science will be able to determine the cause and effects that a myriad of foods will have on the specific condition of almost all internal organs and much more will be known about foods and diseases such as Cancer.

With the use of computer technology (advanced greatly by the year 2010), an individuals nutritional data will be easily calculated and transferred to present a selection of menu items and their portion allowance. Hospitals will of course be utilizing this advancement first, however, restaurants will be following this lead as the business opportunities begin to explode.

Can you imagine?

Mrs. Ontime calling the restaurant by computer link from her office downtown. She slips in her nutritional card which contains all of her families health information necessary to calculate dietary requirements. Next she indicates the code number of the particular restaurant she wishes to patronize. The computer screen shows a variety of menu items which each family member is allowed to consume. Portions and prices are also indicated on the screen.

Now Mrs. Ontime selects those menu items which her family will enjoy, indicates the time she will pick them up or have them delivered.

If there is a change in a menu item or the delivery time she can use the telephone or the computer, using a customer code so that orders are not confused at the restaurant.

Since medical science is already working in a direction which will provide the reality to Mrs. Ontime's routine, and computer technology is rapidly approaching our exampled prediction, it seems that all we need to do is add the consumers interest and need for a more health conscious diet (which is also increasing).

The restaurant owners part in Mrs. Ontime's future will be centered around the computer which will use software capable of calculating the incoming customers data, choosing appropriate menu items and matching portion requirements to the need. The computer will simultaneously print-out the menu items ordered by Mrs. Ontime, providing specific changes to those menu items which may require special handling. The customer code number, method of payment, scheduled time for pickup or delivery (including address information) will also be included.

Since the restaurant will have many such orders during this relatively new type of rush hour business, already prepared foods in refrigerated holding units will be widely used, as reheating through a conveyor-type process, including a semi-pressurized rethermalization unit (with controlled moisture injection), produces an individually packaged meal complete with utensils, allowable condiments and the ordered beverage at the end of the in-line system.

Tastes change in mood and food

As the average median age increases to almost 37 years old (figure 15-Five) by the year 2010, we will witness a shift in menu items, decor, music, and most everything which denotes the likes of a more mature adult. Already we have seen some early evidence of this shift as the softer rock music of 1987 creeps past the harder rock music lovers place on the charts. To stress the point even further we demonstrate statistical data in figure 15-Six that indicates an 82 plus percentage increase in the age group between 45 and 54, which is achieved by the year 2005.

Employed U.S. Workers

Solid=Yearl984 Pattern=Year2Ol0

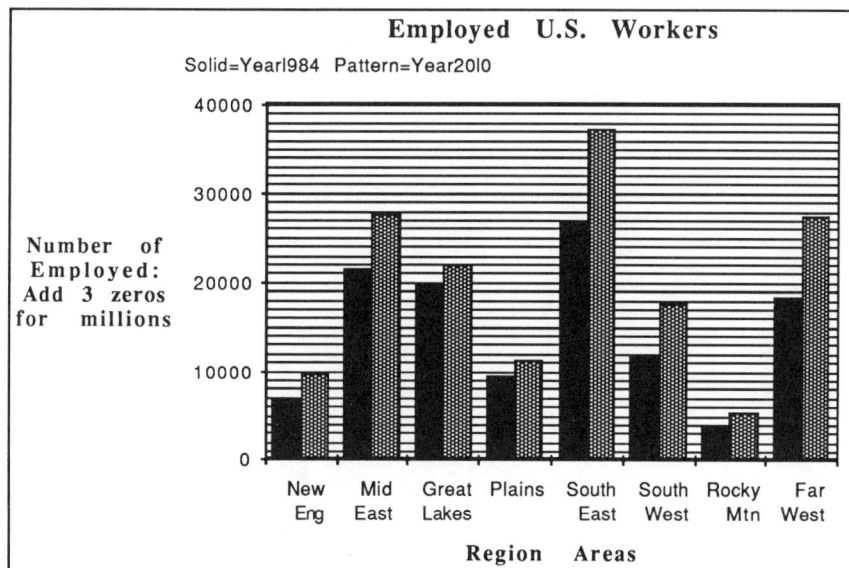

Number   of
Employed:
Add 3 zeros
for   millions

Region   Areas

Figure 15-Four
Source: Woods&Poole Economics, Washington D.C.

U.S. Median Age

Average age of the U.S. Population

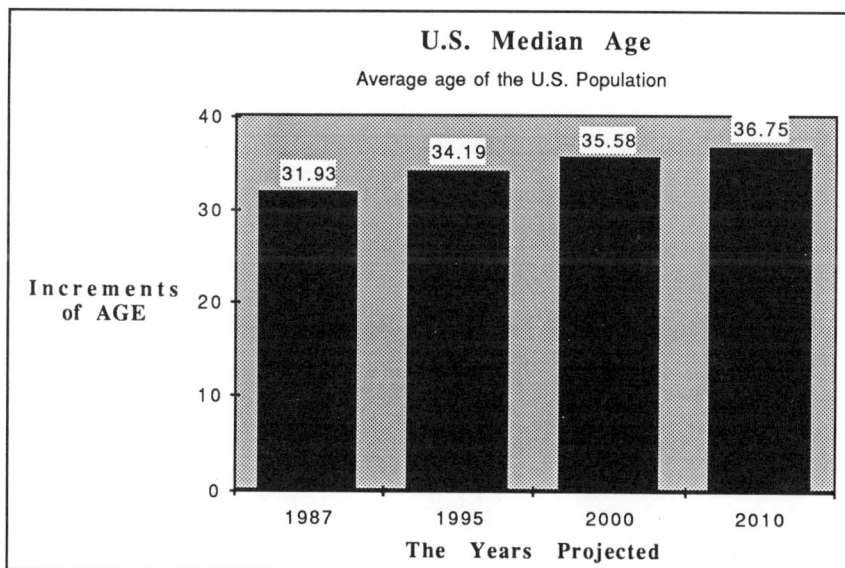

Increments
of AGE

The   Years   Projected

Figure 15-Five
Source: Woods&Poole Economics, Washington D.C.

Food tastes have also started changing in 1988, with the greater demand for salads, hearty soups, back to basic home style meatloaf, and a more critical eye on nutritional value.

U.S. Population by Age Group

Solid=Year1987   Pattern=Year2005

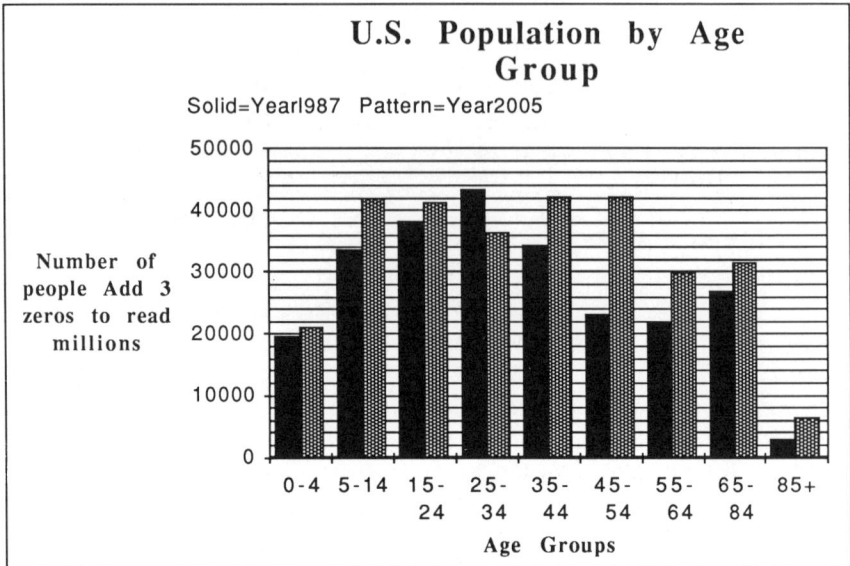

Number of people Add 3 zeros to read millions

Age Groups

Figure 15-Six
Source: Woods&Poole Economics, Washington D.C.

These changes which are occurring, mean opportunities for restaurant owners willing to use their imagination and organizational abilities.

As the median age goes up, the menu prices will be scrutinized more closely by the customer. The extra amount of common sense, education, and experience which normally comes with age, converts to value seeking customers that will increase competition in the marketplace. Restaurant owners will find the need for a higher quality of product, and they must find ways of offering their product at reasonable prices.

REFERENCE SECTION

This section provides some reference to BOOKS, TRADE MAGAZINES, ASSOCIATIONS and EDUCATIONAL FACILITIES that deal with restaurant management.

The benefits of reference information is only seen by those owners who realize that learning just one point, can either save a serious problem from occurring or create an idea which will add to the owners successes.

BOOKS OF INTEREST

If you read one point which inspires an element of success, then there is no question that the book was worth it.

Directory of Food & Nutrition Information Services & Resources: By Frank, Robyn C.,Oryx Press, 1984. Directory lists schools, addresses, eligible clientele, cost of educational programs, and degree programs.

Exploring Professional Cooking: By Ray,Mary Frey., Charles A Bennett Co, 1976.
1. Food Service vocational guidance.
2. Cookery vocational guidance

A Modern Guide to Food Service Equipment;By Avery, Arthur C., Van Nostrand Reinhold Co, New York, 1985.Textbook on foodservice equipment, including equipment specifications, sanitary design and maintenance.Includes information on arranging equipment and energy savings.

Food Equipment Facts- A Handbook for the Food Service Industry; By Scriven, Carl and Stevens, James.,John Wiley & Sons Inc, 1982. Foodservice equipment and supplies.

Food Marketing; By Austin, James E., Marketing Science Institute, 1977. 1. Food, Industry and Trade. 2. Nutrition.

Basic Accounting Standards; By Ninemeier, Jack D., AVI Publishing co, 1984. Foodservice accounting.

Sanitation for Foodservice Workers;By Richardson, Treva M., CBI Publishing Co, 1981. 1. Foodservice-sanitation. 2. Food handling.

Food Service Purchasing; By Kelly, Hugh J., Chain Store Publishing Corp, 1976. Offers purchasing and operating procedures for small independent restaurants to large chains. Covers portion control, purchasing services, strategies and organizational information.

Food Service and Hotel Purchasing; By Peddersen, Raymond B., CBI Publishing Co.,1981. Resource for purchase decision making. Includes development of standards, specifications, procedures and controls.

Quality Control in Food Service; By Thorner, Marvin E and Manning, Peter B, AVI Publishing Co., 1983 Revised edition. Step by step procedures, assisting the operator in analyzing present system.

Principles of Food Sanitation; By Marriot, Norman G., AVI Publishing Co., 1985. Principles of contamination, cleaning compounds, sanitizers, and cleaning equipment, plus how these principles apply to specific instructions.

Increasing Productivity in Food Service; By Peddersen, Raymond B., Institutions/Volume Feeding Magazine. Distributed by Cahner Books,

89 Franklin St., Boston, Mass. 1973. This first edition text deals with equipment arrangement,plus task planning to increase efficiency and productivity.

Food and Beverage Cost Planning and Control Procedures; By Albers, Carl H., The Educational Institute of the American Hotel and Motel Association, at East Lansing Mi., 1981. Contains principles of the managerial aspects to food and beverage cost accounting.

The Art & Science of Managing Hotels/Restaurants/Institutions; By Vallen, J., James Abbey, D. Sapienza., Hayden Book Co. Rochelle Park, New Jersey., 1985. Presents a comprehensive view of management with a special treatment in Chapters 3 & 5 concerning human relations and the employees needs versus the organizational needs.

Profitable Food and Beverage Management: Planning; By Green, Eric, G. Drake & F.J. Sweeney., Hayden Book Co, Rochelle Park, New Jersey., 1986. Book 1 concerns planning and book 2 deals with managing the business. Planning covers strategy, design, accounting, legal questions and laws affecting food and beverage operations. Book 2 on management concerns day to day production, storing, sanitation and security., also contains a lengthy bibliography of additional sources of information.

Fast Food: The Endless Shakeout; By Emerson, Robert L., Chain Store Publishing Corp., 1979. The fast food industry,from its inception, spotlighting specific franchises like; Pizza Hut, McDonald's and Burger King

Foodservice Planning: Layout and Equipment; By Kotschevar, Tendal & Margaret Terrell., John Wiley & Sons Inc. Calls attention to significant points in planning and is more detailed that other texts on the subject. Examples on sound control and lighting are excellent.

Profitable Food Service Management Series 1 through 9; Published by The National Restaurant Association, 311 First street N.W. Washington D.C. A series of nine short, How-to manuals:
1. Job Analysis
2. Employee & Mgmt meetings.
3 .Good Supervision.
4. Reduction of Employee
    Turnover.
5.Job Evaluation.
6. Worker Motivation.
7. Performance Appraisals.
8. Counselling & Inter-
    Communications.
9. Recruitment & Selection of Employees.

Purchasing,Receiving and Storage; By Ninemeier, Jack., CBI Pub Co., 1983. Purchasing management principles in food and beverage operations, plus procedures for improve-

ments. The appendix includes copies of blank forms presented, which may be copied to suit a particular purpose.

The Sale and Purchase of Restaurants; By Stefanelli, John., John Wiley & Sons., 1985. Covers food-service value from the sellers view, from the buyers view and details techniques involving finalizing the sale.

**Menu Design,
Merchandising and Marketing;** By Seaburg,Albin G., Cahners Books., 1971. Complete treatment of menu production, including many examples and pages of artwork.

The U.S. & International Directory of Schools; Published by The Council on Hotel, Restaurant and Institutional Education. Henderson Bldg, University Park, PA.,1985. Lists schools which are CHRIE members and education programs in the U.S. and abroad.

TRADE MAGAZINES

Restaurant Business; Published 18 times a year, by Bill Communications, Inc., 633 Third ave, New York,N.Y. 10017. Free to Restaurant owners who participate in their periodic survey. Write and ask.

Restaurant & Institutions; Published bi-weekly. Cahners Plaza, 1350 E. Toughy ave, P.O. Box 5080, Desplains, Ill. 60017. Free to restaurant owners who participate in their periodic survey. Write and ask.

Restaurant Management; published monthly by Mary Hofer-Clem., Owned by Harcourt, Brace, Jovanovich Publications. 7500 Old Oak Blvd, Cleveland, Ohio,44130.Free to restaurant owners who participate in their periodic survey. Write and ask.

Club & Food Service Magazine; Published by Executive Business Media, Inc., P.O. Box 788, Lynbrook, NY 11563. Magazine has special issues which give excellent market study reports.

Food Service Marketing; Published monthly by EIP, Inc., P.O. Box 1648, Madison, Wisc. 53701. Presents many different types of survey information.

TRADE ASSOCIATIONS

American Culinary Federation. P.O. Box 3466,St. Augustine, FL 32085. This is a professional, educational and fraternal association of chefs and cooks, dedicated to the advancement of the culinary profes-

sion. With over 16,000 member chefs, many educational programs surround the certification of various professional levels.

National Restaurant Association. 311 First Street, N.W. Washington, D.C. 20001. This is the largest trade association representing the restaurant segment of the foodservice industry. The annual convention and exhibition, together with many educational seminars and materials is the mainstay of the organization.

EDUCATIONAL INSTITUTIONS & SCHOOLS

The Culinary Institute of America. Hyde Park, New York, NY 12588. A most widely imitated school for chefs in this country. All 2 year programs are indebted to CIA.

STATES AND THOSE SCHOOLS CONDUCTING MANAGEMENT COURSES:

Alabama: Jefferson State Junior College.

Alaska: Alaska Pacific University.

Arizona: Northern Arizona University. Pima Community College.

Arkansas: Arkansas Tech University.

California: California State Polytechnic University. Pomona City College of San Francisco. Golden Gate University. Lake Tahoe Community College. Oxnard College. United States International University. University of San Francisco.

Colorado: Metropolitan State College. University of Denver.

Connecticut: University of New Haven.

Delaware: Widener University.

District of Columbia: Howard University.

Florida: Florida State University. Tampa College.

Georgia: Georgia State University.

Hawaii: Hawaii Pacific College.

Illinois: College of Dupage. Kendall College. Southern Illinois University.

Indiana: Purdue University.

Iowa: Iowa State University.

Kansas: Washburn University of Topeka.

Kentucky: Murray State University.

Western Kentucky University.

Louisiana: Grambling State University.

Maryland: University of Baltimore. University of Maryland.

Massachusetts: Boston University. Newbury Junior College. Northeastern University. University of Massachusetts at Amherst.

Michigan: Davenport College of Business. Grand Rapids Junior College. Michigan State University. Northwood Institute.

Minnesota: Moorhead State University. Southwest State University.

Mississippi: University of Southern Mississippi.

Nevada: University of Nevada.

New Hampshire: New Hampshire College.

New Jersey: Atlantic Community College. Bergen Community College. Fairleigh Dickinson University.

New York: Cornell University. New York Institute of Technology. Paul Smiths College. Rochester Institute of Technology. State University of New York Agricultural and Technical College. Niagara University.

North Carolina: Rockingham Com-

munity College. Wilkes Community
College.

North Dakota: Bismark Junior College. North Dakota State University.

Ohio: Ashland College. Bowling
Green State University. Ohio State
University. Ohio University. Tiffin
University.Cincinnati Technical Col-
lege.

Oklahoma: Oklahoma State University.

Oregon: Portland Community College. Oregon State University.

Pennsylvania: Central Pennsylvania
Business school. Marywood College.
Harrisburg Area Community Col-
lege.

Rhode Island: Bryant College.

South Carolina: University of South
Carolina. Beaufort Technical College.

South Dakota: Black Hills State
College. South Dakota State University.

Tennessee: Belmont College. Chat-
tanooga State Technical Community
College.

Texas: Del Mar College. Houston
Community College. Wiley College.
University of Houston.

Vermont: Champlain College. John-
son State College.

Virginia: James Madison University. Radford University. Virginia
State University.

Washington: Shoreline Community
College. Washington State University.

West Virginia: Shephard College.
Concord College.

Wisconsin: University of Wisconsin. Nicolet College and Technical
Institute.

Note: *There are many more schools
which offer courses in Restaurant,
Hotel and Institutional management
for the foodservice industry. Check
them out.*

INDEX

*Inherent in the owner is a mix
of Mr. Naive and Mr. Know,
however, more of the latter
will certainly bring that quiet
time, when you realize your
actually learning to calmly
take things in your stride.*